Tin Men

Folklore and Society

Series Editors
Roger Abrahams
Bruce Jackson
Marta Weigle

*A list of books in the series
appears at the back of the book.*

Tin Men

Archie Green

UNIVERSITY OF ILLINOIS PRESS
URBANA AND CHICAGO

∞ This book is printed on acid-free paper.

Library of Congress Cataloging-in-Publication Data
Green, Archie.
Tin men / Archie Green.
p.   cm. — (Folklore and society)
ISBN 0-252-02750-7 (cloth)
1. Tinsmiths—United States—Folklore.
2. Tinware—United States.
I. Title.
II. Series.
GR105.G736   2002
398.2'0973'07—dc21   2001006426

To Julia Ardery and Norman Granz,

who in their own ways made this book possible

CONTENTS

ACKNOWLEDGMENTS

A museum exhibit in 1995 precipitated my thoughts on sheet-metal artistry in general and tin men in particular, and this book took shape. The staff of the San Francisco Folk and Craft Museum and the members of Local 104, Sheet Metal Workers' International Association, received my initial thanks.

In time, I became indebted to many others: curators, librarians, archivists, photographers, folklorists, historians, art and antique dealers, folk-art collectors, apprenticeship-training instructors, trade-union officials, tinshop proprietors, and skilled tinsmiths.

The names of many of these friends appear throughout, marking their activity in unfolding the stories of individual tin men. Many, however, remain unnamed, yet their collective contribution tilts this book toward an exploration of creativity in a community of work. I am aware that no list, long or short, can adequately thank all who helped.

In the preparation of my manuscript into a book, Aarne Anton read an early draft of the text and constantly guided me into new territory. Julia Ardery, Michael Kazin, and Adam Machado carefully read "final" drafts. With a sure hand, Judy McCulloh, Mary Giles, and Paula Newcomb have guided *Tin Men* through the maze at the University of Illinois Press.

Tin Men

Vulcan

Vulcan fut fils de Iupiter et de Iunon et Nacquit extrememenr laid dont Sa mere despitée le ietta en l'isle de
Lemnos de laquelle cheute il deuint boiteux, il est depeint forgeant et un Aigle proche de luy pource quil
Forgeoit les foudres de Iupiter et les Armes des autres Dieux

Cun priuil. Reg.

1. *Vulcan.*

PROLOGUE

Sons of Vulcan have toiled through the ages with precious elements and alloys, among them tin. Contemporary sheet-metal workers and their predecessors—tinkers, tinners, tin-plate artisans, wiredrawers, braziers, pewterers, cornice makers, coppersmiths, and whitesmiths—have long represented their crafts on banners, badges, charters, crests, and signboards or with statuary. In miniature seal and massive sculpture, tinsmiths have portrayed tools (snips, hammers, and soldering irons); fabricated objects (lanterns and candelabra); and the human figure.

Long engaged in producing domestic ware, today's sheet-metal workers heat, cool, and ventilate all manners of buildings, from cottages to cathedrals to space-exploration centers. Although the public does not see much of this handicraft (which remains hidden above ceilings and behind walls), we depend upon tinners' skill for modern society's survival.

I have long sought to "see" the "unseen" gifts of tinsmiths, as well as the living men and women behind the screens and panels that hide their work. Of the many artifacts they have made and continue to make, we glimpse some of their representations of humanity crafted in metal: processional icons, valiant warriors, roadside behemoths, wondrous automatons, and proud mechanics.

Within this universe of saints and sinners, I focus upon one category: tin men fabricated originally as advertising trade signs in and about tinshops and, more recently, as instructional teaching tools in apprenticeship classes. Skilled workers form such figures themselves out of a complex set of motives, some but dimly understood.

Museums and collectors enshrine a few tin men, many are lost or vandalized, and tinshops and trade schools hold the remaining pieces. I explore this differential response to similar artifacts with the instruments of vernacular studies, labor history, and folk-art research. This investigation is part of my ongoing study of the traditions of coal and hard-rock miners, textile hands, mariners, pile drivers, shipwrights, millwrights, and other workers. I have tagged this field "laborlore" and welcome companions.

Tin men have been studied infrequently by popular-culture students or art historians. Such oversight prevails in other academic areas; however, tin men should appeal both to art connoisseurs and enthusiasts, as do ship figureheads, cigar-store Indians, duck decoys, and homemade quilts.

More than esthetic or utopian vision challenges me. Fundamental in my approach to artisanal expressive culture is the life of individual workers—their skill, customs, values, joys, sorrows, and institutions. Who designs and shapes a tin man? How? Why? As background to these queries, I offer kaleidoscopic images from fable and fiction. The poetic or artistic portraits in workers' minds often become a pattern for the object they craft. By this circular process the tinner, template, and tin man exchange features and become one in spirit.

Americans are simultaneously fascinated or repelled by what we do in making our livings. Herman Melville's *Moby-Dick* and Marlon Brando's *On the Waterfront* both illustrate work's traumas. Industrial Workers of the World ("Wobbly") soapboxers railed against capitalism's evils. New Deal muralists painted confident workers engaged in making the proverbial desert bloom. We continue to be mystified and enchanted by legends or ballads about steeldriver John Henry. Did he not die for all of us at the Big Bend Tunnel?

Laborlore students frequently expect to find radical material—contestational and controversial. Among the metal figures (robot, clown, space cadet, knight, cowboy, athlete, and tin woodman of Oz) I have found, no martyred Joe Hill or prophetic Mother Jones marches. Why this lack? Are tinners immune from ideology? Do shop and classroom sculptures lend themselves to polemical messages? My answers to these questions, firm or tentative, lie ahead.

Unlike many folk-art and material-culture students, I devote attention to the labor union to which tin-man makers belong, the Sheet Metal Workers' International Association. Like comparable American unions, the SMWIA has achieved fine wages, fair working conditions, and a degree of shop-floor democracy. It is rightly proud of its century-long struggle for job security and dignity.

I am also deeply conscious (and constantly puzzled) by the relative neglect of history and culture by pragmatic unions. As a trade unionist for many decades, it troubles me to learn of the contradiction between organized labor's ideals and some of its practices. SMWIA tinners are far more aware of their creative heritage than other workers, but, like Oliver Twist, "I want more." I want knowledge about work and workers. Our need for cultural tools is constant: Web-sites, films, broadcasts, exhibits, forums, monographs, and festivals.

In a sense, I view labor's attention to expressive data—tale, poem, drama, ritual, symbol, landmark, and artifact—as a vital elixer, good for body and soul. Essentially, I desire a polity in which "tin-knockers" (their own colloquial label) undertake the roles of oracle, documentarian, curator, and critic.

Perhaps I ask too much of others in that I have tried to combine these plural tasks in daily work. Nevertheless, I am confident that a few tinsmiths will be challenged by my book to explore their own traditions. This gathering can serve as a guide to various techniques, whether close description of existing tin sculptures, compilations of finding lists, oral histories with old-timers of artistic bent, or comparative studies of expressive forms across craft lines.

An anecdote recalled on a tin man's making may open a journey to distant shores; a lone picture may conjure images of realms unexplored. Ultimately, the smallest bit of information (measurement of a tin man's size, photograph of a stage in its fabrication, a tinner's choice among models, or notation of a tin man's origin or meaning) helps in framing the largest moral questions facing working people.

Metalsmiths fashion dazzling church spires, sheath towering skyscrapers, and construct spidery spiral stairways; they continue to shape the human form in metal; surely they can also interpret their craft's legacy. When an inanimate tin man hints at the circumstance of his genesis, we expect the human maker to articulate large values.

Chronological narrative, conceptual analysis, and deductive reasoning on the part of outside savants serve noble purposes, as do less-structured studies: rambling, shadowy, imaginative. The tinsmith's logic is not always visible in his initial design, nor do we always see the miters or seams that lock together his ductwork's units.

I trust that my experience as a worker-scholar have combined to offer a book useful in the academy, union hall, and tinshop. All journeys must begin in time and place. I open my exploration of sheet-metal artistry, and reflection on labor-lore's boundaries, in the year 1995 at a craft museum facing San Francisco's Golden Gate.

2. Museum buddies.

1 FORT MASON'S PAIR

In the summer of 1995, the San Francisco Craft and Folk Art Museum welcomed a pair of tin men to its Fort Mason Gallery. For this unusual "Working Folk" exhibit, guest curator John Turner had selected some forty items (paintings, carvings, miniatures, and artifacts) revealing aspects of everyday work. He included a few pieces by recognized folk artists—Howard Finster, Clementine Hunter, and Ralph Fasanella—as well as many others unknown in museum circles.

Among the show's objects, Turner had paired one of galvanized iron with one of copper. I had seen the copper figure in San Francisco's sheet-metal union hall years before 1995. The two figures juxtaposed at Fort Mason "turned me on." Admiring the skill manifest in making the copper figure, I was not impelled to explore its story. By contrast, the galvanized man was a delightful surprise demanding that I explore its origin. What ties linked him to his museum buddy? Did any documentation exist for these dissimilar sculptures?

Although I had worked alongside sheet-metal mechanics on waterfront and building-trades sites in the 1940s and 1950s, I had no memory of encountering their art objects. Knowing that tobacconists and other shopkeepers announced their wares with figurative carvings or signboards, the juxtaposed museum metal men in 1995 kindled my curiosity. Initially, I questioned the artifacts directly. Gradually, I widened my search to encompass matters of sheet-metal artistry, and in time I viewed the Fort Mason pair as affecting large concerns about the place of workers in American society.

Long interested in the culture of working people and their lore, I visited the tin men many times, urging them to break their silence. Conversing with each, I asked, Who fabricated you? When? Where? Why? What brings you into a museum gallery? How do you add to my sense of identity and citizenship? Defying commonsense knowledge that they could not speak, I likened them to the balladeers, yarners, and gifted artisans with whom I had talked over the decades.

Of course, both pieces never opened their hearts to me. If I could respond to their bulk and flair, why could not they answer my questions? Who might reveal their secrets? Casting about for some plan, I pictured the two as characters in a book. I would "read" the metal pair as I had read Robin Hood or Huck Finn. With each tin man treated as a literary text, I turned pages to decode hidden messages.

One figure, eight feet tall, announced in painted letters on his chest, "Al's the Tin Man." Why did his maker name him a tin man when *Al* was made of galvanized (zinc-coated) sheet iron? For centuries, tinsmiths had used various metals and alloys in addition to tin: lead, copper, aluminum, brass, bronze, pewter, iron, and steel. The old terms *tinker, tinner,* and *tin man* had given way to the modern *sheet-metal worker* to designate a skilled mechanic in the trade. Contemporary craftsmen as well as art dealers and curators voice "tin man" to name figurative sculptures in and around tinshops or in homes and museums.

Al, oblivious to problems in nomenclature, smoked a stubby, iron-pipe cigar as he balanced above his head a red-frame, unglazed skylight. At once, he told me that someone in the shop made, installed, and repaired these objects. *Al* treasured skylights as fellow workers loved baseball bats or fishing poles. I lack such affection, shuddering in memory of past torrential leaks in two skylights at home.

Al could not verbalize that he had "hung out" as a three-dimensional outdoor trade sign since the late 1940s at a tinshop at 7667 Melrose Avenue in Los Angeles. I learned this from Elizabeth Lees of Caskey and Lees, antique dealers in Topanga, California. She did not know the full name of the tinsmith who made *Al,* but she did share a few details.

The skylight-holder had served faithfully until 1983. Upon the shop owner's death, his son moved *Al* to his own tinshop on La Brea Avenue and put him inside its window. About 1988 the son relocated to focus on commercial work, selling the sign to Off the Wall Antiques on Melrose. In turn, the dealer sold the tin man to collector Stephen Johnson, who kept it at home until 1994 and then sold *Al* to Caskey and Lees.

Tracing the intertwined transition, esthetic and commercial, from trade sign to collector's prize to museum star—with names of tinsmith and son still unknown—I posed another question. Did *Al* belong in the folk-art realm of patchwork quilts, duck decoys, fiddle tunes, hex signs, limner portraits, Grandma Moses scenes, and Watts Towers?

Conscious that curators, critics, and ethnographers have not agreed upon a common definition for folk art, stretching from quilt to tower, I felt no urge to "elevate" *Al* to a canonical realm. Instead, I sought to grasp the body of experience

3. *Al's the Tin Man.*

within which a Los Angeles tinsmith fashioned *Al* and whether his gallery-placed companion came out of a similar tradition.

Al's buddy, a sixteen-inch copper figure, held a toolbox in one hand and blueprint roll in the other. Seemingly, he had no name, but he sported a coin-sized emblem stamped on his pullover/jacket—tin snips, soldering iron, and tinner's hammer crossed in a lettered circle—the union seal of the Sheet Metal Workers' International Association. An exhibition card identified the wee man as San Francisco Local 104's mascot.

Visiting the union hall, I met business agent Bob Urbina and training officer Ray Manley. Each expressed pleasure in having placed *Copper Man* in a San Francisco museum. Fortunately, they recalled the mascot's maker, Lewis Wittlinger (1913–90), who had served for decades as a mentor in Local 104's rigorous apprenticeship program. Wittlinger's father had learned coppersmithing in Germany. His son's skill and devotion to unionism led to active membership in the SMWIA as well as a vocational teaching and administrative position at the John O'Connell Trade School in San Francisco.

Pursuing *Copper Man*'s history, I reached a friend of Lew, octogenarian Louis Gold, a retired class instructor for the union. Gold reported that he, Wittlinger, and other teachers had fabricated annual gifts for students or had assigned gift-making tasks to advanced apprentices. He suggested that Lew likely had created the little figure as a teaching tool, a "hands-on" example of superb workmanship.

Although curiosity about *Copper Man* had led me to Louis Gold, I gained from him, in an unanticipated way, a sense of fulfillment at a life in the trade. He had worked from the mid-1930s to retirement in 1975 and had spent two additional decades teaching apprentices. I learned that certain jobs stood out for him—a fabulous pagoda in Chinatown, the Ruth Asawa–designed Origami Fountains in Japantown, and Frank Lloyd Wright's metal ornaments at the Marin County Civic Center.

4. *Copper Man.*

Gold added to such highlights a touching account of the first woman apprentice in Local 104 and his role in helping her devise a strategy of survival against the ingrained opposition of a few diehards. Gold did not name the apprentice, but he reminded me that sheet-metal workers, like other skilled tradesmen, have had to struggle to overcome discriminatory habits in their work communities.

During visits to training centers in Pacific Coast sheet-metal union halls, I viewed projects in various stages of completion as well as a few pieces retained for display purposes. The latter became visible models, readying apprentices for "turning out/topping out" rites (advancement to journeyman status). Because their classrooms held an unstated "heritage" role, teachers expected students to learn by osmosis. Instructors followed an unstated assumption: Well-crafted artifacts, by their presence, would reveal trade esthetics and inspire respect for excellence. An antique lantern or miniature copper figure, when seen, could be built by apprentices who aspired to an honorable calling.

Richard Mikelson served as apprenticeship coordinator after Wittlinger. When I visited Rich at home in Marin County, he showed me one of his predecessor's gifts, a silhouette of the union's logo tools in copper, brass, and stainless steel, framed and mounted on his den wall. Wittlinger had fabricated such items, presenting them to friends and fellow workers on occasion.

Mikelson recalled that Wittlinger brought *Copper Man* into the union office

5. Louis Gold and apprentices.

about 1982 and gave it to Robert Mammini, Local 104's business manager. Wittliger had been Bob's apprenticeship teacher, and a relationship of respect persisted between the two when the latter moved from the trade to elective union office. Neither made a big deal of the gift, for each understood its significance. Both men looked at the diminutive figure's fine seams, close soldering, and accurate details as examples of superb craftsmanship. Indeed, *Copper Man* represented a kind of Bureau of Standards yardstick for fine work.

When I asked Mammini for his thoughts on the figure's meaning, he skirted large matters with an amusing recollection. Because the diminutive figure wore a mustache similar to Bob's, he had accepted it in good humor as a personal gift. Yet when Mammini retired he did not take *Copper Man* home; instead, he left it to decorate the union's inner sanctum.

In Local 104's hall, Wittlinger's present to Mammini took on added value. Just as no individual member could own the union's framed charter or silk banner, no one could claim possession of *Copper Man*. Indeed, over the years its initial association with one teacher, a tinner, gave way to a broad symbolic role. For members who did not know Wittlinger, *Copper Man* stood for excellence in craftsmanship. When displayed at Fort Mason, the only union-labeled piece in the folk-art exhibit affirmed that it had graduated from being a good-work symbol to becoming a goodwill ambassador.

Initially, Fort Mason set me on a path to uncover background information on *Al* and *Copper Man*. As their stories unfolded, additional questions surfaced. After a lifetime of museum attendance, I wondered why I hadn't seen tin men on display before 1995. That led me to search catalogs and investigate the role folk-art enthusiasts had played in enlarging tin men's domain.

Many trails converged upon Herbert (Bert) Waide Hemphill, Jr., a champion of twentieth-century folk art who made his aesthetic codes widely known across the continent by sharing findings through extensive exhibitions. Smithsonian Institution curator Lynda Hartigan pictured his collection's highlights and marked his influence in *Made with Passion* (1990).

A typical Hemphill show included a wildly eclectic mix: visionary paintings, tattoo designs, face jugs, religious tokens, gnarled canes, children's toys, and utilitarian trade signs. I do not know when Bert first displayed a tin man, but Rita Reif noted of an exhibit at Heritage Plantation in Sandwich, Massachusetts, in 1974, "The Oz-like tin man, once the trade sign of a plumbing and heating concern, seems appealingly vulnerable despite its heroic, six-foot-plus size." Her comment, directed at a broad reading public, can be seen in retrospect as a ladder-step in the climb of a Hemphill tin man to the folk-art canon. The Milwaukee Art Museum pictured the same galvanized man, which was from an Ogdensburg, New York, shop, in its 1981 catalog, *American Folk Art*.

The Cincinnati Contemporary Arts Center followed in 1986 with a catalog, *The*

Ties That Bind: Folk Art in Contemporary American Culture, edited by Eugene Metcalf and Michael Hall, influential scholar-collectors. They included a photograph of a metal figure with arms, legs, and neck fashioned from flexible tubing. *Tube Man* had followed a circuitous route to the art world: Ohio tinshop maker unknown, then bought by a picker (someone who seeks pieces for resale) and sold to Akron quilt dealer Darwin Bearley, who took it to a Massachusetts sale where it was purchased by Hemphill, who put it on loan to an Ohio show in 1986, to be acquired by the Smithsonian American Art Museum after Bert's death in 1998.

At this juncture, I return to John Turner at San Francisco and the two artifacts precipitating this study. Including tin men seemed natural in a show about work in 1995. Why? John had "backed into" art when photographing vernacular envi-

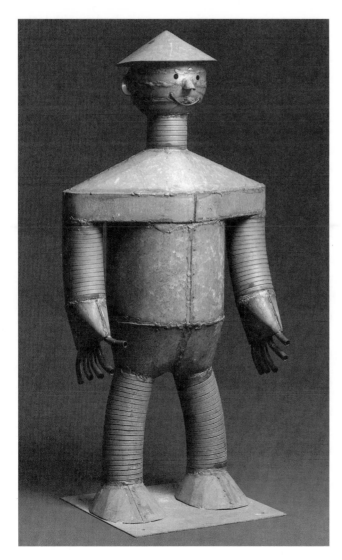

6. *Flexible Tube Man.*

ronments in California during the 1970s. That led to modest collecting and substantial reading. Hemphill and Weissman's influential *Twentieth-Century American Folk Art and Artists* (1974) became a guide for John; on a Manhattan visit, he met Bert. By the time of the Fort Mason exhibit, many professionals had been touched similarly by Hemphill's vision.

I gave little thought at Fort Mason to curatorial influences or museum policy. Indeed, I had no plan to begin a book, but *Al* and *Copper Man* affected me strangely. As the trade sign towered over the mascot, I puzzled over their difference in size. The contrast seemed proper as I delved into their stories. The large one purposely attracted public attention; the other drew students to itself with a hint that it might decipher trade secrets. Despite dissimilarity in "skin and bones," when placed side by side they compelled thoughts on workplace artistry.

Certainly, the tin and copper companions held enough wisdom to confide the secrets of each "father's" trade. How did these silent creatures accept their particular lots as trade sign or union emblem? Could the metal icons reveal the creative impulses of their respective makers? How did they relate to each other, friendly kin or rival tribesmen?

Al proclaimed a shop's location and material offerings: Come inside and order a skylight/flue/furnace/gutter/downspout/ cornice/cupola/finial/lantern/bird cage/cheese mold/whiskey still. By contrast, *Copper Man* marked ideal goals for learners: You, too, can achieve grace through competence. Its blueprint roll anticipated *Al*'s skylight, signifying the shift from abstract drawing to finished product—a transformation built into every tinner's sense of self-identity.

Both figures joined hands in trumpeting skill. *Al*, stepping out front, promoted blatantly. *Copper Man*, backstage, preached quietly. Each called attention to the centuries-long art of fashioning the human spirit in metal. Each joined ancestor figures—saint, warrior, weather vane, and toy—in a fascinating parade. Both called attention to ever-changing language.

I have already noted that *Al* and *Copper Man* are not made of tin, yet both live under the rubric *tin man*. How did that anomaly occur? Leads in the *Oxford English Dictionary* shed light in this regard. *Tin,* a word as old as the English language, has many offshoots, technical and vernacular. "Tin-horn gambler," "Tin Pan Alley," "tin ear," and "cat on a hot tin roof" bear only a faint relationship to the soft, white metal standing behind these and similar expressions.

The tag *tinker* emerged a millennium ago to identify a handcraftsman in tin and has acquired humorous or bawdy undertones. The Irish and the Scots extended the word to gypsies to mark one of their customary occupations, mending pots and pans. On both shores of the Atlantic, ballad singers and audiences enjoyed the droll exploits of jolly tinkers—bunglers, rogues, thieves, and lovers. In America, tinker tales merged with those of crafty Yankee peddlers.

The word *tinner* described an ore miner in 1512, and in time speakers applied it to a tin plater and a tinsmith. Contemporary sheet-metal workers still voice "tinner" but rarely use "tin man" and "tin plater." Another early term, noted in 1302 for a worker in tin, *whitesmith,* has dropped out of everyday speech although it had been used for ages to distinguish tin men from blacksmiths. "Tinsmith," which gained currency in the mid-nineteenth century, is recent compared to its predecessors.

As early as 1611 the term *tin man* appeared in print. It has been used variously to identify a worker in several sites and occupations: ore mine, smelter, rolling mill, tinshop, factory, and retail store. An example from colonial Boston attests to its longevity in America. When the Old South Church was under construction, the pastor noted in 1730, "They raised the vane or weathercock, Shem Drowne, tin-man, made it" (Coffin 1968, 40). Charles Tomlinson (1858, 59) pictured a tin man and helper at work, surrounded by many hand tools.

Known to all in building and metal trades as a deprecatory or humorous term for a sheet-metal worker, *tin-knocker* seldom appears in dictionaries. Maine professor George Chase first included it in a dialect word list in 1914. When it appears (infrequently) in the *Sheet Metal Workers' Journal,* it may be punctuated to indicate that a substandard or undignified tone is being used. For example, the *Journal* reported on participation at the Smithsonian Institution's Festival of American Folklife under the heading "From 'Tin Knocker' to Air Balancer on Washington's Mall" (1973).

A shift in names marks the decline in usage of "tinker," "whitesmith," "tinner," "tin man," and "tinsmith." In 1888 several craft unions in the United States banded together to form the Tin, Sheet-Iron and Cornice Workers' International Association. In 1896 the new union became the Amalgamated Sheet Metal Workers' International Association. In 1924 the IA dropped the word *amalgamated* from its title, bringing the phrase *sheet-metal worker* into present-day prominence.

Some time in the twentieth century, "tin man," used as a term for a worker in the trade, gave way to being the name for a shop-sign figure. Tinsmiths in everyday speech may have applied the latter to a trade sign under construction. Far removed from the shop floor, two characters in literature contributed to the naming process.

L. Frank Baum's Oz books (1900, 1973) included, among other characters, a woodchopper incongruously named the Tin Woodman. As the modern fairy tale circulated widely, readers transformed him. By losing primary definition as a forest worker who made his living with an axe, he became a whimsical figure clad in metal and, ultimately, a ready model for tin men.

From Czechoslovakia, Karel Capek in his play *R.U.R.* (1920) introduced the world to robots (derived from the word *robota* for "forced labor" or "servitude") (Harkins 1962; Kussi 1990). Modern drama enthusiasts in Europe and elsewhere viewed mechanical or automated men dressed in metal suits or costumes as tin men. Inevitably, the Tin Woodman likeness merged with that of Capek's robots. Today, we use the term *tin man* to designate a functional trade sign as well as a likable, Oz-derived simpleton or a sinister, science-fiction creature.

Both Baum and Capek characters serve as models when contemporary tinsmiths build trade signs. No one, however, seems to know who first gave such objects the collective name *tin men.* It would seem that sheet-metal workers named

7. Tinman and tools.

these artifacts as they fabricated them, but we lack firsthand accounts by mechanics of their artistry. Present evidence indicates that folk-art authors used this term in the 1970s. Books by Robert Bishop (1974), M. J. Gladstone (1974), and Bert Hemphill and Julia Weissman (1974) all pictured a tin-shop figure identified as a tin man.

I did not dream of problems in nomenclature at the Fort Mason exhibit. Nor could I sense conceptual issues hidden beneath each tin man's metallic skin—intent in fabrication, ambiguous artistic impulses, and diversity of representative roles. On first meeting *Al* and *Copper Man,* I did not detect that they hailed from terra incognita, a land of toil largely mysterious to scholars or critics. Perhaps good fortune guarded my unseeing eyes.

Sheet-metal workers fabricate tin men, collectors covet them, and curators exhibit them. Because I had not occupied any of these stations but do have some aptitude for asking questions, curiosity about the Fort Mason pair led to this study. I looked for the beginnings of the tin-man-making tradition and figuratively rolled out history's scroll. Analysis and illustrations combined to place these sculptures on a plain of dimly seen social and esthetic horizons. As in my previous writings on laborlore, I assumed an interest in documenting workers' creativity and a commitment to its worth.

Many roads are open to an explorer. I chose a journey of discovery—to dictionaries for word studies, to libraries for history, to archives for papers, to antique and art marts for leads in an esoteric field, to museums for artifacts, and to sheet-metal shops and union halls for present-day trade signs. Above all, I would trace the paths of tinsmiths who crafted tin men. My findings converge in the book ahead.

8. *Der Kupfferschmidt.*

2 History's Scroll

Papier-maché lumberjacks, concrete-cast cowboys, and fiberglass voyageurs beckon today's travelers along the highways. With messages, lurid or sophisticated, these play-giants invite us to eatery and inn, theme park and vacation land. Buy our goods! Stay awhile! Indulge yourself! Beyond such commercial hustle, each colossus—logger, wrangler, and riverboatman—also suggests work's power. See me as more than a pitchman; ask what I do on the job; trust my integrity.

In colonial years on the Atlantic seaboard, merchants and artisans hung decorated wooden signboards or sculptured signs outside their shops to announce distinct craft wares and skills: a blacksmith at his anvil, a dairymaid at her churn, a butcher at his block, a stonemason at his bench. Often the sign maker aimed for realism in objects depicted; occasionally, he hit upon the bizarre. After the Civil War, iron founders cast similar but stereotyped pieces. In modern times, working people have appeared on sheet-metal signs outlined by lightbulbs or neon-filled glass tubes.

Present-day roadside giants look back at antique signboards or sculptured signs as ancestor figures. While aware of such antiquity, when driving across the land or pausing in the city we distinguish a tin man functioning in front of or atop a metal shop from a lodge's ornate, gargantuan figure. What tells us that the former speaks to trade mysteries and mechanical secrets whereas the latter calls us to pleasure in vacationland fantasy? We know that the metal behemoths on North Dakota's vast prairie do not mark a tinshop's presence. In probing the differences between a utilitarian trade sign and a tourist-beckoning colossus, we direct attention to hidden history.

Before settlers reached Jamestown or Plymouth Rock, European guildsmen had used heraldic charters, colorful insignia, and distinctive livery (dress) to symbol-ize their trades and to hint at the mysteries inherent in their callings. Guild rega-lia usually remained hidden but would be publicly displayed on ceremonial days. In eras past, when the populace could not read, outside signboards or shingles also commented on work practices. Shop owners hired artists to execute signs, or at times they might fashion their own out of the material at hand.

As guilds gave way to friendly societies and labor unions, their emblems lived on in banners and badges. Over the centuries, smiths in gold, silver, copper, brass, iron, and tin contributed to designing and fabricating the human figure in metal as well as on cloth and paper. In 1670, for example, London's Worshipful Compa-ny of Tin Plate Workers and Wire Workers chose a coat of arms featuring the guild's own handcrafted product, a ship's spherical lantern topped by a regal crown. Two elegant workmen supported the lamp and crown.

In appropriate language, C. A. Meadows describes the Tin Plate Workers' arms: "Sable, a chevron or, between three lamps (the two in chief, one light each facing each other, the lamp in base with two lights) argent garnished or, illuminated proper. The crest is a globular ship lantern, or lamp, ensigned with a regal crown proper. The supporters are two working tinmen proper, vested in blue coats with red cuffs, lined with fur, blue breeches, red waistcoat, white stockings, black shoes, and silver buckles, and on the head a fur cap" (1957, 86).

In the 1800s, the Worshipful Company gave way to a trade union, the United Tin Plate Workers Society. In designing a new banner for a branch of the society, a sign painter unacquainted with the symbolism of the lightship lantern substitut-ed a globe. Further, he dressed down the supporting craftsmen—from rich attire to democratic billycock hats, knee breeches, and plain stockings (Gorman 1973, 68). This crown-globe, two-journeymen design held firm for decades, gradually giving way to contemporary logos of crossed tools. Ted Brake in *Men of Good Will* (1985), a history of British sheet-metal unions, offers illustrations to mark tinsmith iconography's colorful parade.

I speculate: Did a tin-plate guild-master or friendly-society member ever fash-ion in metal his silk banner's figures? When did an engraved charter or printed-indenture tinman "climb" to a shop facade or roof, thus transforming himself from trade-union symbol to trade sign? Whether examining guild-herald tinners or contemporary neon-clad exotic dancers, we sense that such brothers and sisters trace their lineage back to art lost in time: paleolithic cave-wall incisions of hunt-ers, Egyptian stone reliefs of pyramid builders, and Ostian mosaics of galley boat-men and domestic barrel-haulers.

Over long centuries, the living figure in metal has appeared in multiple arenas as tinsmiths, like other artists with gifts from forge and anvil, have been challenged to represent humanity. Church leaders commissioned statues of favorite saints, mainly in wood and stone but occasionally in beaten copper or other metal. Sec-

9.Union banner.

ular rulers similarly called upon smiths in gold and silver to replicate or miniaturize men and women in precious artifacts symbolizing power and wealth.

Armor, metallic body covering for combat, is the best-known work of early smiths. Relatively simple protective gear in Norman England evolved in complexity and weight until a Huguenot knight complained of being laden with anvils not armor (Ditchfield 1904, 177). Medieval armorers, proud of their skill, organized into guilds. As warfare changed, other craftsmen—blacksmiths, braziers, and tinners—absorbed their mysteries. An early seal of the Armourers Company depicts St. George slaying a dragon. To this day, tinsmith apprentices fabricate replica knights.

European craftsmen have long fashioned weather vanes based upon recognized human figures. In colonial America and the young United States, householders and farmers placed angels, soldiers, sailors, goddesses of liberty, jockeys, and Indians atop roofs to mark wind direction. Such pieces, combining pragmatic and decorative purposes, became prized folk-art examples when collectors and curators acquired early examples for display in elegant parlors and prestigious museums.

Early weather vanes may have been made by individual homeowners, neighborhood blacksmiths, or seasoned tinsmiths in their shops. In time, however, specialized firms mass produced such ware for sale via mail-order catalogs. Seemingly, in handicraft days no tinner honored his own trade by making a weather vane showing himself at work. Could not a leather-clad tinner, snips in hand, have pointed the wind's direction as did a soldier or a sailor? Were no tinshops topped by vanes?

Wooden signboards fashioned for a tinshop by a joiner, carpenter, or cabinet-maker might reveal an object (lantern, rainspout, candlestick, or kettle) made inside. It defies reason to assume that a tinsmith did not ask, Why hire an itinerant painter to decorate my sign when I can do better at my bench? Long ago, an artisan who designed on assignment a saintly icon or domestic weather vane must have stepped easily to the task of fabricating the likeness of a working tinner, either for commercial display needs or trade-union purpose.

Tin-plate guilds and subsequent unions generally commissioned outsiders to design or produce their banners and livery, at times bearing a tinner's likeness. Tinsmiths, however, fabricated their own metal signs. What determined that a banner would be made by an artist with paint on silk and a metal shop icon by an inside artisan? It must have seemed obvious or natural that tinners would depend on their own skills when called upon to fabricate shop figures.

The earliest preserved sign made of tin in the United States is a seven-foot coffeepot from 1858. It did not call attention to a coffeehouse, however, but rather a tinshop. Fabricated by Samuel and Julius Mickey at Old Salem, North Carolina, it advertised their roofing, stove, and sheet-metal firm. It remained in place for a century until the coming of Interstate 40, when Winston-Salem relocated the familiar local landmark on a grassy plot at the dividing line between the old towns.

The Shelburne Museum in Vermont has gathered and shown many early trade signs. Two using tin were made in the shape of a key (for a locksmith's shop) and a fire axe (shop unknown). Such sculptured advertising objects have not vanished from the landscape. In Eureka, California, for example, Pierson's Building Center displays a twelve-foot clawhammer (with a stainless-steel head and wooden handle) on the ground alongside its building. Were early tinshop signs made parallel to those for other proprietors?

In 1897, Silas West in Haverhill, Massachusetts, designed and patented a number of life-sized men made of pressed tin, brightly colored for advertising purposes (Fried and Fried 1978, 93). The figures did not represent particular trades; instead, a painter would letter in the name and location of the firm. Merchants placed these flat tin men on outside walls as well as on barns and buildings, where travelers from Maine to Ohio could see them.

One Silas West sign acquired by the Heritage Plantation of Sandwich, Massachusetts, advertised antiques, old books, and postage stamps until a gentlemen's apparel firm purchased and repainted it. Curators at Sandwich removed the overpaint to restore the sign's original function (if indeed the stamp dealer was first). In the process, they perhaps inadvertently revealed that the antique dealer's sign

10. Pressed-tin trade sign.

11. *Habit de ferblanquier.*

had become an antique itself. As will be shown throughout this book, some tinshop figures also seem destined to become objects prized by curators and collectors.

Makers of the figurative trade signs of the twentieth century—at least those of which we have knowledge—offered sculptured figures, whether dignified likenesses or comic parodies. A few engravings by masters outside the trade also reveal widely varied depictions of metalsmiths, who at times could see themselves favorably shown in realistic or romantic portraits. When the artist chose caricature or satire a tradesman might not be willing to recognize himself.

In Nuremberg in 1568, Jost Amman (art) and Hans Sachs (poetry) collaborated on *The Book of Trades,* an illustrated survey of occupations. A Latin text by Hartmann Schopper also appeared in Frankfort in the same year (Bruno 1995, 129). Previous tomes had shown some examples of craftsmen, but (to use its short title) the *Standebuch*'s use of vernacular language made it groundbreaking. Changed times in Europe prepared new readers for a handbook focused on the mechanical arts. Interest in everyday science had increased during the Renaissance, and artisans needed instructional literature suitable to complex technologies. Amman and Sachs, in sensing these currents, caught the spirit of the emerging Protestant work ethic with poetic homilies and accessible pictures.

In his pioneering volume, Amman included many metal workers, from armorers to wiredrawers, but the woodcut of special appeal to the sheet-metal craft now is *Der Kupfferschmidt.* A coppersmith, hammer in hand, labors in his shop. His dividers, signifying mathematical knowledge, rest in place on the wall. The open window reveals a clear day, marking ease with nature. Surrounded by pans, basins, vats, and wine bottles, the coppersmith personifies honest toil in the production of wealth.

In startling contrast to Jost Amman, in 1695 Nicolas de Larmessin, a Parisian engraver, published *Les costumes grotesques et les métiers* (Fantastic costumes of trades and professions [1974]), an exuberant gathering of three dozen detailed illustrations of men and women clothed in the objects of their calling. They appeared as stylized characters in a costume ball at the court of Louis XIV, far removed from the grime of the workshop. The engraver anticipated the surrealistic wit sometimes seen in today's ballet.

One de Larmessin illustration, *Habit de ferblanquier* (Clothing of the tinsmith/ whitesmith or worker in white metal), reveals a person displaying rather than making objects and implies a switch in interest from the production to the consumption of worldly goods. The vacant-faced tinner wears identifying accoutrements; tinware of every description hangs from his body. We find it difficult today to name all his goods—once practical, now esoteric.

An Augsberg copperplate engraver, Martin Engelbrecht, about 1730 built upon de Larmessin's album in *Assemblage nouveau des manouvries habilles* (New collection of clothing of the trades). He depicted a tinsmith and his wife (with French

12. *Un cofretier* (Ein
Flaschner).

and German captions identifying thirty-five items draped about their bodies):
lamps, lanterns, plates, coffee pots, funnels, tobacco tins, and jewel boxes. Art historians and antiquarians continue to use Engelbrecht for his revelation of handcrafted goods before the days of factory production.

The dual visions of Kupfferschmidt and Ferblanquier have persisted in modern tinshop trade signs. Today, some craftsmen follow Amman, who depicted a
sturdy mechanic engaged in demanding work—indeed, he earned his bread by the
sweat of his brow, toiling before an open fire. Others emulate de Larmessin, whose
subject approached illusion by displaying a dazzling bounty of trinkets and trifles.

In addition to such contrasting portraits, European artists had occasion since
the fourteenth century to render drawings and engravings of itinerant workers and
merchants and have captioned those illustrations according to their subjects' colorful street cries. Poets, playwrights, and composers of topical ballads wrote about
the hawkers and hucksters, chapmen and charlatans, who offered goods and ser-
vices on city streets. In modern times, depictions in old books of cries have been

13. *Une cofretiere* (Eine Flaschnerin).

reproduced on Christmas cards, biscuit tins, and other gift-shop goods. Here, I note two tinker portraits among many.

Marcellus Laroon published *Cryes of the City of London Drawn after the Life* in 1687, and it has gone through many printings, most recently that edited by Sean Shesgreen in 1990. A real-life tinker appears over the caption "A Brass Pott or an Iron Pott to Mend." His unkempt hair, patched trousers, and ragged jerkin reveal his status close to vagabondage. Shesgreen reports a bit of popular etymology—tinkers would announce their trade by beating a pot with their hammer handle, thus making a "tink-tink" sound. They also used several traditional cries or chants. One follows:

> Have you any work for a tinker, mistriss?
> Old brass, old pots, or kettles?
> I'll mend them all with a tink, terry tink,
> And never hurt your mettles.

This cry, dated to 1667 by antiquarian Charles Hindley (1969 [1884], 99), reveals the pot mender's command of wordplay, exemplified in substituting "mettle" for "metal." It also hints at the ambiguous, sometimes erotic, relationship between tinkers and homemakers. The street cry tells us that the tinker in literature was a libidinous character, a predecessor of the whiz-bang traveling salesman.

Thomas Rowlandson, the English caricaturist, made a series of occupational drawings issued in *Cries of London* (1799) and *Characteristic Sketches of the Lower Orders* (1820). Among his plebeian scissors grinders, chimney sweeps, live-eel sellers, and chair menders, he portrayed a tinker wheeling a portable workbench. This street mechanic argues with a woman over a pot that has holes in it. She is far from the enticing creature of fantasy who inhabits much tinker lore, however; rather, Rowlandson depicts an old crone excoriating a tradesman.

No one has inventoried all the graphic representations of tinsmiths that are found in books of trades, ballad collections, street-cry compilations, art portfolios, and technical manuals. One category includes early broadsheets, each holding many cameo drawings of individual street workers. A sheet from the early seventeenth century entitled *Parte of the Criers of London* (artist unknown, in the

14. *Pot to Mend.*

British Museum), for example, shows three dozen men and women, including a stereotypical tinker with his budget on his back (Shesgreen, ed. 1990, 17). This familiar tradesman continued to catch the eyes and ears of diverse artists. I cite only Francis Wheatley's romantic oil painting of 1795, *Pots and Pans to Mend* (Webster 1970, 84), and, by way of contrast in the same period, Thomas Bewick's realistic woodcut *Tinker* (Cirker 1962, plate 181).

With this glimpse of portraits from German trades, French costumes, and English street life, I invoke an additional source of tin-man imagery. We have long been intrigued by the possibility of an artificial human or automaton, alternately benign or monstrous. In the Mediterranean world, the smith-god Hephaistos/Vulcan fashioned Talos out of brass and Pandora out of clay. In medieval Prague, the idea of a powerful servant, also formed of clay, circulated in the Jewish ghetto. This robotlike creature came to life by a charm, the name of God. Constant retelling codified these legends in *The Golem* (Bloch 1972).

Throughout the years, this theme has taken many strange forms—inhuman monsters, mechanical dolls, thinking machines, science-fiction robots, and space aliens. Some are well known: Johann Goethe's poem "The Sorcerer's Apprentice"

15. Thomas Rowlandson's *Pots and Kettles to Mend*.

(Der Zauberlehrling), Paul Dukas's music for *L'apprenti sorcier,* Leo Delibes's ballet *Coppelia,* E. T. A. Hoffmann's story "The Sandman" in *The Tales,* Jacques Offenbach's opera *The Tales of Hoffmann,* Mary Wollstonecraft Shelley's novel *Frankenstein,* and Fritz Lang's film *Metropolis.* Book illustrators and stage or cinema costume designers made these creatures of fantasy highly visible to modern audiences.

Amazing Stories, a pulp-fiction magazine, began publication in 1926. Its lurid cover art helped popularize sinister, machinelike men and women, although, occasionally, sympathetic metal-clad figures appeared as well. In 1977 George Lucas impressed a worldwide audience with his science fiction film *Star Wars,* which featured two likable robots, the computer-brained R2-D2 and the humanoid, gold-plated C-3PO. In the summer of 1998 the Smithsonian Institution staged "Material World," which included four hundred items, from one-armed bandits (slot machines) to Minerva, a laser/sonar/computer–driven robot.

In my attention to graphic portraits used consciously or unconsciously as templates by tinners, I have neglected the area of statuary. Cast-bronze or chiseled-marble figures provided models for a tinsmith, but in the creation of sheet-metal statues metalsmiths participated directly in artistic production. The Statue of Liberty required the art of repoussé (hammering sheets by hand).

In the 1880s, the W. H. Mullins Company of Salem, Ohio, developed a method of die-stamping the sheet copper, brass, or zinc sections of a figure in a drop forge, later joining each separate unit by solder or rivets. Memorial groups commissioned countless statues of Civil War heroes, and the pieces were mass-produced in this way. Augustus Saint-Gaudens's nude *Diana,* a huge weather vane atop New York's Madison Square Garden (1891), came from the Salem shop. We can speculate that a Mullins mechanic adapted this "advanced" technique while making a familiar trade sign.

Sheet-metal workers do not live in a sealed bubble of soap operas and superbowls. Like other citizens, they are daily bombarded by diverse cultural forces. They absorb, applaud, evaluate, or "talk back" to television fare: movies, sports, news, drama, commentary, and music. Merchants appeal with Norman Rockwell sentiment and Andy Warhol parody until the line between these exemplars of popular and pop art becomes indistinct. In this cauldron, art and advertising merge. Both become part of the tinsmith's "other" tools—they come with the territory in modern life.

Before a tinner, crafting a tin man, picks up shears to cut into a sheet of galvanized iron, he has in mind an image of a mechanical figure. As work begins, he translates this mental picture into a physical pattern or template. The tin man's initial idea may date back to feudal legend or romance poetry or be as recent as the robot Minerva (whose name recalls Roman mythology). The tinsmith may not know the precise source for his model in history or literary texts. Nevertheless, he proceeds, confident in his skills.

Photographs and drawings help the mechanic bring back dimly remembered pictures. Movies constantly recycle old narratives and illustrations. If those outside the tinshop are to comprehend a tin figure's messages, they must account for the techniques used in construction, its stated or formal purpose, sources of personal creativity by makers, and the host of templates available to the tinsmith community.

Our past marches into the present in many guises. We read novels, watch television dramas, pause in museums, visit somber memorials, and play in gaudy theme parks. Together, these actions and places bring antiquity into the present. In such varied settings we match personal experience against received wisdom. To employ a literary expression we unwind history's scroll.

16. W. W. Denslow's tin woodman, copyright in 1899 and published in 1900.

3 Oz

Before the San Francisco Craft and Folk Art Museum dismantled its "Working Folk" exhibit, I scoured libraries for background details on *Al* and his copper companion. The Land of Oz seemed the obvious place to start. With the publication in 1900 of L. Frank Baum's *The Wonderful Wizard of Oz,* Americans could visualize a platonic tin man modeled after original drawings by W. W. Denslow. Subsequent books as well as stage plays, vaudeville acts, musicals, and movies confirmed this tin man as an American icon.

The original book about Oz never faded from public consciousness, but the 1939 film starring Judy Garland as Dorothy—accompanied by the Scarecrow, Tin Woodsman, and Cowardly Lion—reinforced Baum's characters in the national psyche. I suspect that many viewers today who see a tinshop's trade figure are but dimly aware of its advertising function or its role as a mark of a sheet-metal worker's competence. Instead, they accept the tin man as a fairy-tale wanderer (alongside the Scarecrow and Lion), searching for a heart, a brain, or courage.

For a century, the Land of Oz has delighted children and intrigued scholars. Leaving aside the diverse meanings in Dorothy's pilgrimage, questions persist about the Tin Woodman's derivation. Despite considerable attention, the origin of Baum's tin man remains a mystery. Humans wearing armor have long coexisted with metal-clad creatures of fantasy and horror, but a tin woodchopper before Baum's is unknown.

Baum's son Harry recalled that his father had worked as a hardware store window-dresser in Chicago. There, "he wanted to create something eye-catching so he made a torso out of a washboiler, bolted stovepipe legs and arms to it, and used the underside of a saucepan for a face. He topped it with a funnel

hat and what would become the inspiration for the Tin Woodman was born"
(Baum 1973, 134).

We can neither confirm nor deny this explanation. Baum had diverse influences available to him when he conceived of a metal man. The skeleton in armor,
the man in the iron mask, and mechanical monsters appeared in fiction, drama,
or art. Writers as diverse as Henry Wadsworth Longfellow, Alexandre Dumas, and
Mary Wollstonecraft Shelley contributed to the archetype.

I cite two pictures of metal men not to "prove" direct ancestry for the Tin Woodman but rather to indicate what was available to Baum. In 1862 Andrew Tuer, editor of the *Paper and Printing Trades Journal* (London), used a drawing of "The New
Steam Compositor," a metal-clad typographer at his case. This human boiler stood
with a fire pot behind him, steam spouting from his kettle head. Tuer poked fun
at shifts in printing technology and, indirectly, at other skilled workers facing
obsolescence. He again ran the satiric cut as the frontispiece of *Quads* (Tuer 1884),
a gathering of trade humor.

An advertisement in *McClure's Magazine* in December 1900 for Sapolio, a widely
popular household cleaning and polishing soap, bore some resemblance to the
hardware-window torso that Baum had contrived before Denslow illustrated *The
Wonderful Wizard of Oz*. The "Man from Panville" steps out in polished gear, ready
for a joyful evening as he views an elegant mansion across the street. The Sapolio
advertisement and *The Wonderful Wizard of Oz* appeared in the same year; one may
have influenced the other. It seems likely, however, that Baum, Denslow, and the
Sapolio artist all drew upon then-current models of metal-clad men.

I have noted that Karel Capek introduced robots in 1920, and the image took
hold quickly. Professor Bugs Mechanical Men of 2029, for example, strutted at the
Philadelphia Mummers Parade in 1929. For that event, a line of men in tin suits
(or cloth or cardboard painted to resemble tin) posed with their leader, distinguished in formal attire. His crew came from the League Island Club, and their
costumes might have been influenced by Capek's vision of robots or Baum's of the
Tin Woodman. Although folklorist Debora Kodish has pursued this matter, no lead
on the source of the marchers' attire has surfaced.

After failure as a merchant and newspaper publisher in South Dakota, Baum
relocated to Chicago in 1891, initially as a china salesman and, subsequently, as
the publisher-editor for a department store window-trimmers' magazine. In *Show
Window* he created a land of fraud and fantasy—in short, an anticipation of Oz.
In these years did Baum encounter a tinshop tin man?

After 1900, books about Oz elaborated the Woodman's story by twice renam-
ing him. He was Nick Chopper to mark forest work routines and Ku-Klip to note a
subsequent transformation into tinsmith. Baum's imagination led to rapid
changes in names and tasks for his characters. Ku-Klip personified skill; beyond
shaping all manner of metal implements and toy tin soldiers, he tried to create

17. Sapolio advertisement.

18. Professor Bugs Mechanical Men of 2029.

flesh-and-blood humans. Critics have observed that Baum's tin man addressed substantial matters, among them industry's march to dominance in an agrarian society and Populism's response to a dehumanized social order.

We can accept or reject such speculations for Baum's Tin Woodman. Yet after seeing similar figures in metal shops and folk-art museums, I believe they do comment metaphorically on American experience. We sense the tin man's diverse meanings by a detour to the Chicago World's Fair of 1933. There, at Enchanted Island, workers erected two "sky-high," Baum-inspired sentinels, Scarecrow and Tin Woodman. Children enjoyed these play-giants, brothers to papier-maché, carved-wood, or cast-concrete loggers, boatmen, and cowboys. Adults were free to ponder how the characters related to the fair's theme, "A Century of Progress." Did the tin man simultaneously decry and applaud technological progress?

In 1981 the Rice family donated a 1907 farm house to the Seward County, Kansas, Historical Society to establish a local museum in Liberal, Kansas, based on Baum's concept of Dorothy Gale's home. Carpenters had only to alter the roof to match his description. Named Dorothy's House, it offers tourists colorful displays and animated entertainment that are incantations of illusion. Similar theme parks and pleasure palaces mix play, profits, and patriotism until these elements become indistinguishable.

Dorothy's House sells souvenir dolls of the Tin Woodsman; he appears on T-shirts, placemats, Christmas ornaments, ceramic mugs, and postcards and as jewelry and a pewter figurine. Oz-inspired collectibles, stocking-stuffers, miniatures, and bric-a-brac pour out endlessly. Hobbyists treasure some items in this tin, tinsel, cloth, cardboard, plaster, and plastic mountain of inanity, but much ends in trash bins.

No one has counted all the tin men derived from Denslow's drawings of 1900. It would be impossible to identify the gift-shop material alone; however, tinsmiths' work lives beyond that of most souvenirs. A few shop figures have employed elements of the Tin Woodman, such as his heart, axe, or funnel head.

Calaveras County in the California Sierras perpetuates Mark Twain's classic tall-tale by staging an annual jumping-frog contest. Hence, the local tinshop might have decorated itself with a logo of a gold miner holding a pet frog. Instead, Angels Sheet Metal chose Baum over Twain. Proprietor Jeri Mills worked twenty-four years as company bookkeeper, learning procedures from front door to loading dock. Purchasing the firm in 1992, she capitalized on the logo of the previous owner, who designed the insignia for his business forms, letterhead, and trucks without building an actual tin man.

To rectify that contradiction, Mills asked foreman Mike Woodberry to fabricate a six-foot-tall tin man for mounting at eye level on the shop building's exterior. One arm up and one down, the trimmed-in-red mannequin wears a candy heart on his rectangular chest. Do all who see him recognize the tiny heart's symbolism?

Perhaps Baum's Tin Woodman has chopped his way into our imaginations and his characters need no explication.

A cautionary note adds clarity: Tin men exist in too many shapes and styles to assert a single source. A gift-shop or theme-park figure, when named and sold as a look-alike for the Woodman, proclaims its intent. The maker has ample incentive to cleave to recognizable models. By contrast, tinsmiths conscious of obligations to their trade are free to disregard the Tin Woodman's lines when fabricating a shop sign.

A Canton, New York, tin man resembles Denslow's model, down to the axe he holds. Milford Howe, a hardware store proprietor, fabricated the man about 1940 (presumably upon seeing *The Wizard of Oz*). Many hardware stores in rural America combined retail sales with plumbing, roofing, electrical, or sheet-metal work.

After Howe's death in 1983, an auctioneer sold his estate and Kate and Allan Newell, folk-art collectors, purchased the tin man. Allan Newell serves on the board of trustees of Traditional Arts of Upstate New York (TAUNY), a regional archive/museum/cultural center. In June 1998, TAUNY exhibited a number of pieces of yard art, garden ornaments, and public-space sculptures, including *Canton Man*.

Varick Chittenden, TAUNY's founder and director, studied folklore under Louis Jones at Cooperstown and assisted Bert Hemphill in annotating New York finds.

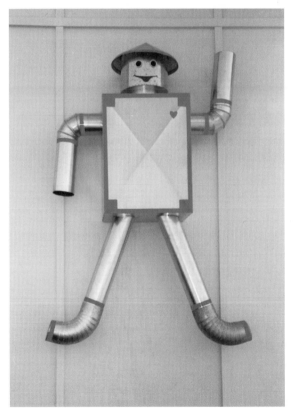

19. Angels Camp tin man.

"Chit" introduced me, by mail, to *Canton Man* and called attention to a problem in analysis posed by this tin man. Although the figure clearly demonstrates the influence of Baum and Denslow's work, we cannot be certain that it functioned in Howe's hardware store and tinshop as a reminder of craft skill. It could have been kept at home for a private reason known only to the Howes. No clear evidence survives, for example, a photograph of the tin man in a corner of the store or shop or, conversely, in the Howes' parlor.

A pair of Duluth, Minnesota, figures, both embellished with tiny red hearts, pay tribute to the Land of Oz but pose additional questions for the curious. D. G. Solem

20. Canton tin man.

and Sons is nine miles out of town on a rural road, and not many casual visitors seek it out unless they have specific sheet-metal needs. About 1994, foreman Brian Linn undertook the making of three tin men. A thief stole one before completion, but the remaining two decorate the shop's roof and the yard of Linn's adjacent home.

The life-sized figure atop the roof is reasonably secure from vandals and the smaller yard man can not be budged, for he is filled with concrete and mounted on an abandoned well-casing. Both tin men have lived through severe winter storms that affect their painted hearts, causing replacement "surgery" at approximately two-year intervals.

I have depended in all phases of my research upon friends scattered throughout the land for visits with tinsmiths and photographs of their trade signs. Accordingly, sociologist Sal Salerno, who visited Brian Linn in August 1999, has supplied several photographs of the Solem tinshop. I was intrigued by a shot of an old metal structure resembling a farm silo at one end of the shop. In a telephone conversation, Don Solem, the shop's owner, explained its presence. Originally, it had been a gasoline station's underground tank, but after developing a leak it became dysfunctional. Solem salvaged the tank for use as a wood-pellet storage space when coal and fuel oil became expensive. At present it has no function other than to share duties with the roof figure and "guard" the tinshop. Both artifacts offer no physical protection but suggest, in their separate ways, that the shop does fine sheet-metal work and that the mechanics within care for old things.

Linn stressed that his roof-piece represented hours of careful work; he built it over several months' "free time." To outside observers, the figure also stands for the

21. Tank, tinsmith Brian Linn, and tin man.

22. *Harvey Gallery.Com.*

Tin Woodman. To Linn, it represents some measure of freedom. Many sheet-metal workers, as well as their companions across trade lines, guard the distinction between "company" and "personal" time.

The fact that Linn fabricated the tin man during his "own time" gives the piece special value. The tank's message is murky and less easy to decode—perhaps it concerns the need to recycle. Not all old equipment need be discarded as junk or put out of sight. An uneconomical object may convey a sense of the past. A rusty tank becomes a local-history text similar to a museum holding.

The few tinshop figures I have described suggest the century-old Tin Woodman, as do many "funnel heads" employed in other enterprises. It seems inevitable that a tin man from the Land of Oz would be caught up in the halcyon days of dot.com ventures. To my delight, Mark Lerner, a New Jersey railroader, found an art gallery in Lahaska, Pennsylvania, that had a tin man perched on its porch roof, his feet dangling inches from a lettered sign: HARVEY GALLERY.COM. How is one of Baum's characters connected to a toney Bucks County art shop? Proprietor Henry Harvey, an artist and sculptor, fabricated the replica himself to suggest the range of objects for sale inside. I ask again, What difference exists between a tinshop trade sign and an artmart advertising figure?

Tin men like the one from Oz, in all their permutations, share honors with pieces who have been influenced in their construction by characters from both life and fiction: space cadets, cowboys, Indians, warriors, dudes, dandies, robots, ath-

letes, hard-hats, Buck Rogers, and Godzilla. Not all sheet-metal workers can articulate what impels them to build a tin man or whether they see their creative artifacts as representing an illusory realm or a tinsmith's everyday practices.

Baum's *The Wonderful Wizard of Oz* continues its inspirational role, but twenty-
first-century children face a rainbow of choices. Each sheet-metal mechanic who
crafts a shop figure draws upon a variety of models and is influenced, of course,
by the physical properties of available material, the economy of the shop, and the
traditions of the trade. We do not know whether the Tin Woodman will serve as a
governing template for future sheet-metal shop signs. Will Baum's character's
enormous importance expand or decline in decades ahead? Perhaps a cinematic
science-fiction creature or a gunslinger for the age of missile defense will capture
the imagination of creative tinners in the future. In 1900 L. Frank Baum and W.
W. Denslow could not have predicted the cultural influence they would have, and
neither do we know who will play a similar role in the twenty-first century.

23. *Grinder Man.*

4 At the Boundaries

In addition to everyday utilitarian ware, tinners enjoyed making toys, often mimicking the human figure—a sparse silhouette, a dignified hourglass, a tubular mass, or an angular shadow. What they produced ranged from commercial products to complex, science-fiction gear to leisure-time trinkets.

In this book, I have separated toys from the domestic and industrial goods built by sheet-metal workers and from tin-can figures, found-object constructs, and folk- or fine-art sculpture. The limits that I have set court problems inherent in classifying an array of artifacts that hold esthetic merit. For example, a tinsmith fabricates a tin man as an eye-catching shop sign, and a fellow worker makes a similar piece for sale in a gift shop, art gallery, or craft fair. By what standard do we mark differences in such look-alike figures?

In an analytic study of tin men we move back in time, seeking answers to questions of origin, category, purpose, and meaning. When and where did anyone in America first fashion a shop figure to announce a craft? Why do these display pieces take so many appearances? Does a trade sign hold visible clues to its maker's intent? Did tin men serve functions other than advertising? In assessing meaning, how is balance achieved between the conflicting perspectives of artisan and connoisseur? Do we judge a tinsmith's creativity by norms applied by artists and critics rather than by shop-floor mechanics?

A little nineteenth-century figure described as a tinsmith pushing a grinding wheel, or, alternatively, a knife grinder, poses such questions. He appears in four books by several authors associated with the American Museum of Folk Art in New York City (Bishop and Coblentz 1981, 114; Hollander 2001, 554; Lipman, Warren, and Bishop 1986, 146; Lipman 1990, 117). Apparently, a tinner in or near Marblehead, Massachusetts, fabricated the thirteen-inch man, who pushes a wheelbarrow-propelled grindstone. *Grinder Man* wears a top hat, smokes a pipe, and sharpens a tool. His creator simultaneously fashioned a whirligig animated by a vaned wind-wheel and connecting rods. Such toys compel interest by their motion—a butcher cleaves a side of meat on his block, a woodsman swings his axe in the forest, or a grinder bobs and bends to his stone as the wheel turns.

Perhaps the Marblehead tin man functioned as more than a toy. He may well have been an advertising artifact, a piece of sculpture calling attention to a tinsmith's ingenuity or a tinshop's wondrous offerings. Elizabeth Warren suggests (Lipman 1990, 117) that trade figures were placed outside buildings as well as in shop windows and on countertops. In short, without knowing something of a maker's intention, we are unable to pigeonhole his or her construct. Time has erased the circumstance of the whirligig's construction. Compilers of folk-art books guess that he was made between 1825 and 1875; Ralph Sessions suggests that the knife grinder's tin can (for water) above the wheel dates the artifact to the post–Civil War era (Hollander 2001, 554). It is beyond *Grinder Man*'s power to answer specific questions concerning his age and purpose or address our large curiosity about the genesis of tinshop trade signs.

In 1974 Bert Hemphill and Julia Weissman edited an attractive folk-art book that pictured, among other treasures, a "tin toastmaster" made about 1900 in Chicago. The little man, forty-one inches tall, wears a formal suit, favors a high hat, and holds a tin cup at chin level. He also has a tin-can assemblage and articulated marble eyes and is welded and painted (Hemphill and Weissman 1974, 37). In 1988 Michael Hall pictured the same piece but with a carefully altered description. He was said to be twenty-one inches tall, formed and painted, have inset glass eyes, and have been made of sheet metal between 1910 and 1920. The articulated little man, Hall told me, hinged in mid-section and could be opened at the waist. Accordingly, the tin-knockers who made him used *The Toastmaster* to hide their whiskey bottles. The story, although unconfirmed, rings true because it represents an apocryphal note in the narratives makers told about their tin men.

It is unlikely that any collector or curator can now uncover this particular drinking story or, more important, reveal the purpose that *Grinder Man* or *The Toastmaster* served. Did a tinsmith craft the whirligig as a child's toy or a shop sign? Did a fraternal lodge officer order a diminutive man to grace his hall? Did a tinner in overalls see himself dressed in "fancy duds" and make an object to suit his self-image? Without facts on origin, we can but speculate on the most appropriate way to label these icons.

I turn to a pair of metal men who function unambiguously as playthings. Collectors Allan and Penny Katz hold a number of antiques in their Connecticut farmhouse, among them two life-sized baseball players close in appearance to shop tin men (Weber 1993, 99). Batter and catcher, ready for electrically precipitated action,

24. *The Toastmaster.*

stare blankly at an unseen human pitcher who endeavors to throw a ball into the catcher's hands without hitting the moving bat.

Inventor Robert C. Turner applied for a "Game Apparatus" patent on September 21, 1927, for his players, and the U.S. Patent Office assigned Strike-Em-Out Base Ball Inc. of Boston patent number 1,731,477 on October 15, 1929. The dates are significant: Coolidge prosperity gave way on October 29, 1929, to the stock-market crash and subsequent Great Depression.

Allan Katz believes that his baseball pair may have served as a working model or prototype of Turner's amusement device before the metal men became ready for manufacture and sales. The set is unique; no others have been found. I assume that Turner had knowledge of the sheet-metal trade or cooperated with a tinner who moved readily from making tea kettles or skylights to sports fantasies. We accept the reality of shifts in production by skilled mechanics, yet we know by sight that the Strike-Em-Out pieces were not intended to serve as tinshop trade signs.

The baseball players, *Grinder Man,* and *The Toastmaster* can be designated as toys even though these three objects may have functioned differently. The word *toy* signifies a child's plaything, a bauble, or a trinket. Tin soldiers have delighted generations of youngsters. "Toy" also describes an amusing act, a diversion, or a flirtation. These various meanings deployed from object to action require that we accept varied responses upon encountering tin men trade signs.

Blacksmiths, boilermakers, plumbers, structural and ornamental ironworkers, electricians, industrial welders, and auto mechanics have also turned pipe fittings, tubes, gears, bolts, wire, radiators, tanks, stock parts, and scrap into whimsical curios, yard ornaments, and trade signs. "Muffler men" are seen everywhere, perhaps because of the dominance of automobiles in U.S. society. Exhaust-system parts, reincarnated as auto-repair markers, both advertise and amuse.

Tim Correll and Patrick Polk, who have studied muffler men, have published

25a,b. Strike 'Em Out baseball players.

their findings in *Muffler Men* (2000). In October 1999 they exhibited artifacts ranging from spotted dogs to extraterrestrial robots in a show at UCLA's Fowler Museum: "Muffler Men, Munecos, and Other Welded Wonders." Correll and Polk, based in Los Angeles, presented pieces largely by Mexican American mechanics. The curators noted the interplay of ethnicity and occupation in the creation of *munecos* (doll, puppet, or mannequin). Critic Rita Reif ("There Can Be Art in Car Parts, Too" 1999) hailed the show for its flamboyant metal icons and pointed to the currency of the sculptures, which dated from between 1970 and 1990.

Self-taught artists whose work is sought by collectors and puzzled over by scholars also exhibit metal figures that often resemble tinshop signs. I limit this study, however, to the tin men made by mechanics who are employed in the sheet-metal industry. An "outside-the-boundary" tin-can man helps establish the contrast between similar objects.

Francis Bellimer's "toy" does not come from a sheet-metal shop or an apprenticeship classroom. Bellimer, a retired Bristol, New Hampshire, electrician in his nineties, has always made "old things"—a model church of copper, a group of singers made of cans, or a bearded man, also of soldered cans. The latter figure could serve as a child's toy or a home-altar or mantlepiece object, or it could be a gadget made for diversion from everyday routine. Only Bellimer knows what guided his hands or stimulated his imagination when he crafted an impish man who wears an elegant high hat—or what he called him. Although I have not learned if Bellimer named his can figure, I favor *The Bearded One.*

To my knowledge, Bellimer has not been discovered by the authors of folk-art books. In attempting categorization, I label him a hobbyist and describe his activity as a pastime. Such terms can trap critics in a well of condescension. I imply no judgment, however. Without further information about Bellimer, I go no further than to use *The Bearded One* as a "book marker."

Two tin men made by workers in sheet-metal firms also help mark the limits of my findings. One hails from rural Iowa and the other from British Columbia. Donco Air Products of Albion, Iowa, manufactures air diffusers for large buildings; its labor force is in Des Moines Local 45, SMWIA. In 1996, Donco's CEO, Larry Raymon, undertook a goodwill project for the Marshalltown Kiwanis Club's Christmas Festival.

Raymon, a Civil War buff, planned *Moses,* a larger-than-life replica of a Union artillery soldier holding a drum. Not only did Donco's shopmen fabricate the drummer, but Raymon also documents its construction process as well as its subsequent appearances. A company handout, for example, notes that he is made of 90 square feet of 24-gauge galvannealed steel, and that he is authentic in detail from boot tip to shako top. In April 1997 *Moses* stood on display in the rotunda of the Iowa State Capitol, serving equally to honor the state's metal craftsmen and veterans of all wars.

In 2001 the *Sheet Metal Workers' Journal* featured the world's largest tin soldier, which had been fabricated by Local 280 members in New Westminster, British Columbia ("Local 280 Members Create World's Largest Tin Soldier"). Welder Tony Hardie also created a Web-site documenting the step-by-step construction process, and the *Journal* included twenty-six photographs that detailed in sequence the giant's birth and growth.

The five-ton figure, thirty-one feet high, is neither a particular shop's trade sign nor a "proof piece" demonstrating an apprentice's competence. Officially, it raised funds for a children's charity during the Christmas season of the year 2000. Painted in the colors of the British Royal Engineers, the tin soldier became an instant

26. *The Bearded One.*

tourist attraction. Possibly, it points to the future, as metal figures move out of tin-shops and training environments to assume public-relations roles.

In presenting *Grinder Man, The Toastmaster,* the Strike 'Em Out Company's baseball players, *The Bearded One, Moses,* and the world's largest tin soldier, we see that tin-knockers, folk artists, and business executives design and construct pieces that challenge esthetic categories. Conveniently, we tag *Grinder Man* and the base-ball players as toys. Does *Toastmaster* also fit that rubric? Did Francis Bellimer confide to anyone his ability to charm through tin-can artistry? How many roles does *Moses* the Civil War drummer play? Could not the Canadian tin soldier be an old-fashioned shop sign as well as a contemporary eye-catcher?

27. Moses.

28. The world's largest tin soldier.

In their particular modes, these varied sculptures stand as sentinels outside this book's boundaries. Of course, the notion of guardians at borders is arbitrary—an academic attempt to impose order on an unruly universe. I will close this chapter by turning to a tin-man "insider" who is unambiguously within trade-sign boundaries.

29. *I'm Your Man.*

In 1939 a Chicago tinsmith fabricated a four-foot tin man actually cutting a duct-pipe, tin snips in hand. The figure radiated bold confidence, and raised, soldered letters on his chest spelled out "I'm Your Man" (similar to *Al's the Tin Man* in chapter 1). The duct-cutter functioned in his shop for more than four decades.

Collector Mark Jackson purchased *I'm Your Man* in 1984, and Michael D. Hall pictured him in a *Metalsmith* article in 1988. In an October 15, 2001, letter to me, Hall noted that the piece now belongs to the Hill Gallery in Birmingham, Michigan. Whatever its ultimate fate, this trade sign states clearly that its figure is in command of his trade. Snips in hand, snips at foot, he personifies work.

30. *Jordan's Squire* on roof.

5   JORDAN'S SQUIRE

Having opened an exploration of tinsmith artistry by meeting *Al* and *Copper Man* within a museum, I set out to locate cousins close to home. Local 104's Ray Manley pointed me to Glenn's Metal Works in Sebastopol, California, and folklorist Maria Hetherton and labor historian Henry Anderson also aided in my quest. We found a conical-hatted figure, holding two unusual objects and seated atop a shop off the Gravenstein Highway. Present owner Dick Aldrich credited the tin man to the original proprietor, John Jordan (1906–86).

Continuing my search, I visited John Jordan, Jr., now retired, in San Jose, California. As training director for the Santa Clara County Sheet Metal Joint Apprentice Committee, he helped youngsters walk the trails of ancient trades as well as drive the virtual highways of Silicon Valley. John recalled with affection that his father had created the Sebastopol figure, *Jordan's Squire,* between 1948 and 1950 and intended him to straddle the ridge of King and Jordan Sheet Metal Work, which has had several owners as it moved from its original location to the present one. Jordan would also parade his creation in the back of a truck during Sebastopol's Apple Blossom Festival.

Weighing 250 pounds, the metal icon conveys Jordan's superb craftmanship in the intricate use of tapered, folded, gored, and circular shapes. The son stressed that his father had soldered all the man's seams. I sat entranced in his office while he sketched and named the many parts his father had teased out of a trade's bounty. He also searched family scrapbooks for early photographs of the trade sign.

Like Ceres, goddess of agriculture cradling grain in her arms, *Jordan's Squire* in Sebastopol continues to posture, an apple in one hand and a chicken in the other. For many years, nearby Petaluma boasted of holding the world's record for

chicken and egg husbandry, and Sebastopol is an important apple-growing center. In saluting early sources of Sonoma County wealth, the tin man also calls attention to intangible matters beyond craft competence and commercial promo-
tion. In the middle of the twentieth century a blue-collar mechanic in a farm
community had fashioned a metal sculpture that celebrated rural modes of living.

Jordan's original sign has served different owners (King and Jordan, Glenn
Klineman, and Dick Aldrich) in succession. After the community became aware
of the tin man's status as a local landmark, Aldrich had a printer design a business
card that used him as the shop's logo. *Jordan's Squire* fills a warm place in my heart
because it was the first tin man I encountered that still functioned as a trade sign
and wasn't a collector's prize or museum piece. Stimulated to find others, I began
an inquiry that has still not ended.

Dick Aldrich urged me to drop in at Aaero Heating and Sheet Metal in Novato,

31. *Jordan's Squire.*

TEL. 823-6019
DICK ALDRICH

Glenn's

Metal Works

SHEET METAL
HEATING - AIR CONDITIONING

THE TIN MAN
LIC. NO. 418086

833 GRAVENSTEIN AVENUE
SEBASTOPOL, CALIF. 95472

32. Business card for Glenn's Metal Works.

California, and check out its tin man. On July 20, 1995, I found a six-foot, funnel-headed, spot-welded figure hanging by a spike on the shop's back wall. Its maker Grant Garl took time away from work to comment on the Aaero creature's inspiration. For some years, the firm had used a business card sporting a tiny tin robot, and in 1979 Garl had projected that image into a life-sized tin man. It was a reverse of the process of a tin man being the source for a card.

Using twenty-six-gauge metal and a single divided ventilating duct for legs and pants, Garl—in about three working days—fashioned a man a bit like the Tin Woodman. To add a special touch, he placed a tinner's old hammer and tin snips in its hands, thus providing utilitarian tools for a creature of fiction. From time to time, the Aaero crew frees the metal figure from its wall and takes it to trade shows, where it serves as a marketing device. After such festive events *Aaero Man* returns to his perch, silently watching the busy hands on the floor below.

Late in the summer of 1998, Ray Manley retired as training coordinator for Local 104. He introduced me to his successor Frank Cuneo, who proved equally interested in my quest. When the latter mentioned a life-sized figure clad in gold on display in Local 104's San Jose training center, he piqued my curiosity. When I went to San Jose on September 24, I encountered a model of C-3PO from *Star Wars* that confirmed that tin-man creativity flourished. I welcomed the opportunity to talk to its maker Dan Collier at home in nearby Sunnyvale.

The film *Star Wars* (1977) had inspired Dan, who initially had conceived of C-3PO as a Halloween costume. Worn on a few occasions, its magic lay more in construction design than use as holiday dress, however. Upon retirement in 1998, Dan moved C-3PO to the apprenticeship training center lobby, where it would be

33. *Aaero Man.*

displayed among antique tools. The contrast with a century-old hand brake as well as snips, hammers, stakes, and soldering irons is startling and underscores Local 104's appreciation of its trade's history.

The shift of locations gave C-3PO meaning beyond that of a popular icon's replication. When he had it in his home, it reminded Collier of a cinema hit and a holiday celebration. At the training center, however, the tin man took on added identity. Young apprentices, for whom *Star Wars* was an old movie, recognized a familiar figure. It is likely that most students had seen the film and would have assumed that a sheet-metal worker had the skill to fabricate C-3PO.

Only a few apprentices would have questioned why the gift graced their center. If pressed for answers, they might have replied that C-3PO was a teaching tool—a guide for those who desire to build their own tin man. Some would see it as a comment on their trade's heritage, and some on its maker's artistry. Because Collier did not fabricate a conventional figure, he included an explanatory sheet for his gift: "Using the sheet metal techniques in layout, reasoning, and forming that I had learned during my years in [the trade], I made Star Wars' C-3PO. The arms are mild steel and gas welded; the torso and legs are fiberglass, using tech-

34. Dan Collier's C-3PO.

niques that I learned while working on fiberglass duct and fittings in the field; the head is store-bought, but highly modified, and fitted with light-emitting diodes to light the eyes; the shoes were also store-bought and modified to fit the project."

In conversation Collier expanded that mechanical description to reveal that he had first became aware of a tin man at the age of eight, when his mother took him to see *The Wizard of Oz.* A few years later in San Bruno, California, he "discovered" a sheet-metal shop sign of a horse-mounted cowboy. During Dan's apprenticeship, instructor John Jordan had brought a photograph to class of his Sebastopol construction and explained its fabrication to the students.

Dan mentioned these details casually, yet they struck me with great force. In talking with tinsmiths I had become aware that most knew of the existence of shop-sign figures although few felt impelled to make one. *Star Wars,* however, had excited Collier. It precipitated emotions gained from viewing *The Wizard of Oz* in childhood, seeing an actual horse-and-rider trade sign, and learning of a teacher's experience in making a tin man.

No specific image linked *Jordan's Squire* to *Star Wars,* yet Collier was confident that when the occasion arose he could make a tin man. For him, skill included "a

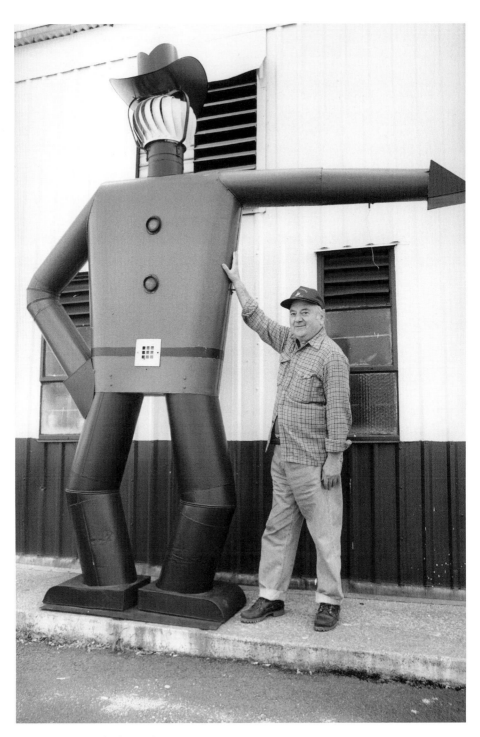

35. *Mr. Dixie,* with the author.

heightened sense of reasoning" (something I take to mean the facility to conceptualize and execute a project). What is the source of such mental power? In part, Dan had always known that he could make "things."

Collier offered an example to account for his inherent mechanical ability. Years earlier, his father had taken a contract in Kingman, Arizona, to dismantle and melt down surplus Air Force aircraft. The grand scene on the ground, more airplanes than he could count, merged into one single airplane. The memory surfaced in 1968 when Dan built a fifteen-foot Curtis P-40 Flying Tiger for his baby daughter. He still prizes the model, which his daughter, now grown, plans to keep in the family.

The steps from P-40 to C-3PO seemed natural to Collier, although the latter is only partially made from sheet metal. Collier had formed fiberglass ducts and fittings on many jobs in Silicon Valley, and thus he experimented with cardboard templates of his own body. Clay molds with complex curves followed, and then Dan brushed many coats of liquid onto each mold. The hardened results resembled a suit of hand-beaten armor. Whether it represents the tin men of the future I do not know, but it is likely that novel figures and new technology will combine to create tin men yet unimagined.

Like other tinsmiths before him, Dan Collier—articulate about his Halloween costume's construction—was reluctant to entertain questions leading to uncharted waters. The connection between the characteristics of C-3PO and those of the Tin Woodman of Oz seems significant, yet neither of us ventured to discuss popular-culture matters. I am conscious of such issues held back and hope for studies by others in the field of sheet-metal artistry.

Ray Manley had sent me to Sebastopol and San Jose, Dick Aldrich to Novato, and Frank Cuneo back to San Jose. Finding tin men but a few hours from home, I queried acquaintances for additional clues. Several suggested a computer search, and that led to *Tin Men,* a 1987 film about aluminum-siding hustlers in Baltimore. Leaving the information highway behind, I reverted to old-fashioned questions. Sightings tumbled in from the Pacific Ocean to the Potomac River.

Across the continent, Nancy Balz and David Taylor led me to *Mr. Dixie,* who stands at ground level in front of the Dixie Sheet Metal Works in Falls Church, Virginia. On November 17, 1995, David and I greeted the eleven-foot giant—who wears a black cowboy hat and red-reflector coat buttons and has bowed, duct-pipe legs, a wind-turbine head, and an outstretched left arm. Fabricated during the 1970s, he attracts attention from strangers eager to purchase him. Shop owner Paul Puckett, obviously proud of *Mr. Dixie,* told us that his tin man is not for sale.

Each tin man commanded me to seek others. The search seemed straightforward enough until I ran into a roadblock in Colton, California. On a visit to Bill Myers, a pile driver in San Pedro, we pursued a lead to Wright's Manufacturing, an air-conditioning firm at the edge of desert country. We met Calvin Wright, president, who years earlier had erected a twelve-foot tin figure on his shop's roof. The piece was, he assured us, far superior to the plaster-cast fat boy at nearby Bob's Barbecue and delighted school children, who would pause in admiration outside the shop before and after classes.

Despite guy wires, however, a severe desert windstorm blew Wright's tin man off the roof. Before it could be repaired and reinstalled, someone cleaning up the shop discarded the damaged man as junk. Wright expressed anger at this act of sabotage, and questions about a photograph or story in a local newspaper only seemed to intensify his loss. Bill and I left the premises before Wright's pain became intolerable.

Perhaps the tin man in Colton represents many others of which we have some knowledge but are now beyond reach. One California figure typifies other mysteries encountered in these pursuits. Tom Carey, a San Francisco librarian, found an intriguing advertisement on page 11 of the Modesto *Farmer-Labor News* of March 16, 1951, for De Wing Sheet Metal in Merced, California, that featured a smiling tin man, snips and hammer in hand. The image, I surmised, stood for a piece on the De Wing shop floor.

Deanna Kobayashi, Merced County librarian, suggested that I contact Mildred De Wing, who confirmed that her late husband had built two tin men. The first, of galvanized steel, stood on a canopy over the tinshop door from about 1945 to 1952; the second, made of stainless-steel and eight feet tall, presided in the shop after 1952. He became a favorite with local children because he was wired to talk and could inflate balloons; he also appeared for many years at the Merced County Fair.

Carl De Wing had learned the sheet-metal trade in his native Wichita, Kansas. Migrating to the Yosemite area in 1936, he followed his trade, eventually establishing a successful firm. Upon retirement in 1976, he donated his prized tin man to Merced College. This act of preserving a piece of tinsmith sculpture without the intercession of a folk-art collector or curator impressed me. Accordingly, I attempted to learn the present status of De Wing's tin man, only to learn that no one at the college knew. Had it been carelessly discarded and, if so, when? Perhaps it is in deep storage, now forgotten.

Colton and Merced represent different losses. Not all tin men share the good fortune of *Jordan's Squire* and survive outdoors for half a century. Sheet-metal shops change hands, advertising with a handcrafted artifact seems a quaint custom in the television age, weather is a constant enemy, collectors buy a few choice pieces, and critics remain ambivalent about blue-collar artisanship.

The Merced and Colton experiences had a subtle influence in expanding the scope of this book. Starting out of curiosity about *Al* and *Copper Man,* I had continued my studies as additional finds surfaced. What would I do if a tinner did not or could not share information on his trade sign? I had assumed that mechanics willingly talked about their construction. Fortunately, most did, but some did not. Underlying the varied responses to my queries stirred large concerns, both esthetic and ideological. Gradually, tin figures and their makers called my attention to hidden problems. It became clear that I would have to combine description and dissection as work on this book progressed.

36. Rene Latour in his garage shop.

6 ENLARGING THE SEARCH

I confess excitement in having encountered tin men atop, inside of, and outside shops across the continent. They impelled me to ask friends to help in my search for tinners' artifacts. In February 1996 I began a continuing correspondence and telephone talks with Aarne Anton, owner of Manhattan's American Primitive Gallery. For two decades he had searched for tin men and related figures, conveying them to museums and into private hands. With tinsmith Irving Dominick, Anton attended the Smithsonian Institution's opening of the Hemphill folk-art exhibit, "Made with Passion," in 1990. There, Dominick enjoyed the recognition accorded his own *Marla* (chapter 9) in the National Museum of American Art.

Anton alerted me to the art of Rene Latour, a gifted tinner in Florida. In turn, I forwarded the latter's address to folklorists Ormond Loomis and Tina Bucuvalas in Tallahassee. Born in 1905 in France, Rene was eighteen months old when he arrived in America with his coal-miner father, who had emigrated to Pittsburgh. Upon his father's death in 1921, Rene entered a steel mill as a bricklayer's helper (hod carrier). From that initial work, lining blast furnaces, Rene advanced to pipe fitter's assistant, making and setting furnace drain pipes.

Stimulated by metal work in the mill, Latour purchased a set of sheet-metal manuals and added welding to his skills. Upon the pipe fitter's retirement in 1924, Rene took his place as a journeyman. To "better himself" he took a sheet-metal class at the Carnegie Institute of Technology. Rene has retained several of the books he purchased during the 1920s, one of which is the sixth edition of William Neubecker's *Universal Sheet Pattern Cutter*.

During the war years, Rene worked as a metalsmith on the Monongahela River fleet, repairing the barges that went from coal mines to steel mills. At the war's end, he moved to New York to open a small shop and found that the majority of his work consisted of replacing rusted gutters. Constant outdoor toil in cold weather persuaded Rene to move to Florida in 1951, where he continued sheet-metal work in seven counties around Daytona Beach.

In Florida's booming space-defense industry Latour worked for Martin Marietta and NASA, joining several unions in organized plants. In 1952 he married Lucia Kuhlmann, a nurse. Their daughter, Darlene Madacsi, lives in St. Augustine, and an adopted son lives at home. Rene and a partner opened a tinshop in Ormond Beach, and after that firm dissolved in 1959 he set up his own business, Ormond Sheet Metal and Roofing, on U.S. Highway 1. Gradually reducing his scope of outside work, Rene continued on creative projects. He retired in 1995.

It has been as difficult for Rene Latour (as for many other tinsmiths) to explain the sources of his artistry. In May 1961 he fabricated his first tin man designed to advertise his shop. To authenticate that act he prepared a plan, mailing it to himself in order to claim "self-achieved" copyright status. When Aarne Anton, on a Florida trip in 1978, saw the trade sign he offered to buy it. Latour refused but relented the next year. Anton carried it back to New York on the roof of his car, and eventually art dealer Stephen Mazoh purchased it. It now rests in Mazoh's garden in Rhinebeck, New York.

About 1976 Rene saw a roadside business sculpture on Nover Road in Ormond Beach. At that time, the city had enacted a fee ordinance for outdoor signs. Thus, Latour crafted a metal cowboy to serve as his second trade sign as well as to avoid the fee. Wearing skintight boots and a huge Stetson, the wrangler sported the numeral 200 on his chest, not as a rodeo number but rather to mark the South Yonge Street address. Sadly, neighbors objected to a sign, however artistic, on their residential street, thus forcing Rene to remove his sculpture or be accused of zoning-law transgression. That painful act helped push the quiet tinsmith into a shell of withdrawal from neighbors as well as from local journalists who might pursue an artist in their midst.

As Aarne and Rene became friends in the late 1970s, Rene entrusted him with a number of pieces for his Manhattan gallery. The dealer had spotted *Cowboy 200* fastened to a curbside pole at the edge of Latour's driveway. Because zoning laws made it impossible to keep the shop sign in place, Anton bought it and sold it to Bert Hemphill, who, in turn, donated it to New York's American Museum of Folk Art.

Buoyed by the knowledge that his metal sculptures had gained recognition as well as good homes, Latour designed other special figures. For two decades he fabricated a series of tin objects: girl with sphere, ballerina, clown, dog, cat, sheriff, rodeo cowboy, moonwalker, and baseball player at bat. After seeing a geodesic dome at a Las Vegas shopping mall, Rene sought out a book by the "father" of such domes, R. Buckminster Fuller. Sharing ideas on domes with a Florida architect,

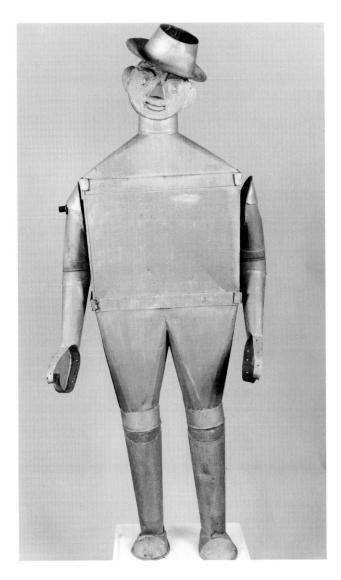

37. Latour's first trade sign.

Latour developed a configuration blending Fuller's fantasies with the funnel patterns used for decades at the tinner's trade. These experiments with spherical shapes evolved into heads for cowboys and clowns, cats and dogs, and a planetary system—the sun with nine revolving planets.

Latour labored on individual sculptures for months at a time. Ideas jelled slowly, and each part had to be custom-made. Rene viewed his creations as more than technical problems to be solved, for they held conceptual challenges. He favored twenty-six- and twenty-eight-gauge galvanized steel, joining parts with screws. Many of his human figures had movable arms and legs, thus allowing a choice of articulation for his "children."

Ormond Loomis has provided a fine description of Latour's garage shop,

frustrum of cone pattern lay out.

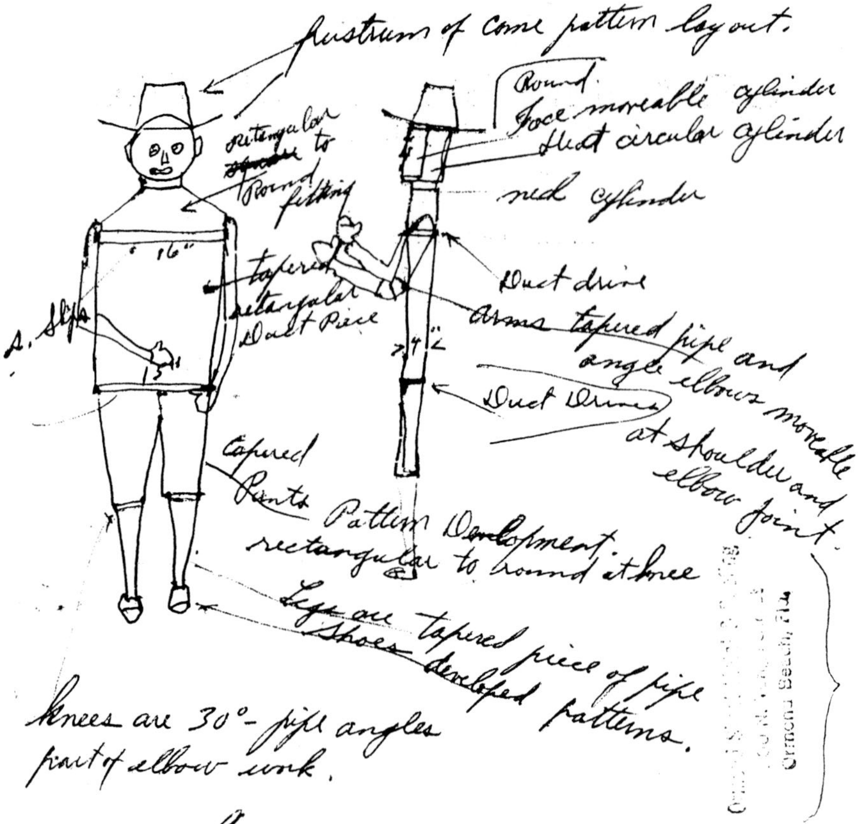

rectangular to Round fitting

16"

tapered rectangular Duct Piece

s. slips

tapered Pants

Round face moveable cylinder
flat circular cylinder
neck cylinder

Duct drive
arms tapered pipe and angle elbows moveable at shoulder and elbow joint

Duct Drums

Pattern Development. rectangular to round at knee

Legs are tapered piece of pipe
Shoes developed Patterns.

knees are 30° - pipe angles part of elbow work.

This metal man was completed before May 12th 1961

This Idea is mailed thru the U.S. Mails to be sent back to me postmarked in an unopened envelope, sealed. to be kept to substanciate the date and make of the metal man. to be used by me.

Signed May 15 1961
Rene V. Latour.

38. Latour's copyright claim.

39. Latour's *Cowboy 200*.

diagonally behind his house shaded by live oaks and palms. It reflects similar work environments built at home by mechanics across the United States. Inside the garage, a workbench wraps around the wall. A jumble of partially completed tin parts, scraps, wood and cardboard templates, notes, sketches, pictures, pamphlets, and small tools covers all free space. A brake, a major piece of sheet-metal equipment that bends and folds flat sheets to desired angles, fills most space in the center of the shop. Some retired tinners cannot live without these machines, others are happy to leave the shop's noise and clutter far behind. Rene, however, is a hand-craftsman who uses his brake and other tools as extensions of sight and mind.

When Latour explained his shop layout to Loomis, and again to Tina Bucuvalas, he showed them the brake, crimping tool, shears, and other gear. As he did so, he related his life story, illustrating choice episodes with digressions on equipment and mementos scattered about. Many more such descriptions interspersed with biography are needed for all tinners mentioned in this book.

As Latour reminisced he pulled out of the past one possible thread, curiosity, commenting on his artistry. In early employment at age eighteen he had been transferred from the hot mill to the tin mill. There he observed that huge sheets of coated tin, when cut and trimmed, yielded scrap, "waste" that the crew carefully saved for shipment to an unknown customer. Eyes and ears open, he soon learned that the scrap went to Japan and was used in making tiny metal men and similar toys. Rene was able to laughingly relate his own trade signs and their companion tin men to the toys made from "his" steel-mill scrap in Pittsburgh seven decades earlier.

During years at home Rene Latour remained hidden to academic scholars—a spell not broken until 1996. In my view, he deserves attention similar to that accorded such stars in the folk-art firmament as Kentucky wood-carver Edgar Tolson or Georgia painter Howard Finster. The Florida tinner has achieved little recognition in his lifetime, however. Critical acclaim walks a long and convoluted road with many detours.

To indicate the scope of Latour's achievements, Aarne Anton, Tina Bucuvalas, and I have compiled a preliminary checklist of his sculpture. We are aware that our findings are incomplete. Rene has not kept a list, or even photographs, of all his creative output. He recalls, for example, making a college graduate in cap and gown but does not know its present location. Much effort remains to describe each individual piece before any slip into the "maker unknown" bin. Our list includes only those items for which I have photographs.

1. *Ballerina*
2. *Baseball Player* (Airport Museum, San Francisco)
3. *Cat,* bent tail (Myron Shure, Chicago)
4. *Cat,* spring tail
5. *Cat,* vertical tail (Aarne Anton, New York City)
6. *Clown* (Myron Shure, Chicago)
7. *Cowboy,* rodeo buckle (Muriel Karasik, Great Neck, New York)
8. *Cowboy 200* (American Museum of Folk Art, New York City)
9. *Dog* (Aarne Anton, New York City)
10. *Fisherman* (Darlene Madacsi, St. Augustine, Fla.)
11. Geodesic spheres
12. Geodesic sphere, sun, and nine planets (Myron Shure, Chicago)
13. Geodesic sphere, with cross (Archie Green, San Francisco)

14. *Girl with Ball* (Myron Shure, Chicago)
15. First tin man (Stephen Mazoh, Rhinebeck, New York)
16. *Man,* arms akimbo (Allan Katz, Woodbridge, Conn.)
17. *Moonwalker* (Mennello Museum of Folk Art, Orlando)
18. *Sheriff with Gun* (Myron Shure, Chicago)
19. *Sphere-Headed Man* (Allan Katz, Woodbridge, Conn.)

Three of Latour's tin men—the first shop sign, *Cowboy 200,* and *Sphere-Headed Man*—show his range in subject matter. He worked slowly, lavishing attention on details of the piece at hand. Although he used some standard parts, such as rectangular duct sections and duct pipes, much of his work consists of "custom-made" parts he imagined and fabricated for each item.

Because Latour remains unknown except to a few folk-art collectors, critics have not analyzed his work. If and when such a belated discovery occurs, his innate

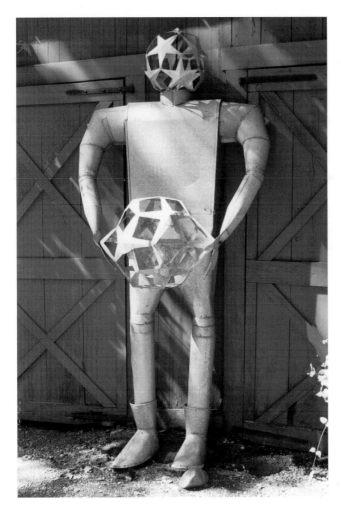

40. Latour's *Sphere-Headed Man.*

creativity, the craft skill demanded of all in the sheet-metal trade, and his status as an artist/mechanic will have to be considered.

Art historian Melissa Dabakis's writing (1999) on labor sculpture offers a possible lead. Among many pieces, she treats the Haymarket Monument (Chicago), the Mechanics Fountain (San Francisco), and the Gompers Memorial (Washington) as three diverse representations of workers, ultimately united in heroic endeavor. The Haymarket statue memorializes radicals as martyrs; the Mechanics group salutes skilled tradesmen and manliness; and Gompers, surrounded by mythic figures, personifies organized labor—formal, ceremonious, and stately.

As the son of an immigrant coal miner, Rene Latour's pedigree as a proletarian is sound. His intimate knowledge of work flows directly from a lifetime as a steel-mill hand and sheet-metal craftsman. Seemingly, as a metal sculptor he could be classed with artists commissioned to create labor monuments in bronze or granite. His pieces, however, do not resemble conventional, union-lauded statuary. His clowns and ballerinas portray entertainment-industry workers, not typical "labor" heroes or martyrs.

Latour's figures convey no obvious polemical messages. Drawn largely from popular culture, his men and women reflect a cheery view of American society. His pieces neither trumpet large causes nor approach the realm of myth. Each possesses, however, an inner dignity that elevates it above much tinsmith art. He pushes his skill to the physical limits inherent in sheet-metal material. Perhaps his years at the trade have taught him that a flat sheet is not fluid bronze ready for casting or textured stone awaiting the chisel. Absent his own words in explanation of artistry, we are left to describe his pieces and speculation on his philosophy.

In time, Latour's figures may receive the attention of art historians able to answer the many questions hidden in his work. In September 1998 the Historical Museum of Southern Florida (Miami) opened an exhibit of contemporary folklife, including his *Moonwalker*. In April 1999 the San Francisco Airport Museums presented his *Baseball Player* in an exhibit, "Gearing Up: A Look Back at Sports Equipment." These two shows, a continent apart, cast light on how museum staffs assist in transforming tin men into folk art.

Knowing Rene Latour only through the visits of others, I reflected on the distance from Pacific to Atlantic shores and my lack of a magic carpet. How would I ever meet tinners scattered from hamlet to metropolis? The best alternative to direct travel seemed to be correspondence with colleagues in workers' culture. Perhaps they would help find tinsmiths and bring their creativity to light.

I have been fortunate in the goodwill of friends who have shared findings with me. Martha Cooper, a Manhattan photographer; Varick Chittenden, a Canton, New York, folklorist; Dick Case, a Syracuse journalist; and Dennis Heaphy, a Syracuse tinsmith helped me uncover the story of a family of tin men.

In 1892, D. J. Heaphy, the son of Irish immigrants, opened a shop in Syracuse on Clinton Street alongside the Erie Canal to make wagon mudflaps for teamsters. His business grew as he expanded to include hardware, paint, roofing, heating, and sheet metal. Some time after Heaphy and Son moved to 133 North Geddes Street, a worker—perhaps Charles Penfield—made a six-foot-tall tin man that had a spinner-ventilator head and placed it in front of the new shop. Fortunately, the firm issued a picture postcard of the trade sign (printed by Ernest Countryman), probably in 1908 or 1909. It represents the earliest photograph of a tin man that I have seen and is the only one that, to my knowledge, can be traced to the first decade of the twentieth century.

The Heaphys passed on the business within the family for four generations. After the firm opened a wholesale hardware on the corner of Richmond Avenue and Geddes Street, tinsmith Jim Gallagher, about 1946, built a second tin man who

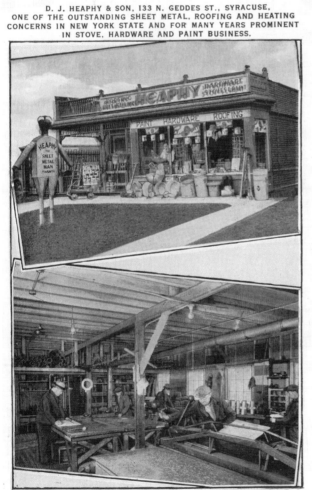

D. J. HEAPHY & SON, 133 N. GEDDES ST., SYRACUSE,
ONE OF THE OUTSTANDING SHEET METAL, ROOFING AND HEATING
CONCERNS IN NEW YORK STATE AND FOR MANY YEARS PROMINENT
IN STOVE, HARDWARE AND PAINT BUSINESS.

SHEET METAL OF ALL KINDS IS FABRICATED HERE

41. Postcard for D. J. Heaphy and Son.

was distinguished by a cowboy hat. The Everson Museum of Art showed it in a 1996 folk-art exhibit on loan from Dennis Heaphy, great-grandson of the founder.

After an automobile "took out" the ventilator-head tin man in the mid–1960s, shop mechanics fabricated another to resemble it and anchored its sheet-metal legs in a patch of grass. Cast-iron sewer pipe and smaller pipes inside reinforced the legs, and the assemblage was set in concrete. In 1984, however, another auto ran into that mass of cement and iron pipe. At the death of the president of the

FOLK ART AT THE EVERSON

Out of the Ordinary— Community Tastes and Values in Contemporary Folk Art

Central New York Folk Art Sampler

On View Through March 3rd

EVERSON MUSEUM OF ART
401 Harrison Street
474-6064
Hours: Tuesday-Friday noon to 5 pm
Saturday 10 am to 5 pm
Sunday noon to 5 pm

TIN MAN SIGN (D. J. Heaphy & Son Inc.), ca. 1946. Arthur Heaphy, designer. Loaned by Dennis Heaphy.

Photo by Hugh Tifft.

Both exhibitions sponsored in Syracuse by Herald-Journal / Herald American and The Post-Standard and members of the George Fisk Comfort Society.

Media sponsorship provided by Adelphia Cable Communications

"Out Of The Ordinary" is sponsored by the Lila Wallace – Reader's Digest Fund and circulated by the Gallery Association of New York State. Other contributors to the exhibition include the New York State Council on the Arts and the National Endowment for the Arts.

42. Folk art at the Everson Museum of Art.

firm, James Heaphy, in 1997, the Onondaga Historical Society acquired the tin man as a gift in his memory.

This bare-bones account does not include the many acts of vandalism against Heaphy's tin man, a fate suffered by all forms of outdoor art, public and private. I am impressed by the care that the company's owners gave to their trade signs. After each car crash or theft of a head, tinsmiths made repairs. In addition, shopmen repainted the tin man every two years, altering the sign's lettering from time to time.

Heaphy's men, as part of the local landscape, inspired imitations. Joseph Saya, a tinner at the General Motors plant, built one in the 1950s. Inheriting the figure, his son placed it outside the Saya tinshop. This tin man wore a bold red and blue *S* on its chest, prompting children to name him Superman. Lincoln Supply placed its man, advertising pipes and fittings, inside its premises. About 1980 Krell Dis-

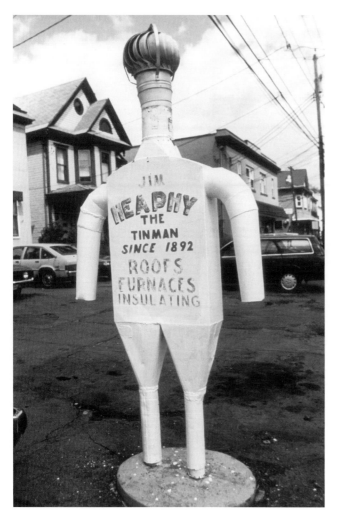

43. Heaphy's tin man.

tribution designed an unusual tin woman "because everyone else had a man" (Davis and Sweet 1985).

Confident that tin men waited to be found, I appealed for friends to enlarge my search. Rachel Epstein (1996) has devoted a book to unusual home mailboxes made of a variety of objects—mufflers, wagon wheels, farm machinery, tools, and gasoline pumps. Among other colorful photographs, she included a happy tin man, slotted oilcan in hand, in Rayville, Louisiana. Because it looked like a tinshop figure, I telephoned A. O. Doughty, its owner, to ask why he had decorated his home instead of his shop. The question intrigued him. After forty years in the sheet-metal business, he could give no simple answer.

In pursuit, I called upon a colleague, Susan Roach, a folklorist at Louisiana Tech University in Ruston. She has been active in charting local traditions and presents her findings at festivals and forums. She had never taken up tinshop "fieldwork," however. Accepting the challenge, she netted photographs and a two-hour audio-taped interview with Doughty and his wife Marie on March 30, 1998. Susan reported on her visit at the American Folklore Society's annual meeting in Anchorage, Alaska, in 2001; here, I offer a summary.

44. A. O. Doughty's mailbox.

Born in Tullos, Louisiana, in 1939, Alvin O. Doughty worked through high school and college summers as an oilfield roustabout, learning to weld. His father had been a "tool pusher" (driller) on rigs, and his grandfather a farmer and preacher. Desiring to be on his own after college, he started in the grain-elevator business, handling soybeans and cottonseed oil. Soon he switched to a small sheet-metal shop, fabricating specialized ventilating and air-cleaning systems for gins, mills, and elevators. The firm, B&D Sheet Metal, proved highly successful and now employs fifty people in a modern plant at Rayville.

Doughty does not fit stereotypes of big-city, blue-collar tinsmith, rural handcraftsman, profit-driven entrepreneur, or southern cavalier of fiction. He has three grown children, lives in the country, participates in the Masonic Order, has two catfish ponds on his land, hunts in the nearby woods, worships in the local Baptist church, and constantly "makes things around the house." Susan Roach listed some of the sheet-metal and stainless steel objects he made for his home: a martin house, barbecue pit, coffee table, fireplace woodrack, windmill catfish feeder, deer stand, duckblind, wind chimes, wood stoves, and a flag pole.

All these objects can be purchased, and Doughty has the means to do so. He derives great satisfaction, however, from his "things" and their sturdy construction and functional lines. At a subliminal level they bridge shop and home. The mailbox conveys the feeling of comfort in both realms. Made in the shop, it works at home. When pressed for the source of his initial idea, Doughty gave no single one. He had seen a muffler mailbox but thought it did not belong in front of a sheet-metal man's residence. Other tinners with whom I spoke also felt it inappropriate to be represented by an auto part.

Conscious of Oz books and film, Doughty provided his tin man with a big red heart. Before fabrication, he sketched the figure, established a seven-foot height, and assisted his shopmen in construction. He used his hands as patterns for the cutout, so, he says, "there is a little of me" in the piece. Of his major industrial installations and decorative objects for home use, the mailbox attracted the most attention. After feature stories in local newspapers brought it some fame, Charles Kuralt presented it to his television audience in 1984. Doughty plans to construct a tin man outside his shop. Unlike the mailbox figure, *Mr. B&D* will not have a visible heart.

In this chapter, and elsewhere in this book, I have viewed tin men through the eyes of others. In lieu of travel and direct observation, friends have conveyed fresh stories, others have sent photographs, and some have challenged my formulations. Here I acknowledge the help of Julia Ardery—poet, scholar, and critic. At every turn she has shared with me the broadest issues raised in folk-art research.

In correspondence, Julie alerted me to Larry Hackley, a Berea, Kentucky, gallery owner who holds a twenty-eight-inch-tall tin man of unknown origin. We speculate that a tinsmith fabricated it because of the special equipment it wears—

45. *The Goggle-Wearer.*

goggles and protective earmuffs. The figure may reflect its maker's consciousness of safety rules or, perhaps, memory of an industrial accident. Hackley's find returns to the question of maker's intent. Unless this tin man's history can be reeled backward, like an audio tape, we will never know all that remains hidden about its message.

I have used the little tin man, purchased by Larry Hackley at a Heartland Antiques Show in Richmond, Indiana, from a New England dealer, and Julia Ardery's provocative questions to focus upon ambiguities in cultural studies. Despite their efforts, Hackley and Ardery do not know who made *The Goggle-Wearer.* By contrast, Aarne Anton or Susan Roach, for example, had the opportunity to talk directly to Rene Latour and A. O. Doughty about their motives in creating eye-catching tin objects.

Whether a tin man reaches a crossroads flea market or posh antique shop, its origin is often a blank. Confronted by such reality, scholars grope for answers to issues of creativity and theorize wildly on assigned meaning for art. We indulge each other endlessly in definitional games. At times, in the name of research we push tinsmiths (and mates in other trades) in unfamiliar directions: commercial market, museum realm, and cloistered academy. We are not always sensitive about meddling in the lives of those from whom we draw strength. Despite such detours, however, our road stretches ahead.

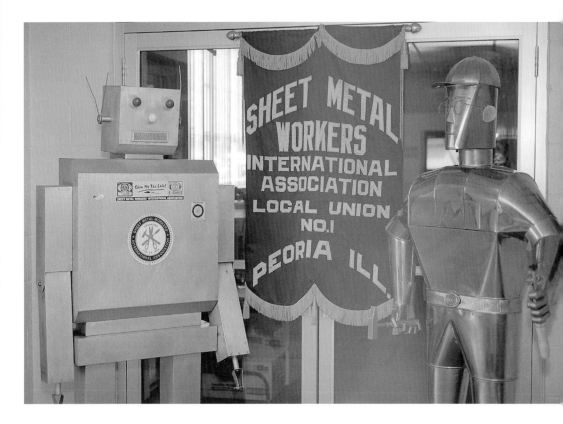

46. Local 1's tin man and copper man.

7 UNDER UNION BANNERS

Many friends will find their discoveries in this book. Among them, Bill Butler in the Washington office of the Sheet Metal Workers' International Association, steered me to the *Sheet Metal Workers' Journal.* Subsequently, the January–February 1996 issue featured "'Tin Men': The Sheet Metal Worker's Human Touch in Metal." *Journal* publisher Phil Airulla used a cover photograph of *Jordan's Squire* in Sebastopol, apple and chicken in his hands, perched atop his shop roof. Airulla also gathered sixteen pictures of shop sites and crews on parade from Anchorage to Boston. He showed the great variety in tin men, leaving open matters of origin. It deepened my wonder at sheet-metal creativity to leaf through back issues of the *Journal.* Under varied names, the publication ran from 1895 to 1933, suspended publication during depression years, and resumed in 1948. The photographs and articles that appeared in the *Journal* and are relevant to this volume are cited in the Appendix and References.

Tin men appeared in the *Journal* sporadically as local unions sent in snapshots of parades, trade shows, or apprentice classes. For example, on Labor Day 1949 Detroit members marched with a "Metal Dingers Band" that rode along with a life-sized tin man in a float pulled by a truck ("Detroit Labor Day Parade Units" 1949). Previously, at the Western Idaho State Fair, Boise apprentices exhibited two men made of standard fittings ("Idaho Local Exhibits Apprenticeship Work" 1950). The *Journal* used photographs of these events to report on a successful apprenticeship program and a Labor Day parade but did not feature the tin men themselves. In May 1951, however, the *Journal* carried a picture and an accompanying column, "'Mr. Sheet Metal,' Robot, Made at No. 124." The story, submitted by the Milwaukee Joint Apprenticeship Committee, is the first I have found that uses the word *robot* to identify tin men.

The relationship between the advertising function of tinshop trade signs and tin men as classroom teaching tools constantly piqued my curiosity. The *Journal* did not explore such parallel uses, but it did offer tantalizing clues. In October 1951 it used a snapshot of the Lueck Sheet Metal Shop on Whidbey Island at Oak Harbor, Washington. A flying horse and a rider are suspended just below the roofline of the shop building. Moreover, the editor requested photographs of "other sheet metal signs which indicate unusual application of the craftsman skill" ("At the Sign of the Tin Horse" 1951).

Future issues carried photographs of many signs but none of tinshop figures. In a two-page spread on the Electrical Products Corporation of Los Angeles, however, the *Journal* ran a photo feature on neon signmaking ("Neon Sign Fabrication" 1958). Three mechanics are shown hovering over a huge metal figure ("like a scene out of Gulliver's Travels") splayed out on the shop floor. Another shot reveals the figure to be a janitor—bucket in one hand and broom in the other—erect on the roof of the American Building Maintenance Company. I admired the bold sign but confess that I wished it to be a tinner holding the tools of his trade.

Earlier in this book, I described *Al's the Tin Man* and *Copper Man* as being made for separate purposes. In detailing the mascot's origin, I noted that instructor Lewis Wittlinger helped advanced students fashion ornamental gifts (lanterns, beer steins, watering cans, flowers in a vase, and picture frames). While selecting their projects, some apprentices also chose utilitarian items such as toolboxes.

The making of an object as a symbol of the completion of a training period dates to the Middle Ages when apprentices often lived but a step removed from servitude. Becoming a journeyman freed an apprentice to wear a guild's livery, travel in search of employment, and, if fortunate, set up his own shop. Regulations demanded a "proof piece" or a "master piece" at the end of indenture. A lightship's globular lantern (depicted on the charter or banner), when crafted by an apprentice at the close of "his time," became a favorite emblem of the longed-for passage to freedom.

The *Journal*'s coverage of tin men focused on instructional or celebratory projects, putting aside the commercial use of trade signs. The emphasis on apprenticeship revealed union labor's long commitment to skilled-trade technical education. Youngsters who favored a medieval lamp, practical toolbox, or whimsical piece could and did step easily to the tasks involved in fashioning a human figure in metal.

Reports on SMWIA training history do not indicate when apprentices were first assigned tin-men fabrication projects. Similarly, no one knows what happened to all the tin men that have been pictured in the *Journal* since 1948. Fortunately, I did learn the history of Seattle's "robot" ("not a man from Mars"). To prepare for the city's Centennial Exposition in 1952, Local 99 instructor S. R. (Bob) Hansen at the Edison Technical School and preparatory student Jack Miller crafted an eight-foot figure, forty-three inches in girth and holding an extended battle lance ("No. 99 Apprentice Makes Robot" 1952). Over the years, the warrior (*Lance Man*) has ridden in labor parades and presided at community rallies.

47. *Lance Man* and Jack Miller.

During the 1980s, the Sheet Metal Workers' International Association consolidated many small unions into statewide or regional locals. In this process, Local 99 and several other units emerged as Local 66. Miller, the former apprentice who by then had been a member for four decades, advanced through the ranks to become Local 66's president. On December 31, 1996, he told me something of his life story as well the origin of *Lance Man*.

In visits with tinsmiths, I seek to learn the setting for their artistry and am continually amazed at the variety of circumstances that surround each item's genesis. Thomas Jackson Miller, born in Seattle on June 16, 1934, knew poverty as a child. When he dropped out of school at age sixteen, a wise social worker steered him to the Edison School. Showing aptitude for mechanical drawing, Jack gravitated to the sheet-metal class. Good fortune intervened when S. R. Hansen selected him to work on the holiday mechanical man.

A newspaper photographer caught teacher and student, their "robot" under construction, and an accompanying story noted that Edison radio and electrical students would give the tin man a head that swiveled, eyes that blinked, and a recorded verbal message ("Edison School Robot" 1951). He would be displayed at the National Guard Armory show from November 12 to 15. Jack labored for two weeks on the "barker," fitting each lock and seam by hand. Hansen stressed line mastery—the ability to transfer parallel, radial, and triangular lines from sketches on paper or blueprints to three-dimensional, lifelike forms.

Miller served a hitch in the army before his initiation into Local 99 on November 15, 1956. For many trade unionists, military service seemed but a preliminary stage to formal apprenticeship. Throughout Jack's decades of membership and over a remarkable variety of jobs spanning good and bad times he has looked back with wonder at his early good luck in having tapped into a happy tradition—replicating the human figure in sheet metal.

When the Seattle SMWIA apprenticeship office moved from the Edison School to the Sno-King (Snohomish and King counties) Sheet Metal School in Kirkland, Washington, *Lance Man*'s guardians substituted ski poles for weapon. His altered appearance marked more than a school site's name change, for the 1951 warrior had tended to tip over. With his new ski poles in each hand he gained considerable stability. The ski poles brought good fortune. The figure has not wrinkled with age, nor has he suffered accidents on the slopes. Safe in a skill-training center and surrounded by modern tools, he has emerged as a symbol of continuity for generations of sheet-metal workers in the Northwest. Jack Miller's creation belongs to a union of men and women who can hang a gutter on a cottage and move on to install sophisticated heating and ventilating gear in a Boeing plant designed to assemble 777 jets.

On March 5, 1997, I visited the SMWIA Kirkland office and training facility. Miller came directly from work to give me the grand tour and show me a series of treasures that included his tin man. By coincidence, Scott Thurnan, a Local 66 organizer, was present that evening and added a significant detail to the figure's history.

Some years earlier, a senior business agent had decided to purge the old Local 99 hall of "junk," including Miller's piece. Fortunately, Ted Eastman, the owner of Advanced Sheet Metal Shop in Lynwood, Washington, volunteered a new home for the orphan. When a few shop mechanics wanted to use the tin man for target practice, Thurnan rescued it by returning it to the Sno-King hall. Thurnan modestly denied any heroism in this preservation effort, yet he reminded me that the life of any tin man is dependent upon the devotion of its makers and guardians.

Chicago Local 73 joined the tin-man procession with a prize-winning St. Patrick's Day parade float built in 1988 at the Washburne Trade School ("Committee Awards First Prize to Local 73" 1988). Union instructor Gene Williams had apprentices take body measurements from each other and design patterns for life-like metal characters. The float marks the entrance of women into the sheet-metal trade; students fabricated six men and women in hard hats and baseball (labor-insignia) caps. The figures, placed amid a garden of tinshop shamrocks, saluted a century of SMWIA craftsmanship. Between festive events, the union's apprenticeship officer, James Slovey, houses the "Chicago Six" at a modern training facility in Bellwood, Illinois. He loans them out for other celebrations, and, sadly, not all have been returned. Whatever the motives of their "liberators," tin men and women generate deep possessive instincts within some people.

48. Local 73's St. Patrick's Day float.

Although I have not canvassed all SMWIA training facilities from coast to coast, I believe that many hold at least one tin man. Gene Yale, Colorado coordinator, has gathered details on men made by Local 9 students in their Denver quarters. Instructor Bob Boosinger initiated the custom in 1986 when he petitioned the Joint Apprenticeship and Training Committee (JATC) to allow apprentices to fabricate "something different" for their fourth-year projects. Traditionally, each graduating student had fabricated one figure, thus guaranteeing continuity in a craft tradition as the union's journeymen move beyond the bounds of Colorado.

Some Local 9 apprentices have taken their tin men home to decorate dens and basement workshops or to serve as garden scarecrows or mailboxes. Wisely, the union has retained a half-dozen figures for use in parades and celebrations and at high school career fairs. The "Denver Six" include a pair of men who are three feet high and "break out" annually to be pulled in red wagons at Labor Day parades.

Local 9's "home" figures constitute a sheet-metal group: *Daddy, Mommy, Baby Boy,* and *Baby Girl. Daddy* (made by apprentice Ben Anthony) sports a head that swivels, and his eyes blink and his heart beats. This "Union Family," assembled for Labor Day and state fair exhibits, also has been put to educational use at career fairs in Denver's Convention Center. The group calls attention to skill in fabricating

49. Local 9's wagon men.

metal products as well as commitment to family values long before that phrase formed a political slogan.

Wichita, Kansas, Local 29 apprenticeship coordinator Dan Ruebbelke has been especially interested in tin men construction and in documenting its tradition. The *Journal* ran two photographs of graduates with three of their "offspring" (Airulla 1996, 7). Ruebbelke photographed his students to celebrate their achievements as they advanced to journeyman rank. One figure that impresses viewers has a massive SMWIA shield on its chest, recalling the tiny union seal embossed on San Francisco Local 104's copper mascot. Labor emblems on tin men function similarly to painted trade-sign messages—for example, "Al's the Tin Man," "Find Us Fast," and "I'm Your Man."

A photograph of a Local 29 Labor Day parade float featuring a tin man placed against a pegboard backdrop had appeared earlier in the *Journal* ("Local 29 Captures First Place" 1984). Four members (Tom Murray, Presley Johnson, Marvin Evans, and Don Hansen) rode on the float, and spectators could view their movements as they mocked the tin man they had built to parody themselves. A second photograph adds complexity to the occasion. Alongside the float's tin man, Tom Murray, in a hard hat, poses with his son Scott, who is dressed like the Tin Woodman. Who, we ask, is real, and who is acting? Still more photographs record the first-place trophy and the Local 29 members and their wives who built the float. In sending the photographs to his national magazine, Local 29 business agent Ron

50. Local 29's Labor Day float.

Weems had noted that Wichita had revived a tradition dormant for three decades. The trophy marked craft skill (assumed as natural by its possessors) and the survival and revival of belief in a Labor Day parade's significance.

In a telephone conversation on November 28, 1996, Don Hansen told me about Local 29's tin figure. Hansen, who had worked at Boeing Aircraft in 1984, had accepted responsibility for the float. He crafted the tin man out of discarded ductwork, rolled out a funnel hat, and added welders' gloves painted silver. Hansen and his mates improvised their mimicry as the parade took its course, and their entry won first prize. Hansen modified the piece for Labor Day 1985, and after 1986 Local 29 displayed the tin man in the window of a sheet-metal shop for several years. Next, a few members took it to their homes for safe-keeping. The tin man finally earned a secure retirement when the union placed him in a new apprenticeship training center in 1997.

In continued correspondence, Dan Ruebbelke reported good news about the new quarters, which had rooms for drafting, reading blueprints, welding, and using advanced shop machinery. To illustrate the new facility's utility, he enclosed photographs of individual apprentices fabricating tin men—altogether a cluster of seven pieces. To complement those portraits, Dan included eye-catching shots of bison welded from discarded automobile bumpers and a tin-can man perched in the corner of a room. By moving visually from classroom tin men to a decorative tin-can man to shaggy-maned bison mounted in an outdoor setting, we see metal artistry put to divergent ends.

The SMWIA rigorously maintains the skills of its training officers, who are called together for frequent sessions. At one such event in San Jose on June 15, 1999, I met Dan Ruebbelke and confirmed my appreciation of his qualities as an instructor. He was highly skilled, curious about trade history, and modest as well. After "turning out" in 1990 and some years in construction, he became the sheet-metal apprenticeship coordinator in Wichita.

Many union teachers assign tin men as fourth-year projects, and Dan Ruebbelke seems especially conscious of the multiple roles these constructs play. He has retained and displayed a baker's dozen of his students' tin men in his classroom and shop, including the 1984 Labor Day figure, as "recruitment agents." A photo feature (Garcia 1998) yielded unanticipated and humorous consequences, however. Dan had wanted local publicity in order to attract additional youngsters to the trade; instead, readers called to request that he build tin men for their homes, gardens, and offices.

In accounts from Seattle, Chicago, Denver, and Wichita I have shown representative examples of tin men made in formal apprentice-training classes. Similar reports tell of their use in related events. Unionists date the origin of Labor Day parades to 1882, although workers in guilds and friendly societies had celebrated saint's days and special holidays for centuries.

51. Dan Ruebbelke and class projects.

The trappings of early festivities appeal to tinsmiths. At the time of Queen Victoria's coronation in 1838, for example, Tin Plate Workers walked in the Liverpool procession dressed in "tin helmets and carrying tin battle-axes and led by a member—clad in full armor—and riding on horseback, they made a medieval and picturesque show. The Braziers displayed the articles they manufactured, such as copper kettles, urns and many other useful domestic and commercial goods in demand at that period" (Kidd 1949, 105).

Craftsmen in all trades still use trade accoutrements for parades and festivals. Each float or construct, enlarged or miniaturized—whether a giant loaf of bread or a model of a castle, cathedral, construction shack, or skyscraper—links messages of pageantry and ideology that the uninitiated sometimes find difficult to read. At one point, a tinsmith replicated the human figure and placed it on a parade float.

Illustrations of early Labor Days show cornices and other fancy architectural ornaments made by metalsmiths. On occasion, the *Journal* runs old photographs, useful now for tracing this custom, sent by members. The 1910 parade in Mt. Morris, Illinois, included "tin hats made of furnace metal worn by the craftsmen on the float" ("From a Bygone Labor Day" 1958). In 1913 marchers in Joliet, Illinois, sported metal shields, and Denver paraders posed in 1916 carrying tin umbrellas ("Putting on the Ritz" 1961; "Labor Day Paraders Sport Tin Umbrellas" 1966). Tinners stepped easily from hats, shields, or umbrellas to entire costumes made of tin. In 1968 seven members (and a child) in Local 220 of Aurora-Elgin, Illinois, won first prize on Labor Day for their robot dress. They repeated their success in 1969 by dressing as space cadets and standing in front of a flying saucer.

During the 1960s, tin men became associated with science fiction, just as images from *The Wizard of Oz* had taken hold after the 1939 film. In 1982 apprentices in Grand Rapids, Michigan, fabricated a Tin Woodman holding an axe for the United Way "Have a Heart" campaign. In its account of the event, the *Journal* first used *tin man* as a naming term ("His Heart Is in the Right Place" 1982). The *Journal* noted Cleveland's Labor Day parade in 1988 with a photograph of Local 33's Ralph Heimburger in a tin suit. Flexible tubing for arms and legs and a ventilator headpiece set him apart from the figure from the Land of Oz. Detroit Local 80's David Reginek, also in a tin costume, greeted guests at the 1995 AFL-CIO Union Industries Show (Airulla 1996, 7). As the custom continues, the line between making a tin man and dressing like one becomes blurred.

Massachusetts Local 17 strutted in a Dad's Day parade at Boston dedicated to diabetes research. Business manager Joe Nigro seemed especially jaunty in a funnel hat, flamboyant necktie, flag decal, and tin boutonniere as he gathered coins for his community's afflicted (Airulla 1996, 8). In addition to good deeds, the human tin men relished the circularity that their costumes implied—tinners who make tin men dressing as the figures they have made.

52. Labor Day robots, Local 220.

53. Living tin men, Local 17.

For some years, Labor Day has declined in importance as a workers' holiday. It now marks the end of summer, a vacation weekend, or department store sales. Yet the need persists to honor toil, display craft skill, reveal commitment to cause, dress outrageously, and march in unison. Occasionally, however, other events serve these purposes, and locals, large or small, find novel ways to celebrate.

New York Local 28, for example, is well aware of its early origins. Colonial guilds of whitesmiths, coppersmiths, and tin-plate workers gave way to "modern" trade unions in the Civil War era. The Knights of Labor emerged after the war as the dominant workers' organization, and after 1886 the American Federation of Labor overshadowed the Knights. For many decades, New York's tinsmiths actively participated in internal battles within rival sheet-metal unions. Local 28 traces its roots far back to the soil of New Amsterdam's fur traders, but its present charter dates to 1913. Because of centuries-old traditions and Manhattan's pivotal role in national life, New York tinners have experienced all the problems faced by workers in urban and industrial America, whether boom, bust, technological change, shifts in work-force composition, conflict over membership, challenges to status, or political earthquakes.

I leave Local 28's history to others; here I report only on its use of tin men in more recent celebratory events. In a Labor Day 1998 photograph by Joe Doyle, a tin man towers over a float that carries models of many sleek buildings. The symbolism is superb. From the erection of the first steel-frame structure, Manhattan's sheet-metal workers, alongside other crafts, literally left their handprints on the

54. Local 28's entry in
Labor Day parade.

island's skyline. Local 28's training instructor Nicholas Maldarelli, assisted by apprentices, fabricated its Labor Day tin man and innovative float.

During June of 1999 the local recycled the float for New York's annual Puerto Rican Day parade. A tin-suited member marched alongside, a substitute for Maldarelli's mute metal man stored safely at the union's Jamaica, Long Island, training center. The marcher engaged spectators in banter as the float progressed along the parade route. The contrast in parade strategies is instructive. Labor Day called for a tin man symbolizing Local 28's place in the city's physical growth; Puerto Rican Day, however, required attention to the union's participation in the turbulent life of the community at large.

In New York and elsewhere throughout America, native-born workers and immigrants together manned industry and built labor organizations. Often, however, the "ins" and "outs" bitterly contested the very meaning of trade unionism. Occasionally, idealists led the fight to open membership to those previously excluded. Thus, replicas of skyscrapers accompanied by a man in a tin costume tell us that the Puerto Rican Day parade float saluted one of the local's constituent groups and also marked the long internal struggle over minority rights in trade unions.

Here, I digress to comment briefly on how outside scholars and activists influence union activity. Elsewhere, I have described my role during 1971 in bringing industrial-urban workers to the Smithsonian Institution's Festival of American Folklife on the National Mall (Green 1993). On completing this book, I was equally surprised and delighted to learn that Local 28 members, along with their tin man and buildings float, had participated in the event in 2001.

Photographer Martha Cooper had shown several shots of Local 28 at Labor Day and Puerto Rican Day parades in Manhattan to Nancy Groce, a Smithsonian curator. Subsequently, Groce invited the union to demonstrate its skill as part of the Masters of the Building Arts Program. Members fabricated a sparkling new skyline for the float's trip to Washington, adding copper and brass to "dress up" its skyscrapers. Instead of rolling in a street parade, however, the float remained stationary at its site on the Mall. Behind it, a backdrop of tents housed tinners who explained job techniques and trade customs to spectators. Festival staff and Local 28 members led open-air workshops at which old-timers explained matters as diverse as fabricating a tin man or how Local 28 opened it rolls to newcomers.

55. Local 28's float at the Festival of American Folklife.

The event can be interpreted in several ways, one of which follows: New York tinners had established strong unions before the 1888 chartering of the SMWIA. Local 28's members had made trade signs for a least a century but never documented that custom. A photographer and a folklorist sensed the educational potential in the tinsmiths' float on the National Mall. What meaning do we ascribe to a tin man who neither announces a shop nor reflects the training of apprentices?

Sheet-metal workers now participate in folk festivals as well as in Labor Day and various community parades, such as those for Dad's Day and St. Patrick's Day, and the Puerto Rican and West Indian carnivals. That involvement deserves full commentary and analysis, although I will focus only on a few SMWIA locals to suggest the range of expression that tin men convey.

Workers often grope for the appropriate words to convey pride or skill. Tinsmiths who have mastered the science of reading blueprints become strangely inarticulate at describing their genius. "He's a good mechanic" sums up much virtue, and "it just comes naturally" explains the most advanced techniques. Not everyone on a shop floor or in a classroom makes a tin man, yet the command of enough requisite skill to do so is widespread in the trade.

Those who build tin men for a celebration or an advertising sign can also dress in metal and march in a parade. It is fun to flaunt bright costumes and strange accouterments and act the wise fool in miming life or to mask mechanical cunning. Tinsmiths, like other workers, find it satisfying to give play to creative impulses. Under union banners the roles of parader and artisan merge.

Sensing such convergence, I have been puzzled by the distance between the art domain (artists, dealers, collectors, critics, and curators) and the Sheet Metal Workers' International Association. I have met many skilled craftsmen who are fully aware of their creative talents, yet they remain uncomfortable when tagged as "folk artist" or "modern sculptor" and usually avoid both terms. For some, the word *folk* seems to connote crudity, simplicity, and lack of command in trade discipline. At the other pole, the word *sculptor* seems to imply strange vision, artificiality, and an inability to make a living.

Because they have long created objects of esthetic appeal, tinsmiths temper their ambivalence, however. Art and artisanship meet on many jobs. For a century, the *Sheet Metal Workers' Journal* has reported upon or depicted objects of unusual beauty made by members. Sheet-metal workers who heat and cool museum galleries are not blind to exhibitions of folk or fine art. A few mechanics speak directly to curators; others craft artifacts to mimic or complement gallery items. Occasionally, gifted tinsmiths work collaboratively with artists or architects within museum walls.

I have treated tin-man signs as constructs sharing utilitarian and artistic roles. We cannot always discern one use from the other, but sometimes there are features that help in analysis. Only a few of the figures pictured in these pages have visible marks of being crafted by unionists, although Local 104's *Copper Man* lives with a tiny union label embossed on his chest. I am not concerned, however, with establishing formal credentials for all tin men; indeed, I am conscious that tinners unaffiliated with organized labor have also fabricated such icons.

For more than a century, the SMWIA has supported rigorous apprenticeship training in metal-trades shops on construction sites and in industries as diverse as railroading, shipbuilding, space exploration, and information technology. Individual students have many venues in which to relate craft skill to the intangibles mentioned by instructors: heritage, legacy, artistry, and respect. Perhaps those outside the skilled trades find it difficult to grasp the full meaning of union apprenticeship programs for those who seek both practical knowledge and a sense of tradition. As soon as enrollment begins, apprentices feel that they are immersed in an ancient, if not holy, circle.

We glimpse this esoteric realm in a little guidebook issued in London in 1747: *A General Description of All Trades, Digested in Alphabetical Order. . . .* Aimed alike at parents and youngsters, it gave prospective hours, wages, and conditions for many occupations, including the Company of Tinplate Workers, which was incorporated in 1670 during the reign of Charles II. Although that guild preceded the Sheet Metal Workers' International Association by centuries, the latter group depends as heavily on formal apprenticeship for institutional continuity as did the former. Contemporary apprentices who encounter the book might be puzzled by indenture articles and survivals or other ancient rules. Those trappings are now preludes to demanding modern training in mathematics, blueprint reading, computers, and working with other cutting-edge equipment. Teachers who show their versatility by adding tin-man fabrication to advanced design problems serve their trade well.

Tin men studied in isolation do not demonstrate the full range of creative endeavor within SMWIA ranks. Craft artistry lives in many union programs beyond apprenticeship. In January 1988, for example, the SMWIA celebrated its centennial with a dramatic exhibition at Washington's National Building Museum, which had originally been designed by Gen. Montgomery Meigs to house the pension office for Civil War veterans. For that show, as a centerpiece to contrast with the site's formal setting and highlight the evolution in building practices, Los Angeles architect Frank Gehry conceived of a spiraling, geometric structure of copper, brass, zinc, aluminum, and galvanized iron.

Gehry's "flower" had no name. It "grew" between ornate Corinthian columns to dazzle critics and casual visitors alike. Gehry had squeezed a modern offshoot of the Eiffel Tower into a decorated, candy-box space—the old building's Grand Hall. To erect the monument, the SMWIA brought together a pick-up crew of outstanding competence, hard-hats eager to turn blueprints into a soaring wonderland.

Years later I was fortunate in meeting Frank Ulrich, a SMWIA retiree whose career had spanned "dingbatting" (working on jerry-built tract housing), a stint as San Francisco Local 104 president, and "membership" in the crew selected to build the Gehry project in Washington. Ulrich recalled wryly that the flower was not fastened to the rug-covered marble floor but rather rested on plywood sheets. Being asymmetrical in design, it swayed and quaked under construction, reminding the tinsmiths of a ship in stormy seas.

Ringing Gehry's tower at floor level, the curators displayed a set of tools and artifacts, ancient and modern. Snips, shears, soldering irons, hammers, cornice, cupola, barn-roof ornament, ventilator, downspout, duct, and a majestic lion's head—perhaps from a hidden garden—pulled viewers from fantasy above to objects at eye level. Gehry or Chase could also have called for a tin man to greet museum visitors at the door. Come inside! See what we have fashioned! Marvel at our craft!

At the end of the centennial show the SMWIA marvel came down sheet by sheet, unit by unit. Curators David Chase and Carolyn Laray had edited a handsome catalog, *Sheet Metal Craftsmanship: Progress in Building* (1988), to commemorate Gehry's centerpiece. Before the show's opening the *Washington Post*'s Paul Hendrickson interviewed some of the sixty-five tin-knockers, including Ulrich, who had translated architect's sketch into physical plane and angle (Hendrickson 1988). Similarly, Nick Carter, editor of the trade journal *Snips,* featured the exhibit in his February issue.

Despite the unexplained absence of a traditional trade-sign figure, the SMWIA centennial exhibit—riveting artistry to job skill—was a comment on the experience of every tinsmith who has touched the wall that divides worker from artist, intellectual, or antiquarian. At the show's close, the museum staff dismantled the Gehry structure and scattered the complementary artifacts. An unusual chain of circumstance preserved one object from the exhibit, however—a palm tree—and it can still be seen. The wondrous tree stands in the atrium of the Carlough Plaza, the headquarters of the Sheet Metal Workers' National Pension Fund in Arlington, Virginia. It could have grown in Camelot. Instead, it arrived from Kansas City, Missouri, fabricated in A. Zahner's shop by members of SMWIA Local 2. In 1981 New York architect Robert Stern had designed a pair of palm trees to be made of brass, stainless steel, and anodized aluminum for a swimming-pool pavilion. In 1988 the exhibition planners replicated the trees but from a new product—colored stainless steel made through light-interference technology in which a wavelength of light undergoes changes induced by an encounter with another wavelength.

At the centennial show's end, Frank Bonadino, a retired union officer, won the tree in a fund-raising raffle and donated it to the Sheet Metal Workers' National Pension Fund. In turn, the fund "planted" the tree at its Arlington headquarters. The abstract palm, safe in an atrium that houses other metal sculptures, overlooks

56. A lion's head, Sheet Metal Worker's International Association's centennial exhibition.

the Potomac River. Its association with architect, fabricators, curators, and donor has receded. No utilitarian tin man has yet matched the palm tree's good fortune in being accessible to viewers.

A visit to Garden Grove, California—Local 102's Orange County Joint Apprenticeship Committee—on April 14, 1997, reinforced my sense of the impact of association when artists, architects, and shop mechanics meet on common ground. Training officer Leslie Reinmiller has a copy of the National Building Museum's poster marking Gehry's 1988 construct. One of the few women apprenticeship teachers in the international union, she sets high standards for her charges. Her students may or may not know the storms stirred by Gehry's designs, but the poster sends a powerful message about innovation to all who see it.

The commemorative poster remains as a visible reminder of the union's centennial and its cooperative venture with a distinguished architect. By good fortune, the Baltimore Museum of Industry acquired some of the tools and artifacts that had been displayed in Washington and added them to its Sheet-Metal Gallery collection. The permanent exhibit includes a palm tree that is a twin to the Zahner tree in the Carlough atrium; some fine examples of decorative tin cans for Christmas fruitcake, plug tobacco, candy, and cosmetics; and a proud weathervane rooster. The gallery also displays a functional shop equipped with a full supply of tools and several items produced (skylights, ducts, and a ventilator, leaderbox, and gutter). Sadly, however, no tin man from Maryland shares museum space in Baltimore.

In the same year as the Gehry exhibit, Peoria Local 1 celebrated its one-hundredth anniversary on March 26, 1988. A century before, Robert Kellerstrass, secretary of the Peoria tinners' union, had called for a national organization. Seven locals responded, and in January 1888 they formed the Tin, Sheet-Iron and Cornice Workers' International Association (predecessor of the present SMWIA) in Toldeo, Ohio. Like other natal events, the Toledo gathering generated several markers. When Frank Nolden, who had been Peoria's oldest member, died on December 28, 1931, his obituary stated that he had won the coveted designation of Number 1 for his local in a drawing at the 1888 convention. Hence, Peoria tinsmiths have been especially conscientious in celebrating their anniversary.

An unusual object appeared among mementos displayed at the centennial party: a tin "mister" used to moisten tobacco leaves before they were rolled into cigars. For the purposes of this book, I would have preferred a tin man to a mister and a recollection of having crafted a shop sign rather than a memory of a lottery. We report what comes to hand, however, in our studies.

Local 1's business agent Jerry Pyatt noted in a June 17, 1998, letter that apprentices "fabbed a robot about twenty-five years ago," and recently that year fourth-year apprentices had "fabbed a more impressive copper man." Mike Matejka of the *Livingston and McLean Counties Union News* photographed the pair standing in the

Peoria hall with the local's banner between them. The union does not hide its sculptures as do some private collectors, but neither does it consider them to be "public art" and available to everyday viewers.

By contrast, St. Louis Local 36 and the area chapter of the Sheet Metal and Air Conditioning Contractors' Association also possess in their jointly owned training facility a tin-man pair that function dually as both sculpture and costume. The pair resides inside the center on private display and, on occasion, outside on public display under a miniature of St. Louis's graceful arc of stainless steel. Six-hundred feet high, the Gateway Arch at the Mississippi River's edge commemorates western migration in the United States.

Sheet-metal workers, along with other skilled tradesmen, built the Arch in 1965, and they are justly proud of their part in erecting Eero Saarinen's masterpiece. Appropriately, Local 36 members have fabricated a twelve-foot model at its training center to remind apprentices and the public of tinsmiths' contributions to the cultural landscape. Although tinners as a rule do not document their tin men and related artifacts, training officer Dan Andrews, in response to questions from outsiders, is seeking information about the age of his local's sculptures, who designed them, and who conceived of the Arch as a fitting backdrop.

When the miniature Arch and tin men go outside, the pieces "open up," permitting apprentices to dress in the stiff clothing. The *Ste. Genevieve Herald* described the costumes worn at the training center's metal ribbon-snipping ceremony as a "cross between the famed metal man in the Wizard of Oz and some of the more flamboyant mythic metal heros of Japanese cartoons" ("New Location" 1988). Chris Duspiwa, fitting a tin-man suit on fellow apprentice Adam Andrews, captured the convergence of play-at-work and work-as-play built into a tinner's ethos.

To my knowledge, except for a few items in the *Journal* no SMWIA member has written critically about tin men. Among sculptors and collectors, only Michael Hall has studied the aesthetic codes of tinsmiths and raised questions about tin men as they moved from union hall and tinshop to art mart and museum gallery. Seeking to pin down sources, Hall asserted in 1988 that ready-made shapes in shop bins or racks suggest "figurative forms" to workers. Like carvers who see faces longing to be free in wood or stone, tinners see body elements in flanges, ducts, elbows, and other standard parts. Beyond such "special sight," Hall noted, tinners also possess the skill to "translate information from flat patterns into forms in the round." The process is similar to sewing a contour-hugging gown from a bolt of cloth and a paper pattern.

With shop parts at hand, the tinner adds imagination and skill to his tin-man design and fabrication project. Fortunately, he has old tools at hand—hammer, snips, and soldering iron—as well as shop machines. Brakes fold metal, shears cut it, beaders add ridges to tubes, and crimpers texture metal. Whether working with hand tools or computer-guided machines, the mechanic envisions a tin man styled

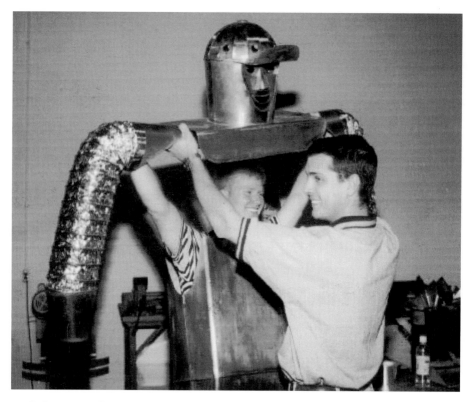

57. St. Louis Local 36 apprentices "dress up."

upon popular images (mental templates) before and after Oz: clown, cowboy, as-
tronaut, robot, warrior, athlete, runway model, and movie queen. Some resemble
Frank Baum's Tin Woodman. Others, elegant in modernity, might have been born
under Frank Gehry's construct in the National Building Museum. Still others,
antiques in their own time, seem to have been destined for folk-art status. We accept the different appearances in the knowledge that all crafted for shop display
have shared a common goal: Come into my lair!

The *Sheet Metal Workers' Journal* has pictured tin men made as teaching tools
made in apprenticeship classes. Like their counterparts in commercial shops, they
also have wide contrast in shape and style. Perhaps I have challenged some colleagues in linking pieces made in tinshops with those made in classrooms. Purposes do differ, although fabrication techniques are similar. In correspondence
with collectors, I have learned that some purchase their finds at flea markets and
art fairs. In such cases it often becomes difficult, if not impossible, to identify a tin
man's source.

Assessing the meaning of trade signs and teaching tools demands close attention, as it does for other art objects. Over the years, advertising has become a less
important function of trade signs. Among the many factors that have contribut-

ed to the decline is the fact that tinshops have moved from city centers to the outskirts of town and no longer depend on passers-by to see their trade emblems. Meanwhile, the tin man as an instructional aide has thrived in SMWIA classes after most commercial shops abandoned the practice of crafting their own figures. Current apprentice instructors know that by assigning tin-man projects they prepare their charges for varied work, for integrating skill and imagination in these tasks, and, ultimately, for membership in an ancient guild linking artistry to artisanship. We glimpse such antiquity in the chapter ahead.

58. *Hephaistos.*

8 HEPHAISTOS AND AUTOLYCUS

Tinsmiths concerned with the realities of making a living also deal on occasion with intangibles in their culture. Some mark celebratory events—a local's anniversary, an old-timer's retirement, a Labor Day parade, or an apprenticeship skills competition—by noting respect for the trade's longevity. It seems easier to articulate "my trade is ancient" than to boast "I am special."

Technical manuals and apprentice-instruction guides add to workers' esteem by citing classical passages. Guild, labor, and industrial histories, too, call up myth to certify antiquity. Philip Flower's *A History of the Trade in Tin: A Short Description of Tin Mining and Metallurgy* (1880) is as much at home in the classics as it is in technology. Flower, writing in Queen Victoria's era, opens by citing a passage from Lord Derby's translation of *The Iliad* concerning Vulcan, the Roman god of fire and metalwork:

> He left her thus, and to his forge returned;
> The bellows then directing to the fire,
> He bade them work; through twenty pipes at once
> Forthwith they poured their diverse-tempered blasts;
> Now briskly seconding his eager haste,
> Now at his will, and as the work required.
> The stubborn brass, and tin, and precious gold,
> And silver, first he melted in the fire,
> Then on its stand his weighty anvil placed;
> And with one hand the hammer's ponderous weight
> He wielded, while the other grasped the tongs.

And first a shield he fashioned, vast and strong,
With rich adornment; circled with a rim,
Threefold, bright gleaming, whence a silver belt
Depended; of five folds the shield was formed;
And on its surface many a rare design
Of curious art his practiced skill had wrought.

Thereon were figured earth, and sky, and sea,
The ever-circling sun, and full-orbed moon,
And all the signs that crown the vaults of Heaven;
Pleiads and Hyads, and Orion's might,
And Arctos, called the Wain, who wheels on high
His circling course, and on Orion waits;
Sole star that never bathes in the ocean wave.

And two fair populous towns were sculptured there;
In one were marriage pomp and revelry,
And brides, in gay procession, through the streets
With blazing torches from their chambers borne,
While frequent rose the hymeneal song.
Youths whirled around in joyous dance, with sound
Of flute and harp; and standing at their doors,
Admiring women on the pageant gazed.

Flower assumed that readers of a book on tin-plate manufacturing were familiar with Homer's *Iliad*. They would appreciate an account of Vulcan's skill in decorating a metal shield and understand the reference to "sole star." Contemporary readers curious about the connection of tinsmith artistry to an ancient deity (Vulcan in Rome and Hephaistos in Greece) will find Richmond Lattimore's edition of *The Iliad* (1962) instructive.

Book 18 takes up the fatal dangers that Achilles faced at Troy. His sea-nymph mother Thetis approaches Hephaistos, god of artificers, to make a stout shield for her son. At the forge, the smith toils with precious gold and silver, valuable tin, and enduring bronze. The shield becomes a universe of earth, sky, sun, moon, and the constellations. On its decorative surface, plowed fields and abundant vineyards scatter their riches, towns enjoy feasts and festivals, and young people dance. Hephaistos has wrought defensive armor of sacred power, but, sadly, the shield cannot save Achilles from death.

We expect Homer to treat the smith-god with reverence; he who tames fire, lives in volcanoes, and builds implements of war and peace deserves respect. Over the span of centuries, the power of Hephaistos/Vulcan declined, along with that of related gods. With the rise of new religions, Christians and other believers reduced the deities to characters in children's stories.

Vulcan, son of Mighty Zeus, had been depicted as a lame artificer faithfully toiling at forge or anvil. By Chaucer's time, however, the image of an actual tin worker had devolved into a ragged itinerant, mender of kitchenware, or peddler. In time, the word *tinker* itself acquired negative tones—gypsy, bungler, knave, rogue, and lecher. It was said that to mend a kettle "to cure one hole, the tinker makes two."

William Shakespeare's *Winter's Tale* introduces Autolycus, a tinker/peddler/con-man/ballad-seller (IV, 3). He enters singing "when daffodils begin to peer" to mark spring's arrival and the joy he anticipates in thievery and tumbles in the hay with "aunts" (whores). Autolycus punctuates his song by claiming past princely service and resumes with a vagabond's stanza. He closes:

> If tinkers may have leave to live,
> And bear the sow-skin budget,
> Then my account I well may give,
> And in the stocks avouch it.

Dual readings follow: Custom allows tinkers to live by carrying tool bags, obvious symbols of recognition. If punished in the stocks for vagrancy, I'll vouch for my true calling as a tinker (artisan) and seek release (Shakespeare 1963, 81). The word *budget,* an early term for a tinner's leather bag, recalls a time when it was cheaper to secure pigskin than to construct a metal toolbox. Peddlers also extended the word to mean an ordinary pack or a purse. Autolycus may never have worked with tools. Thus, in the stocks he'd vouch that he was a peddler and that his pigskin pack held trinkets, linen, ballads, and such delights (Shakespeare 1995, 126).

Autolycus served Shakespeare as a tinker/trickster, handy with song and jest but ultimately ambiguous as an occupational figure. Did he ever wield hammer and snips, or is it more likely that he lived only by his wits? At one point he acknowledges having married a tinker's widow—probably a cynical ploy to gain her late husband's tools and trade credentials.

Beyond questioning Autolycus' place as tradesman, I ask whether Shakespeare had observed tinsmiths filling new roles in society as work conditions altered with feudalism's decline. Without firm answers at hand, we remain free to pair Hephaistos and Autolycus as polar models for workers today. I do not imply that only Homer praised the smith-god or that Shakespeare alone portrayed the rogue-tinker. Deities and vagabonds appeared in European literature; four English works are among those that reflect the then-prevalent portraits of tinkers.

Thomas Harman's *A Caveat or Warning for Common Cursetors, Vulgarly Called Vagabonds* (1930 [1566]) includes "A Drunken Tinker" who carouses when he is not stealing kettles, chafers, or pewter dishes. Robert Greene's *The Second Part of Conny-Catching* (1966 [1592]) recounts a "true and merry tale of a knight and a tinker that was a picklock." A knight tricks a thieving tradesman by sending him with a sealed letter to a Lancaster jailer, who in turn hangs the dupe. Thomas Dekker's *The Wonderfull Yeare* (1966 [1603]) tells of a tinker who honors the god Pan by striking his copper cauldron so sweetly that bees empty their hives and swarm after him. Hired by an innkeeper to dispose of a Londoner dead by the plague, he happily strips the diseased's body of clothes and purse and exits with a song.

An unknown London author in 1630 published six tales in a volume entitled *The Tincker of Turvey,* which was based on an earlier gathering, *The Cobler of Canterburie* (1852 [1590]). Both were ultimately derived from Chaucer's *Canterbury Tales.* The use of Turvey as the Tincker's home is choice, for it invokes the realm of topsy-turvy—Cockaigne, Alice's Wonderland, and the Big Rock Candy Mountain. In this upside-down land, tradesmen do very little work. As tricksters, they enjoy goblet, jest, or sport as well as carnal pleasures. In popular literature, tinkers hammered out music while roaming the countryside with disreputable companions.

Parallel to tales of pot-menders, hole-stoppers, and kettle-beaters, composers built upon the theme of tinkers as lusty lovers. In 1616 John Trundle registered in England's Stationers Office (copyright) a black-letter ballad, "A Pleasant New Songe of a Jouiall [Jovial] Tinker." Under related names ("Room for a Jovial Tinker," "Old Brass to Mend," and "Jolly Tinker") it has been sung for four centuries, sometimes as a bawdy narrative entitled "The Highland Tinker." Variants are found among the Roxburghe and Pepys collections of ballads as well as in modern collections (Kennedy, ed. 1975, 405; Pinto and Rodway, eds. 1957, 279; Warner, ed. 1984, 177).

The manufacture of paper and the growth of printing technology made it possible to issue cheap, single sheets of ballads, usually called "broadsides" or "street ballads" and often decorated with a crude woodcut. Among these illustrations is one of an Elizabethan tinker, first used in Trundle's "Pleasant new Songe." The tradesman, a budget over his shoulder, holds a hammer in one hand and a pot in the other as he contemplates a candlestick, flagon, and teapot on a nearby table. Does he see the tableware as potential work to either savor or dread? The woodcut has been recycled and used with other song texts, and it remains one of the few representations of tinners in the Shakespearian era.

Early in this book I introduced Kupfferschmidt and Ferblanquier as representing dual tinsmith traditions. Poets, playwrights, novelists, and artists have all limned workers as heroes, villains, or humans caught between these poles. We can imagine that the German coppersmith acted out Hephaistos' godlike virtues while the French whitesmith lived in Autolycus' flawed shadow. Not only were this pair, seen in prints, obviously old, but they also symbolize attitudes governing work today. Kupfferschmidt produces and Ferblanquier promotes. Despite a consumption-based economy, the biblical injunction of honest toil still guides many workers.

I do not suggest that contemporary sheet-metal mechanics spend their evenings reading the Scriptures, deconstructing Homer and Shakespeare, leafing through rare books of trades and costume histories, or resolving problems that

A pleaſant new Songe
of a iouiall Tinker.
To a pleaſant new tune, called, Fly Braſſe.

There was a iouiall Tinker
  dwelt in the towne of Thurbie,
And he could mende a Kettle well,
  but his humors were but ſcuruie.
Yet ſtill would he cry,
  Tincke, tincke, tincke,
Tara ra ring tincke, tincke,
  Roome for a iolly drinker:
He would ſtop one hole, and make two,
  was not this a iouiall Tinker.

He was as good a fellow
  as Smugge, which made much laughter:
Full little would you thinke that in his drinke,
  he would beat both his Wife and Daughter.
Yet ſtill would he cry,
  Tincke, tincke, tincke,
Tara ra ring tincke, tincke,
  Roome for a luſty drinker:
He would ſtop one hole, and make two,
  was not this a iouiall Tinker.

He walked about the Countrey
  with Pike-ſtaffe and with Budget: (Rat,
Full little would ye wat, when he was drunke as a
  how trimly he would trudge it.
Yet ſtill would he cry,
  Tincke, tincke, tincke,
ra ra ring tincke, tincke,
Ta Roome for a luſty drinker:
  e would ſtop one hole, and make two,
  was not this a iouiall Tinker.

There's none of his profeſſion,
  was ere ſo ſkull'd in Mettle:
For he could mende your Frying-pan,
  your Skellet, and your Kettle.
Yet ſtill would he cry,
  Tincke, tincke, tincke,
Tara ra tincke, tincke,
  Roome for a luſty drinker:
He would ſtop one hole and make two,
  was not this a iouiall Tinker,

Hee'd toſſe the iolly Tankard,
  the Blacke-pot, and the Pitcher:
No Ale or Beere for him was deere,
  to make his Noſe the richer.
Yet ſtill would he cry
  Tincke, tincke-&c.

Hee walked to Fayres and Markets,
  to furniſh his red Noſe:
And when he was drunke, would beat his Punck
  and make her pawne her Clothes.
Yet ſtill would he cry,
  Tincke, tincke, &c.

Who was it durſt moleſt him?
  his Braſſe did him inuiron:
Sargeants arreſt, yet he was bleſt,
  for he was baylo with Iron.
Yet ſtill would he cry,
  Tincke, tincke, tincke. &c.
    FINIS.

59. An Elizabethan tinker.

have confounded philosopher-kings. They do, however, under certain circumstances feel morality's voice and antiquity's hand in classroom, workshop, and union hall. On occasion, instructors employ literary allusions as they display a handcrafted piece or help apprentices in patterning and assembling a special project. Normally, the blueprint, building-code manual, cost "specs," and union contract govern work. Nevertheless, on a few jobs a sense of the past still echoes.

Particularly on preservation work, ancient wisdom guides today's practices. In the mid–1950s, for example, I worked on the restoration of St. Mary the Virgin Episcopal Church in San Francisco. Conscious that it was the oldest such church in California and built of native redwood, the crew gave every detail special care. Whether encasing new structural-steel columns in redwood trim, rebuilding the bell tower "as before," or installing and disguising modern heating and ventilating gear, we gained, as if by osmosis, something of theological thought. Strange as it sounds, we were touched by our environment.

St. Mary's might have been bulldozed and a new church erected in its place, but parishioners decided to save the old. The mechanics on the job, hired regardless of creed, performed superbly. We knew this to be a once-in-a lifetime project. It carried great prestige and provided something to talk about. Workers do distinguish among jobs, usually as good or bad, hard or easy. At times, however, the contrast is old against new. The former includes preservation, restoration, remodeling, and disaster repairs.

Although some new work lodges in memory, much old work—however difficult or challenging—is memorable. The tag "blue-collar preservationist," whether on cathedral, cottage, or clipper ship, ensures continuity against large forces of change. Sheet-metal workers have long had the skills to maintain and restore old structures. As every experienced hand knows, a metal roof or gutter begins to deteriorate the day it is installed. Hence, an instinct for preservation comes with a tinsmith's first days at the trade.

While reading the *Sheet Metal Workers' Journal,* I was impressed by the number of articles that dealt with members' participation in preservation work. For example, Lucy the tin elephant, built in 1881 to promote a beach in Margate, New Jersey, near Atlantic City, had deteriorated and was facing demolition ("Local 43 Members Restore 'Lucy' the Elephant" 1978). Concerned citizens raised funds to save the landmark. Tinners for Thomas Roofing and Sheet Metal clad it with twelve thousand square feet of tin and lead, fabricating Lucy's "skin" on-site, piece by piece. Even Lucy's tusks were made of sheet metal. No one knows how many photographs visitors have taken of the elephant since its original construction, but five accompanied the *Journal*'s story. Like other outdoor metal structures, Lucy demands constant attention against physical deterioration. A picture postcard issued by the Save Lucy Committee has aided in preservation efforts. The editor of the *Journal,* commenting on the contribution of tinsmiths to the endeavor, noted that

60. Lucy the Elephant.

Lucy "stands as a symbol of the Victorian Era in America, which was a time of gilded opulence."

Trade-union magazines do not often comment on Victoria, Homer, or Shakespeare. I do not suggest more than a metaphoric tie between Lucy the Elephant, the god Hephaistos, and the scoundrel Autolycus. Taken together, however, they illustrate one of the ways in which sheet-metal heritage operates. A trade as old as metalsmithing never succeeds in escaping antiquity's hand. Mechanics who cope daily with science-fiction techniques sense that ancient voices guide them—whispering advice, offering tips, chiding bad practice, reminding tested precedent, and cheering fine work. The language of the classics in all its majesty flows from library shelf to shop floor to outside job and back again. Hephaistos, Autolycus, and their many peers in legend and ballad live.

61. *The Dean.*

9 COLLECTORS AND CURATORS

Only a few collectors and curators have explored the tin man legacy, and few have gone beyond fragmentary reports. Michael D. Hall (1988) provides the best overview in a pioneering study that combines technical detail, cultural history, popular iconography, and visits to sheet-metal mechanics at their places of employment. Hall, who seems at ease within a tinshop's confines, talks to tin-knockers as one creative artist to another, seeking to comprehend the "vocabulary of shapes" they share in common.

Hall lends meaning to the terms of a tinner's lexicon; circles, squares, and ellipses are described as being "rife with figuration." The ability to comprehend the visual aspect of language is vital to interpreting work to outsiders. Carefully, Hall leads readers in understanding how a tinsmith transforms something intended to be used for heating or cooling into a tin man's arms, legs, head, or torso. The process involved in completing a job—design, fabrication, and installation—puzzles and intrigues observers.

Hall's background as a sculptor, teacher, collector, ethnographer, and critic has made him a persuasive champion of twentieth-century folk art. Collections of essays or lectures have spread his often-provocative views; two catalogs from the Milwaukee Museum of Art (1981, 1993) call attention to items he gathered for each exhibition. From his home in Hamtramck, Michigan, Hall continues to spark ideas and enthusiasm.

Hall's *Metalsmith* article features a photograph of a gentleman identified as *The Dandy,* elegant in top-hat and tailcoat and with a cane draped over his arm. He stands with stock sheet-metal parts cluttered at his feet in the window of the West End Sheet Metal and Roofing Works in New York City. Although he is not dressed in conventional work overalls, he advertises his shop and craft as do his plebeian brothers.

Apparently, this tin man was among the first discovered by New York folk-art enthusiasts. I have never seen *The Dandy;* I know him only through the eyes and pens of others. However, on starting my exploration, he appealed by virtue of his obvious quality, coupled with my desire to understand the process whereby a functional shop sign becomes an art object. Although curiosity led in several directions, I am uncertain that I have untangled *The Dandy*'s entire story.

This tin man, yet unnamed, first appeared in his new role in 1970 at the Winter Antique Show sponsored by the East Side Settlement House in Manhattan's famed Armory. Dealer Gerald Kornblau presented the metal man; collectors Elaine and Eugene Cooper purchased it. In October 1974, Amherst College staged a comprehensive exhibition entitled "American Folk Art." Its published catalog included a photograph of the tin man and identified it as being made around 1900 and lent by Eugene Cooper. Curator Lewis Shepard acknowledged the help of other lenders, including the Gerald Kornblau Gallery. It has taken me many years to trace the journal from an initial New York showing to its present museum home.

I have listed published citations for *The Dandy* in the Appendix; here I note that

62. *The Dandy.*

most authors date the figure to 1894–1900 and attribute it to J. Krans, tinshop proprietor. When a photograph of the tin man appeared in the *New York Daily News* announcing the Whitney Museum's Bicentennial exhibit, "Two Hundred Years of American Sculpture" (March 16–September 26, 1976), Rochelle Spielvogel challenged the Krans notation and nineteenth-century date. She telephone and corresponded with collectors Elaine and Eugene Cooper, Jennifer Russell at the Whitney, and Jean Lipman and Elizabeth Warren at the American Museum of Folk Art.

It is unusual for a family member to persist in documentation efforts, but Spielvogel asserted that her grandfather, tinsmith David Goldsmith, had fabricated the trade-sign tin man. Her view prevailed, and Jean Lipman and Helen Franc, in *Bright Star* (1976), accepted Spielvogel's impressive factual record.

David Goldsmith (1901–80), born in the Austro-Hungarian Empire, had learned the art of metalsmithing in Krakow, Poland. Emigrating to America in 1920, he followed his trade, eventually opening his West End Sheet Metal and Roofing Works in Long Island City on the depression's eve. With time to spare, he crafted a figure of Uncle Sam from galvanized iron sheets, using his own clothes as a model. He then poured concrete into each leg, ensuring that the sculpture would stand erect in the window. Goldsmith retired in 1964 and sold the shop, including the trade sign, to Adolph Schloss of Brooklyn. Schloss retained the old name for his new shop.

Authors have given the Goldsmith/Schloss figure various names (*Tin Man, Tinsmith, Dandy,* and *Uncle Sam*). Like any piece of provocative art, it has attracted commentary and been compared to Abraham Lincoln, a cigar-store Indian, a snowman, and a scarecrow. It has been likened to the precisionist works of Charles Sheeler and Charles Demuth. To Elizabeth Warren, the tin man resembles a New York nightclub patron of the 1920s or 1930s: "His boxy, square-jawed style—a combination of sharp edges and rounded forms—is also typical of the Art Deco period in the decorative arts" (Lipman et al. 1990, 117).

In previous case studies of ballads and tales, I have been confident that enough facts would surface to permit a coherent narrative. I lack such confidence, however, regarding tin men. Documentation is missing, leads remain contradictory, and trails run cold. Although Elaine and Eugene Cooper deserve thanks for protecting their tin man from decay, other pieces, uncollected, rust away, fall prey to vandals, or are sold at flea markets. Some ended life on wartime scrap piles before it became fashionable for fold-art buffs to combine pleasure and virtue in buying sheet-metal sculpture.

Did the Coopers question the age of their tin man or his dignified appearance? Were they conscious of errors in attribution in fold-art books? Did they evince any desire to meet its tinsmith maker, very much alive in the 1970s? These are more than rhetorical questions; they can be asked about many of the tin men described throughout this book.

Fortunately, I learned from Aarne Anton that Gerald (Jerry) Kornblau had presented the tin man at the Armory Show in 1970. Upon reaching Jerry by telephone at home in Claverack, New York, on August 10, 1999 and again on December 29, 2001, he treated me to a raconteur's account. Clearly, he enjoyed describing the figure's adventures.

Kornblau had noticed a tin man in a Brooklyn tinshop window one morning after taking a wrong turn during the commute from his home in Queens to his gallery in Manhattan. Intrigued by his find, he visited the shop several times, asking the owner, Adolph Schloss, if the figure were for sale. Schloss, asserted that he would never sell his own handcrafted object. Kornblau though that response ambiguous, however. Without challenging the tinner directly he asked Schloss to make an exact duplicate and sell it to him. Thus, they could each have a tin man. Should a complication arise, Kornblau offered to buy both pieces.

Put to the test, Schloss undertook to fabricate a second tin man but failed to meet the demanding workmanship of the original. He eventually confessed that he had purchased the entire tinshop, including the trade sign, in 1964, allowing Kornblau to acquire his prize. Jerry Kornblau recalls the sequence of events as having some of the inevitability of a Greek drama: His Brooklyn discovery, sustained offers to Schloss, the failed test, Schloss succumbing, and a transaction consummated on Kornblau's birthday.

I have yet to clear up the matter of how and when Krans entered the picture. I assume that after Schloss parted with the tin man, he then sold the West End shop to tinner J. Krans. Perhaps Kornblau or the Coopers let the misattribution stand. In time, the Coopers divorced, and their collection was broken up. Kornblau again became involved in the tin man's fate, arranging its sale to Ralph Esmerian, a private collector and president of the American Museum of Folk Art in Manhattan.

In December 2001, the museum celebrated its new building by displaying hundreds of paintings and objects that had been given by Esmerian, including Goldsmith's tin man. An accompanying brochure featured a photograph of Goldsmith's debonair creation. In a full-color exhibition catalog, *American Radiance* (2001), curator Stacy Hollander described the Esmerian collection. Ralph Sessions's catalog comments correctly relate the tin man to previous shop and cigar-store figures. In this spirit, I have selected the photograph of *The Dandy* (named by Michael Hall) and originally taken by Jerry Kornblau at the West End shop in Brooklyn to document his finding a choice item of "true folk art."

Satisfied that Goldsmith's tin man is secure in a New York museum, and having told something of its story, I will move on to other icons. In *Made with Passion* (1990), Smithsonian Institution Lynda Hartigan included photography of three tin-man figures. One, in Bert Hemphill's apartment, is shaped like a stove made from an oil drum; two others are at the National Museum of American Art. That pair is entitled *Galvanized Man,* a larger-than-life worker made by Gerald McCarthy at his Ogdensburg, New York, shop, and *Marla,* a spirited girl fabricated by Irving Dominick in Spring Valley, New York.

Comparing three-dimensional signs designed for tinshop display, we complement visual sensation with a query: Is a museum-held figure a folk item by virtue of institution ownership, esthetic appeal, or scholarly standards? Although sheetmetal mechanics constitute a stable occupational community, not all tinsmiths fabricate tin men. Those who don the "sculptor's apron" do not readily identify themselves as artists, either fine or folk. Yet most tinsmiths view their emblematic signs as part of a shared artisanal legacy—natural, timeless, and traditional.

A transcontinental comparison of Melrose Avenue's *Al,* created and valued within a work community, to the Smithsonian's *Galvanized Man* reveals whimsy, satire, and considerable scope for individual variation in traditional artistry. Nevertheless, *Al* and *Galvanized Man* function as twins. Both announce their respective shops and the skill of those who made them. We assume that a tinner called Al named his storefront skylight man after himself. Similarly, Gerald McCarthy painted "Plumbing Heating Cooling" across his tin man's chest to affirm competence in related crafts.

In linking *Al* and *Galvanized Man,* I am aware that one is in a museum and the other is in a book. Both appeal to collectors and curators who willingly shared interest in their possessions with the public. In addition, their owners helped *Al* travel from Topanga, California, to San Francisco and back and *Galvanized Man* from Ogdensburg, New York, on the St. Lawrence River, to Manhattan, then Washington, and then Santa Fe and several other museum sites before his return to the Smithsonian.

In Santa Fe, long associated with native American art, the Museum of International Folk Art mounted "Recycled, Re-Seen: Folk Art from the Global Scrap Heap: in 1996. In the show's catalog, museum director Charlene Cerny and anthropologist Suzanne Seriff comment on worldwide trends toward reusing industrial trash for pleasure and profit (Cerny and Sheriff 1996). Curators placed McCarthy's piece (on loan from the Smithsonian's National Museum of American Art) on a platform with three other figures made from mufflers and assorted scrap metal. I have imagined midnight conversations among this quartet as they compared notes on the idiosyncrasies of their respective makers and asked how they themselves had come to be in an elegant New Mexico museum.

I am pleased that Gerald McCarthy's *Galvanized Man* journeyed, via many hands, from Ogdensburg to Santa Fe and points beyond. I am uncertain, however, about the figure being displayed as recycled art. An eye-catching show title that has great cachet in museum circles may not apply in the world of production and commerce. McCarthy assembled standard new parts to build *Galvanized Man*— exhaust duct, flashing, Y-junction, and roof ventilator. All sheet-metal shops have scrap piles, but tinners usually prefer new material to used whey they fabricate tin

63. *Galvanized Man* and companions in Santa Fe.

men. Stock once used may be rusty or otherwise damaged. There is little incentive to search the scrap heap when constructing complex heating and cooling systems.

Unable to resolve the matter, I resume imagined conversations with various tin men. They whisper knowingly upon sharing secrets and chuckle when joking with me. They reach across the continent to compare notes. *Al* at Fort Mason proclaims for all, "I transform blueprint into soaring skyscraper; I sketch, cut, fold, brake, crimp, beat, braze, heat, solder, weld, rivet, place, and fix." Local 104's *Copper Man* adds, "Honor our trade, be patient with time, get it right, keep eyes peeled for each job's appearance, watch miters, stick to the union, and guard our traditions."

On another level, *Marla*'s hairstyle denotes electrical energy, and her demeanor is as suggestive as Madonna's. Clearly a young woman facing life's adventures, she is and is not a sister to *Al* and *Galvanized Man*. Her "skin" marks her as having a generic relationship to trade-sign metal men, but she does not advertise a tin-shop's location or wares. Instead, she points viewers to realms of statuary and portraits of feminine beauty. *Marla* can not alter her tin exterior, but she knows in her heart that she is worthy of veined marble.

We have met *Marla* and several of her brothers because they have been in museums and thus accessible to the public. By contrast, a commanding shop figure, *The Dean* remains hidden in a private collection. It represents future tin men yet to be welcomed by a second audience.

64. *Marla.*

For many years, customers of George Dean's shop in Terre Haute, Indiana, admired his multicolored sign—a huge figure standing on a sheet-metal platform that bore the word DEAN in raised letters. The tinsmith had mounted the construct on a sloping shed roof in front of the wood-frame building at 3426 Park Street. If that did not call enough attention to the work inside, the sign projected a huge shears, a tool used in the fabrication of Dean's tin man. The larger-than-life piece, arms outstretched, stood like Odin in Valhalla.

In a telephone conversation on August 29, 1998, George Dean told me that he had been born in 1923. During World War II, he enlisted in the U.S. Navy as an aviation metalsmith and learned the fundamentals of the tinners' trade. In addition, he enrolled at Indiana State University, preparing for years as a vocational education instructor. In 1956 Dean opened his own shop. Like other proprietor-mechanics, he kept his membership in SMWIA Terre Haute Local 7 (now merged into Local 20, Indianapolis). He retired from ownership in 1985 but occasionally does fine copper work in his home shop. George Dean is too modest to claim anything special for his giant trade sign. Fortunately, art historian Michael Tingley took a series of interior photographs (that remain unpublished) while the shop was still open. In one is Dean's hand-lettered motto, "Learning by Seeing and Doing," a reminder of a craftsman's essential credo.

When Dean's shop closed, Elli Buk, a New York antique dealer, purchased its ten-foot-tall sign. Because of its size, *The Dean* rests in storage in a Soho-district warehouse. On occasion, Buk rents props to play and film producers, so perhaps it will appear in a television show or onstage. It is too dramatic to remain unseen. At present, *The Dean* occupies an ambiguous place, no longer serving community residents as a shop sign but not yet displayed in a museum or a folk-art book.

Following my lead, Nan McEntire, an Indiana State University ballad scholar, visited George Dean, seeking to explore the life story of an Indiana folk artist. Although her findings have yet to be published, one detail is of interest. Dean, unlike many tinsmiths, made his shop sign because he did not want to waste the scraps left over from previous work. His children, also involved in the process, saw the figure evolve and suggested changes. Again, an unpretentious tinner is unwilling to claim too large a role for his artistry.

The act that transforms functional artifacts into esthetic ones, or discarded scraps into provocative art, intrigues collectors and curators. Essentially, these viewers place material items in novel settings and ask how the new environment influences artistic judgment. A well-crafted tin man fills multiple roles. It serves alternatively as an advertising aid, symbol of skill, teaching tool, conversation piece, marker of antiquity, and prize possession.

In recent decades, dealers, critics, historians, and ethnographers have contested, heatedly and without resolution, the substance and spirit of folk art. I'll not enter the debate. Julia Ardery's *The Temptation: Edgar Tolson and the Genesis of Twentieth-Century Folk Art* (1998), an incisive study of the Kentucky wood-carver, takes up such briar-patch issues. She traces the growth of public attention to folk art; the art's appreciation, both monetarily and symbolically; and the consequent conflict that occurs among constituent partisans.

In this volume, I have discussed trade signs without dwelling on the personal routes of journeymen who move, whether subtly or dramatically, from fabricating a functioning tin man to creating a metal-sculpture abstraction or artistic treasure. I have already discussed Rene Latour, whose pieces ranged from a Florida shop sign to a graceful ballerina to a platonic set of geodesic spheres. Irving Dominick represents a similar breadth in artistry.

Private collectors and museum curators helped move several of Dominick's figures beyond his tinshop into their domain. Dominick was born in 1916 and began work in his father's Bronx tinshop when he became a teenager. Herman Dominick had studied metalsmithing in Vienna before migrating to America, where he opened his own shop in 1918. After their father's death in 1960, his sons Irving and Sidney moved the family business to Spring Valley, New York.

On looking back at his work and art, Irving Dominick told local reporter Cathy Maroney (1982) that his father, upon seeing *The Wizard of Oz* in 1939, had determined to make a huge trade sign to be placed on his shop roof. He modeled the piece after a foreman who had "large shoulders and a thin waist." The result, which seemed more indebted to Frankenstein than to Oz, proved highly popular with customers and also attracted the attention of daily elevated-train passengers.

In the move to Spring Valley, the tin man descended from the Bronx roof to the new shop's storefront, where it acquired a name, *Tiny Tin,* as well as a patina of untold tales. Some stories about it are contradictory, others unended. Irving Dominick's son Gerald recalled that the film *The Day the Earth Stood Still* (1951) served as inspiration for making the tin man and that the figure stayed behind, bolted to the shop roof.

Sometime in the 1970s, James Kronen, a Madison Avenue antique and folk-art dealer, persuaded Dominick to sell him the original *Tiny Tin.* In turn, Kronen sold it to Muriel Karasik, also a Madison Avenue gallery owner. She moved the tin man to her home at Great Neck, placing it in the garden, facing the Long Island Sound. Susan LaGrande has sent me a large, framed photo of Karasik's *Tiny Tin,* taken years ago at the Sound's edge. Eventually, Karasik sold the piece to a West Hampton resident who remains anonymous.

Although Dominick seemed reluctant to part with his shop mascot, the tinsmith knew that he could easily fabricate a replacement. In time, Manhattan folk-art dealer Aarne Anton purchased the second tin man. He sold *Tiny* to Chester

65. *Tiny Tin.*

Denten, who, in turn, sold it to Gil Shapiro, proprietor of Urban Archaeology, an New York firm that deals in architectural ornaments. Shapiro sold it to a collector, who remains unknown.

Anton believes that Dominick made a third *Tiny Tin* and left it behind when he sold the Spring Valley shop. Clearly, the tinsmith enjoyed creating artistic forms to relieve the routine of run-of-the-mill work. By 1990 he had put his tools away, retiring to Delray Beach, Florida. He died on July 3, 1997.

I have tried, without success, to trace the present location of three nearly identical *Tiny Tin*s. The pursuit doubles back to *Marla*. After purchasing the second *Tiny,* Aarne Anton asked the tinner if he would consider making a tin woman. Accepting the challenge, he modeled the figure after his granddaughter, Marla. It was not an easy assignment; he labored for months on her eyelashes, ears, earrings, and wavy hair, twisting each strand until he had formed a metal halo. Anton's daughter accepted the tin child as a companion. When she outgrew it, Anton sold *Marla* to Bert Hemphill, and it now rests in the Smithsonian's American Art Museum.

Seemingly, Irving Dominick had traveled a long road from daily sheet-metal tasks, to *Tiny Tin* replacements for enthusiasts, to *Marla,* a "nonfunctional, imaginative form" (Hartigan 1990, 91). At what point in his life, if ever, after contact with dealers Kronen and Anton, collector Hemphill, and Smithsonian curator Andrew Connors, did Dominick add to his identity the label *folk artist?*

Few tinsmiths know, or are accustomed to, that term, yet an unpredictable chain of circumstance brought *Marla* into a prestigious national gallery. I have focused on known pieces of sculpture by Dominick; others may exist. An exotic tin man reminiscent of a Japanese warrior, offered for sale in 1977 by Garry Cole in Manhattan, may have been made by the Spring Valley tinsmith.

Arbitrarily, we distinguish Dominick's *Marla* from *Jordan's Squire* because the latter still sits on a Sebastopol, California, roof. We assign Jordan's figure, with apple and chicken in hand, the name *trade sign* because it salutes the community as an advertising item. By any standard of craft skill or imaginative conception, the *Squire* ranks with *Marla*. Both the metal-working and folk-art communities share responsibility for sorting out matters of definition for sheet-metal artistry.

A tin man on Route 112 in Massachusetts addresses some of these issues. George Duensser, a German immigrant working for the Hampshire Engineering Service, a home-fuel heating company in Northampton, built the fifteen-foot-tall figure in 1952 for outdoor display. He used aluminum to prevent rust; the proprietor wanted the figure to "show the public what we could do with sheet metal." When Hampshire Engineering closed in 1972, Elbert Ulshoeffer, familiar with the tin man since childhood, purchased the figure for his Goshen, New Hampshire, home. He considered it a "piece of American folk art" (Burrell 1991).

At its new location, teenagers armed with hacksaws beheaded *Goshen Man.*

Richard Richardson, who restores antique stoves, took the headless man in trade and sent it to be repaired by John Lind, who taught at Smith Vocational High School in Northampton. Years later, Ulshoeffer found the long-lost head in Chicopee (the location of the original head is unclear). Eventually, the tin man received an Oz-inspired heart transplant of red glass and a stainless-steel frame shaped by Thomas Fern of Chesterfield (Winters 1995).

Goshen Man, who wears an anomalous cowboy hat and holds snips in his hand, stands sentry in front of the Good Time Stove Company on Route 112. He achieved folk-art fame while still serving his original, eye-catching purpose. When Kristin O'Connell, an Amherst College architectural historian, told me of *Goshen Man,* she noted that folkloric subjects have long been taught in several prestigious colleges in New Hampshire. Students and staffs value folk art, and many early discoveries of New England antiquities have occurred in the region. Therefore, neighbors and visitors who encounter *Goshen Man* have a ready-made concept of folk art in mind.

Would *Goshen Man* have received similar attention had he been fabricated or displayed elsewhere? His dual status as advertising symbol and folk-art piece depends upon the shifting judgments of sheet-metal workers, the traveling public, and collectors or curators in the art world. *Goshen Man* may or may not end up in a museum gallery. At present he announces the presence of the Good Time Stove Company. He also tells viewers that he serves another role—as a symbol of a tinsmith's creativity.

66. *Goshen Man* at Good Time Stove Company.

In attention to sheet-metal artistry, I have named collectors and curators and skirted intractable problems in definition built into the term *folk art.* I have assumed that Bert Hemphill, Lynda Hartigan, and their peers represent the fraternity that treasures, comments upon, and displays tin men. Thus, it may come as something of a surprise to learn that the largest accumulation of metal men in America belongs to New Yorker Alex Shear, who is neither a sheet-metal worker nor a shop owner, vocational-school or labor-management apprenticeship instructor, or folk-art dealer or collector. According to his count, however, he has thirty-five tin men, not all of which are tinshop trade signs.

I have tried for several years, without success, to persuade Shear to allow me to list and describe his tin-man trade signs in this book's Appendix. He asserts that flea-market venders and similar traders often provide scanty or unreliable background information for their merchandise. When making purchases, Shear relies on personal, visceral, reactions much more than upon the details or histories offered by sellers. The diversity of his eclectic accumulation provides context for his method of gathering sheet-metal artifacts. He lives in a Manhattan apartment crammed with "stuff" that spills over into a Westchester County warehouse. Over the years, he has purchased immense mounds of cast-off and out-of-date goods, including ceramic animals, transistor radios, manhole covers, and Tupperware.

At the end of 1992, the Park Avenue Atrium exhibited some of Shear's "Favorite Things." The show's announcement revealed the scope of the collection. Contents included "The Kitchen of Tomorrow"; salesmen's samples, including model swimming pools; tin men; streamlined sleds; roadside and house trailer artifacts; antique toys and games; military panorama photographs; Coca-Cola memorabilia; transportation folk art; and more.

David Owen (1999) has profiled Shear's motives and values. Describing a Children's Museum of Manhattan show in 1992, Owen categorized Shear's "Tin Can Art" as consisting of "anthropomorphic sculptures and other items that anonymous craftpeople had fashioned from scraps of metal, lengths of electrical conduit, sections of galvanized ductwork, and similar bits and pieces of industrial detritus." "Metal men" might be a better label than "tin can art" because few of Shear's figures are actually made of cans. Sheet-metal workers are reduced to anonymity by collectors uninterested in stories beneath the surface of each piece.

Tin men, a minuscule portion of Shear's massive collection, are among his choice treasures and sometimes treated as props to demonstrate his passion. A photograph of him with a dozen metal companions heads the *New Yorker* article. Similarly, the *New York Times* used a shot of his Oz-like figures displayed on the Capitol's lawn during the 1994 meeting of the American Zinc Association ("Pay No Attention to That Man behind the Curtain"). Features by Melissa Milgrom ("The Nostalgia Broker" 1998) and Olivia Snaije ("Collector of Americana" 1997) also use pictures of Shear's tin men. Shear is not particularly concerned with the disparate origins and functions of his metal men. He defers to Aarne Anton, of Manhattan's American Primitive Gallery, who keeps such information on file as he accumulates the figures.

At a Massachusetts flea market some years ago, Anton purchased a tin man that he sold to Shear in 1998. Made of stock parts, it has two distinguishing features: a 1950s' thermostat embedded on its chest and a pair of claws or pincers for hands. Although sheet-metal mechanics install thermostats in homes and offices, the use of one in tin-man fabrication is unusual. Neither Anton nor Shear know where the figure was made nor how it journeyed from a heating and cooling shop to a flea market.

Perhaps *Thermostat Man* is more representative of the tin men described elsewhere in this volume than *Jordan's Squire* or his companions. We know something of the *Squire*'s genesis and function but can only guess at the former's. I am challenged by Shear's many tin men and hope that their stories can still be unearthed.

My interest in tin men as indicators of sheet-metal workers' culture narrows this inquiry. No matter the questions asked, the figures raise large aesthetic and social concerns for those involved in the nature of art. Homeowners who buy gutters for their tract houses or urban developers of skyscrapers do not concern themselves about whether a local tinshop or corporate firm has a tin man on the premises. A

67. *Thermostat Man.*

shop's output must be cost-effective and meet civic codes of safety. Proprietors face many issues that touch upon the profits of their enterprises. Although the commercial/financial economy relegates cultural concerns to its margins, a relationship, however dimly perceived, does exist between craft artistry and workers' identity.

Collectors, curators, historians, and ethnographers need to pay attention to present-day tinsmiths employed in a demanding trade. Sheet-metal workers pursue everyday tasks, largely unaware of the lives of those who inhabit folk-art literature. I invite critics who favor terms such as *naïve, self-taught, visionary, untutored, iconoclastic,* and *schizophrenic* to visit one of the apprenticeship classes jointly run by the Sheet Metal Workers' International Association and its employers in their respective trade associations. Apprentice tinsmiths come from widely varied backgrounds and represent the multiple strands in blue-collar life. In training centers one sees young workers—normal by standards of community and citizenship—who combine skill and artistry in their daily routines and who will continue such practices for decades to come. These recruits absorb the "vocabulary of shapes" necessary both for utilitarian jobs and the fabrication of tin men.

The often-hidden connection between the spheres of industry and art requires continuous analysis. A sheet-metal worker crafting a tin man that reaches a museum gallery creates wealth for folk-art enthusiasts. In turn, dealers and their peers give artistic definition and market value to the work of tinners. Although tinsmiths and collector-curators are not well known to each other, perhaps the stories that follow will create a path of mutual respect.

68. *The Drummer.*

10 STORIES SHARED

Conversations or correspondence with sheet-metal workers help demystify the web of association that links utilitarian shop sign with decorative object d'art. Some mechanics fabricate tin men solely to serve as advertisements; others make similar figures for sale at craft fairs or art venues. A few, in designing figures, combine both functional and artistic strategies in their work. Many find tinshop assignments sufficiently satisfying that they have no need to express creative impulses on the job. Others separate the domains of work and art.

Although I am chiefly concerned with tin men, they do not make up the totality of tinsmiths' artistic expression. The *Sheet Metal Workers' Journal* constantly ran photographs and brief reports on a range of objects made by "hobbyists." For example, Joseph Lukes of Mason City, Iowa, finished a pair of intricate copper and stained-glass lanterns that he donated to his church ("Hobbyist Demonstrates Art" 1955). And Bert Barnum of Kansas City, Missouri, made a watering-can knight's helmet as well as a giant eagle and a tombstone "for use against the inevitable day when it will be needed" ("Member Puts Skills to Good Use during Retirement" 1968).

Generally, the *Journal* featured such objects as typical of tinsmith skill without attempting to set off craft from art. I have observed that some who make tin men find it easy to comment on their creative choices, whereas others find it difficult to explain their gift or, in their words, their "natural" skill.

I have heard a few colorful tales surrounding tin men, but each figure is not fortunate enough to have been fabricated by a gifted wordsmith. When I worked as a shipwright, I partnered with bull-slinging yarn-spinners as well as with silent journeymen who poured all their creativity into plumbing a bulkhead, horning (squaring) a hatch, or carefully fitting a set of recalcitrant hawse pipes. Some mates talked constantly, but others shunned hyperbole. Coming to the sheet-metal trade as an outsider, I wondered if I would be able to find storytelling tinsmiths.

Although I have claimed the capacity to read tin men trade signs as books and converse with them as between-cover characters, I know that ability to be a writer's pretense. As friends have alerted me to "new" artifacts at distant sites, I have tried to bring factual knowledge and literary imagination to the descriptions in these pages. Fortunately, in some instances I have been able to reach the tin men's guardians, who have related exciting narratives about their charges.

In the spring of 1995, Karin Nelson of San Francisco's Craft and Folk Art Museum was passing through Centralia, Washington, and photographed the outdoor sign of a tin man beating a "drum" with a tinner's hammer. His other hand pointed to a shop shaded by large trees. The drum's circular rim announced "L. Stoffer & Son Sheet Metal." With Karin's snapshot at hand, my letter to the shop netted a reply on June 25, 1996, from Louis J. Stoffer. There were two figures, he said, one inside the shop and one outside:

> Jasper, the tin man in our show room, was built in 1932. He began his career standing in front of Mr. Louis Stoffer, Senior's, tin shop right in the middle of Centralia. At that time, business was in the height of the Depression. With a lot of time on his hands, Dad made Jasper. Dad would haul him in and out, 8:00 A.M. and 6:00 P.M.
>
> Sometimes, forgetting to take him in at night, on several occasions Jasper would be kidnapped and dropped off elsewhere. During Pioneer Days, he would be arrested for no beard and taken to a Kangaroo court. Because he could not speak in his defense, he'd be thrown into a Kangaroo jail.
>
> In 1936, Mr. Stoffer moved to a bigger location, and, at that time, he installed a radio in Jasper. Also, he made his lips move with a motor. This caused a sensation as Jasper was ahead of his time. Our tin man remained outside with the radio blaring until 1942, when we went into war work, moving to a new location outside the city limits. As we had very little walk-by traffic, we stored Jasper in a shed for about twenty years.
>
> A customer then borrowed Jasper to use as an eye-catcher at a mall display. This person repainted him and kept him for a year. Upon return, we put him in our office show room; children love him. Jasper now stands guard over the place, silently.
>
> In 1945, with war work ended, we went back to civilian business, thus needing a new sign. Dad designed a large square billboard to be placed across the street with Louis Stoffer & Son Sheet Metal on top, and several things we made or installed—below. This billboard held a tin man with a long arm (ten feet) pointing to our shop.
>
> At this time, Centralia annexed our property, zoning it residential. Though the tin man billboard sign was complete, we could not install it. We had to make a smaller sign for our side of the street—a round sign like a big drum with a tinner's hammer as beater. This fit our new residential area.

Drummer Man stood for twenty years until 1970 when we moved again to a building out of town. In 1983, vandals struck by tearing off our tin man's arm. A year later they returned tearing the drummer all to pieces. He had been built of light sheet metal, twenty-six-gauge, and soldered together.

At this point, we built an exact replacement of much heavier material. The present drummer's arms are ¼" well casing. The body, head, and hands—sixteen-fourteen-gauge galvanized. Fortunately, the original vandals were caught, and we got all the parts back. Later, we caught two girls from the gang trying to twist off the tin man's head while sitting on his arms. On another occasion, at 4 A.M., an individual beat our drummer with a big hammer, but caused no damage.

Our present shop (1410 Harrison Avenue) stands on original Highway 99, Vancouver, BC to the Mexican border. We get much traffic every day, and our tin man receives countless beer bottles, pop cans, and rocks. Once in a while, he is decorated with crepe or toilet paper, but through it all he stands his ground.

69. *Jasper.*

Louis Stoffer's letter is priceless because it documents tin-man history from an inside perspective and helps move this discussion from the norms of folk-art esthetics to the prosaic matters of civic zoning and urban vandalism—the real elements framing the lives of many tin men. Stoffer also reveals great pride in his father's work, as John Jordan, Jr., does for his father's Sebastopol, California, squire with apple and chicken. I suggest that both sons speak for many second- or third-generation tinsmiths who equate family with trade tradition.

Among the rich details in Stoffer's letter is the fact that his father remedied *Jasper*'s speechlessness by planting a radio in the tin man's body and electrifying his lips to give him voice. When that novel feat brought added attention to *Jasper,* the tinsmith explained his creativity to a *Daily Chronicle* reporter. He had built his tin man "to prove to the world that a lot of things can be done with a sheet of tin."

With Stoffer's letter at hand, I visited the family's shop on March 8, 1997, accompanied by Olympia, Washington, folklorists Jens Lund and Willie Smyth. We marveled at *Jasper* and *The Drummer* as Louis Stoffer intertwined personal and shop history. His father had been born into a family of five generations of coppersmiths in Alsace-Lorraine. Shipping out to America, the young Alsatian jumped ship in Tacoma to seek a new life. In 1932 he opened his own tinshop in Centralia's Eagle's Building, fabricating *Jasper* to mark his work.

Born in 1924, Louis Stoffer, Jr., learned his trade by imitation backed with a belief in work's value. At the start of World War II he went to Portland, Oregon, to work in the shipyards as a coppersmith. "Graduating" to an Army Air Corps B-17 bomber (398th Group), Stouffer, an engineer-gunner, earned a Purple Heart after a Christmas Eve 1944 crash at Royston, England. Back in Centralia, he continued in his father's firm through its various moves to the Harrison Avenue location announced by the outdoor *Drummer.* Louis Stoffer's son Gary now manages the seven-man tinshop.

These facts stand behind Stoffer's report on *Jasper* and *Drummer,* including when they were made and how they have functioned. While visiting the shop office, I could see Stoffer's artistry in the form of a magnificent brass model of a 1907 Rolls-Royce—sixteen inches long and intended for his granddaughter. He had made three other miniature cars (a 1918 Model-T Ford, 1907 Stanley Steamer, and 1907 Model-K Ford), each for a grandchild. Responding to our wonder at the Rolls's detailing, Stoffer modestly noted that he worked either from model plans or from drawings he scaled from photographs of antique cars.

Louis Stoffer's neighbors view him as a good citizen and successful small businessmen. To these designations I would add master metalsmith. Beyond matters of identity, I have reflected on a memory he shared. Some years ago, he journeyed to Alsace-Lorraine to visit his family's ancestral copper shop. In nearby Colmar, he noted a monument to Frédéric-Auguste Bartholdi, sculptor of the Statue of Liberty. Somehow, Stoffer intuited, a thread of skill stretched from Colmar to Liberty

70. Advertisement.

Island to Centralia, where *Jasper, Drummer,* and brass model automobiles for grand-children represented the craftmanship built into Liberty's hammered-copper skin.

I have not been fortunate enough to meet all the makers of tin men noted in these pages. As I listened to Louis Stoffer, I could sense his innate creativity and appreciation of craft heritage. He also alerted me to the continuity of tinsmithing, and it occurred to me that I would encounter similar stories across the continent.

Narratives find their way to the surface as streams meander across plains—often submerged in quiet pools but at times exposed by rising above protective banks. Only a few observers eye the pools and their banks. Karin Nelson alerted me to a huge, sheet-metal figure on Route 8 in St. Croix Falls, Wisconsin. Literally, this giant beckons customers to the Tin Man, a firm of two parts—a sheet-metal shop and a new auto-stereo and mobile-electronics unit. The latter division's business card features the big piece of sculpture.

When I received Nelson's report, I asked folklorist Tom Walker to visit the current owner, Sam Deering, and he, in turn, suggested that Tom and I telephone the

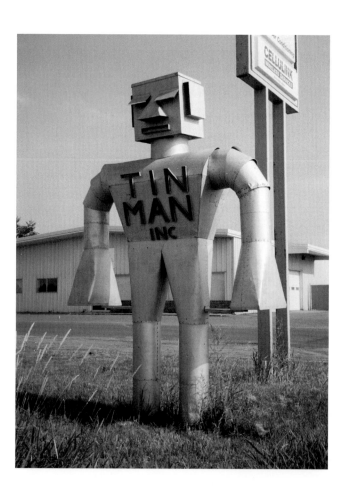

71. *Tin Man.*

original makers of the piece: Harold Bishop in Osceola, Wisconsin, and David Carlson in Tucson, Arizona. Tom reached Bishop, and I talked to Carlson.

Both men were from families of tinsmiths. Carlson's father-in-law, Clarence ("Mac") McSherry, had built a quarter-scale, sheet-metal man some fifty years earlier. When Bishop and Carlson joined as partners in St. Croix Falls, they wanted a large tin man in the spirit of Paul Bunyan—fourteen feet tall and nearly a ton in weight. With the help of McSherry, they fabricated the piece in 1967 and erected it atop the shop at the intersection of Highways 88 and 87. When the tin man became a tourist attraction, its owners found themselves promoting their distinctive sign as much as their heating and ventilation work.

Halloween pranksters "loved" the man to the point of cutting his guy wires and tipping him off the roof. After Bishop and Carlson moved the business "up the hill" to its present site, they reerected the trade sign in front of the shop. Undaunted, vandals tied ropes to the tin man, toppling him. Responding, the tinsmiths anchored their man in cement. Some of the anecdotes that clustered around the figure dealt with its voice. When the partners placed a loudspeaker in the sign, Bishop, in the office, would converse and joke with tourists and photographers.

A telephone conversation with Carlson on November 28, 1996, netted a detail about the continuity of tin-man fabrication. Carlson had moved to Tucson about 1989, where he assisted his son in opening a modern tinshop. McSherry, Carlson's father-in-law (who winters in Arizona), promised to build a tin man for the new shop. Completed early in 1997, it now guards the Carlson Company's showroom.

The St. Croix Falls and Tucson tin men are similar in appearance other than the fact that the one in Tucson is only eight feet tall and holds a red Stillson wrench. The outdoor version faces Wisconsin winters; its indoor companion laughs at Arizona summers from the comfort of an air-conditioned lobby. "Both tin men were fabricated from flat sheets only," Carson told me. The Tucson figure required six sheets of forty-eight-by-ninety-six-inch, twenty-eight-gauge stock. "They were completed using triangulation, tremulation, and some swearing," he added. "My father-in-law 'Mac' is one of the last of the great sheet-metal workers." Many of the mechanics cited in these pages share the same compliment.

I learned something of the St. Croix Falls and Tucson pair through telephone conversations and letters. Following a second path, I "met" a stainless-steel man in Flint, Michigan, by reading an account of him in a technical publication ([Carter] 1990b). A crew from Dee Cramer, Inc., a Flint, Michigan, heating, cooling, and sheet-metal firm, had fabricated a six-foot-eleven-inch creature to "attract attention, stimulate conversation, and demonstrate talent" at the Flint Builders' Show. Several Cramer employees joined in making the figure. Cliff Casabon of the service department suggested the project, in part because it drew on the popularity of the Tin Woodman. Welding foreman Robert Hammond made a rough sketch of the design. Gil Loudon and Gary Hutchinson, shopmen, handled forming and

72. Tucson tin man.

welding tasks as they used two sheets of number 304 stainless steel, number 4 finish. Among other gear, the mechanics used a Cybermation cutting machine for plasma arc fittings and a Lincoln 400 Square Wave TIC Welder. The project took fifty hours to complete at a cost of $2,000.

Folk-art enthusiasts wedded to norms of handicraft integrity may be unable—or unwilling—to grasp the command of modern machinery used in making the man. Similarly, the Dee Cramer journeymen might be amused or puzzled by a folklorist's attention to their sleek display object. Yet a stainless-steel man born in 1990 has ancestors fabricated by Homer's smiths and Shakespeare's tinkers. The creators at Dee Cramer, Inc. in Flint hark back to armorers and artisans, blacksmiths, and whitesmiths whose collective spirit informs contemporary work practices.

A union training officer I visited in Orange County, California, passed along a photocopy of an announcement from the "Lantern Man" (Pete Lyzsewski) in Buffalo, New York. I responded and soon received sheets of plans, patterns, and step-by-step instructions on how to craft eight metal objects: a lantern, sailboat, woven basket, bushel basket, coal bucket, copper boiler, can opener, and tin man (that could be built of copper). The last item caught my attention. It seemed to be related to Lewis Wittlinger's *Copper Man* shown at Fort Mason. I asked for additional details.

Pete Lyzsewski had joined SMWIA Local 71 in 1949 after wartime work in aircraft plants, among them Curtiss-Wright and Bell Aircraft. Attending night school,

73. *Stainless-Steel Man.*

he received credentials to teach sheet-metal classes at Erie Community College. After seeing the appealing Tin Woodsman in the *Wizard of Oz,* he became aware of one that stood in front of a Bailey Avenue tinshop. The dual models lodged in Pete's memory, and when he began teaching Local 71's apprentices he devised a class project that he described in a letter of July 16, 1997:

> Students would think they were building a toy, but in reality they learned many different sheet-metal operations such as layout, scribing, cutting, rolling, breaking, riveting, soldering, filing, and learning to read graphic language. The thirty-four-inch tin man was made of galvanized iron. I also used copper. Occasionally, the seniors assembled a six-foot tin man.
>
> The copper man has been around for over twenty-five years. I used him for sixteen years at the AFL-CIO Union Industries Show to demonstrate excellence in craftsmanship. The adults loved to see him standing proudly, all polished up, with a tool tray in one hand and a duct in the other. The youngsters kept asking if he was a moving robot.
>
> I also used the copper man as a retirement gift for SMWIA officers, as well as others who made extraordinary contributions to the sheet-metal industry.

The Union Industries event, an educational effort of labor unions, is also a trade show that is infused with a "Buy American" spirit. Held annually, it moves to a

Plans are now available to craft eight unique projects made of metal. Shown above are the hurricane lantern, the three sailing boats mounted on a tapered wave, the scaled down replicas of the traditional rectangular woven basket and the ever so popular bushel basket and the "Tin Man" that stands 34" high. Also the oval copper boiler with a cover and the coal bucket that your grandparents remember so well. Added to the list is a 22" giant size can opener. Try your sheet metal skills and your ability to solder. They really make wonderful hand crafted gifts for all occasions. The projects are designed to craft by Pete Lyszewski, SMWIA Local 71, Buffalo, New York.

To acquire the detailed, step by step plans and instructions, check the ones you desire and send $9.97 for each individual project shown above to:

○ Lantern
○ Sailing Boats
○ Woven Basket
○ Bushel Basket
○ Tin Man
○ Copper Boiler
○ Coal Bucket
○ Can Opener

THE COPPER CRAFT COMPANY
POST OFFICE BOX 334
BUFFALO, NEW YORK 14223

Name_____

Address_____

City State Zip_____

(Note: Price includes postage)

74. Pete Lyszewski's announcement.

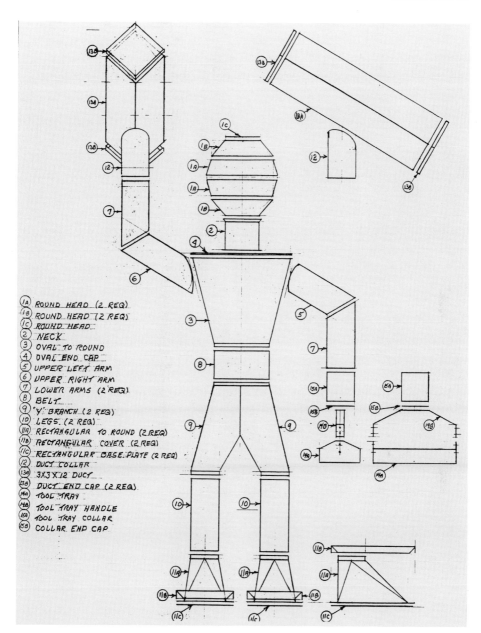

75. Plans for *Copper Man*.

different city each year and draws huge audiences. Lyszewski participated regularly from 1974 to 1989 under the auspices of the National Training Fund for the Sheet Metal and Air Conditioning Industry, a joint labor-management program. At each event he would set up a workshop and booth containing handcrafted lanterns, copper men, and other attractive products, meanwhile answering questions from spectators.

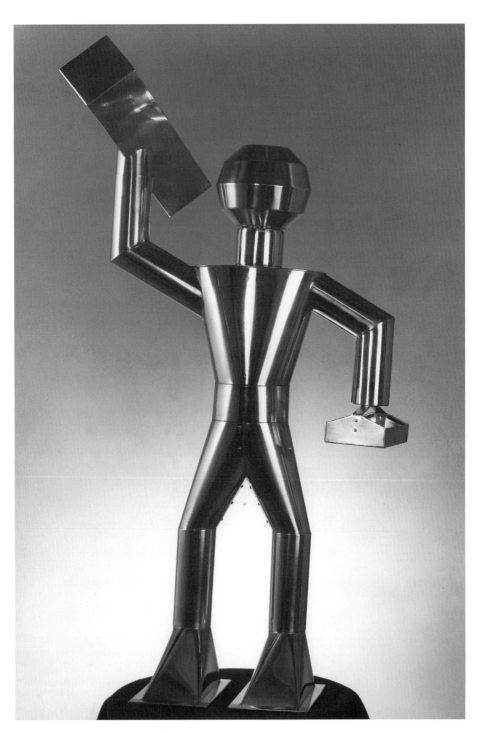

76. Pete Lyszewski's *Copper Man.*

Lyszewski did not sell his wares. Each item became a door prize or gift, a token from the trade. President Jimmie Carter, for example, received a hurricane lantern for the White House. It would be interesting to follow the travels of each copper man given away at the shows. Pete knows where a few of his "children" are, but most are beyond his ken. During the Union Industries shows he became a good-will ambassador for the union. In July 1976, for example, he was pictured in colonial dress, crafting a lantern ("One If by Land"). The *Journal* also published a long letter from Lyszewski, expressing solidarity with Lech Walesa in Poland ("American Sheet Metal Worker" 1981).

Pete Lyszewski's journey—from war worker to teacher, craft demonstrator, union spokesman, and hobbyist—has spanned more than eighty years. He has given many apprentices a good start in life. In retirement, he and his wife, Faustina, winter in Florida and travel extensively. Of the union he says, "Most of our work is hidden above ceilings" (Ritz 1987). Historian Michael Kazin suggests that Pete's comment points to a significant compensatory motivation for crafting tin men—to achieve visibility. At public events, Lyszewski has performed tin work for all to see. Our correspondence, and my subsequent telephone conversations with his son-in-law, Glen Gibson, also a tinner, confirmed my appreciation of Lyszewski's belief in the demands and rewards of his trade.

Through personal visits and telephone conversations I was able to reach a union veteran and two men long established in family firms. All shared personal biographical information that would provide backgrounds for their particular tin

77. Display at AFL-CIO Union Industries Show, Denver.

men. What perspective would I obtain from a young mechanic, however? By good fortune, I reached Scott Hultgren, a member of Minneapolis–St. Paul Local 10. Scott had become interested in sheet-metal work when he was a teenager and had enrolled at the Dunwoody Industrial Institute in Minneapolis in 1982. It was during an unstimulating refrigeration class that he began to plan an armored man. Before his apprenticeship ended, he had fabricated three knights. On April 15, 1998, he described the projects for me:

> It took about one hundred hours to make the first tin man. It was made of twenty-six-gauge galvanized sheet metal, channel iron (in knights feet), pop rivets, and 50/50 solder. My wife made an outline of a friend's child to obtain the proportions. I completed the second man in the spring of 1988. His proportions were better than the first one. His legs were longer and his head looked better. This one was a wedding gift (two years late).
>
> The third man, by far the hardest, was a masterpiece project required during my fourth year apprenticeship. Part of the requirements included: to submit a blueprint to the coordinators and upon approval, complete it before the fourth year. In July 1990, the fun began. I received a letter from the committee that my employer would be forced to lay me off since I hadn't fulfilled my fourth-year requirements—the masterpiece project.
>
> I was out of work because of the unfinished project. The blueprints had taken too long a time. Patterns, in scale, were nonexistent—only sketches and photocopies of articles on armor. I used the *National Geographic World* (March 1981), and a photo in a National Training Fund apprenticeship book (1985) to make the patterns.
>
> The fabrication of no. 3 began as I taped paper patterns together. No longer having a workshop, I had to gather tools: a small sheetmetal brake, a small rolling machine, a stake, some odds and ends. I broke up the big pieces, and headed up north to my grandparents' place to fab it up in their garage. In August 1990, I had finished the project and by September I turned out as a journeyman.

Hultgren understates his achievements—an early interest in the sheet-metal trade, a fascination with armor, and persistence in completing his qualifying project. The third figure was made of sixteen-ounce copper, 95/5 solder, brass button rivets, lead, and twelve stainless-steel, blind pop rivets. The photograph in the National Training Fund's apprenticeship book had come from the Metropolitan Museum of Art—a suit worn by George Clifford, Earl of Cumberland, and made about 1590. Like most mechanics who do layout work, Scott is computer-literate, and he included a printout of the Metropolitan's Web-page about the Clifford armor. Clearly, Hultgren has more than enough talent to make a trade-sign tin man, but armor had a stronger, more personal appeal for him, and no employer has asked him to fabricate a sign. Scott now works for a shop in Eden Prairie, Minnesota. Perhaps such an assignment will yet come.

Scott Hultgren has drawn attention to one of the unresolved matters in this study: Who wills a tin man into existence? The decision to make a tinshop trade sign presumably belongs to a proprietor who wishes to advertise or who recognizes that a sculptured figure on the premises would distinguish his shop from others. The owner of a small firm may have worked, or continues to work, at the trade and thus is able to construct a tin man or participate in its design and placement.

The origin of a decision to make a tin man can become difficult to identify in large enterprises, and the task of ferreting out information can be challenging, whether from a conglomerate or from a tiny tinshop. The Master Lock Company of Milwaukee, for example, held a handsome piece made by a team of sheet-metal mechanics. Standing in the main entrance foyer, it was a cousin to a trade sign, having been made for a 1991 Christmas parade. It welcomed VIP visitors by means of a programmable LED sign. Someone high in the firm's corporate ladder retired the figure in 1988. I do not know who at Master Lock thought it appropriate to fabricate a tin man for a parade, to display the artifact produced, or to retire it.

78. Scott Hultgren and his knight.

Whether or not that executive knew how to craft a tin man had no bearing on its actual construction.

Sheet-metal mechanics have diverse motives for making creative objects not called for in everyday work: curiosity about the past, a strong sense of the ownership of free time, exposure to artistic norms, and conviction that fine work signifies personal autonomy. Often hidden or unverbalized, the impulse to fabricate a tin man or a suit of armor is left to the finished object. The maker assumes that the piece will speak for itself and that motivation is observable. In the early 1960s, the *Champaign-Urbana Courier,* for example, ran a feature on tinsmith Harold Pope (Osborn 1963). An employee of the University of Illinois physical plant and a member of SMWIA Local 230, Pope had fashioned to scale a suit of armor made of lightweight aluminum for his five-year-old grandson. His purpose was clear: a gift for a family member. I am struck by Pope's manifest skill as well as the depth of this research. He borrowed Charles Ffoulkes's *The Armourer and His Craft* (1912) from the university's library. It is not unusual for tinners to consult books (Scott Hultgren did so as well). Ffoulkes, who completed his bachelor's degree at Oxford University in 1911, blends technical detail and social history in a volume that is also filled with superb illustrations.

Old books partially explain the appeal of armor-making to some contemporary sheet-metal workers. To know how to fabricate a piece that is obviously arcane is to display skill that will be respected. In addition, armor is associated with strong values—chivalry, valor, romance, and heroic deeds as portrayed by St. George slaying the dragon of barbarism. Hans Burgkmair's woodcut *The Workshop of Conrad Seusenhofer* appeared in *Der Weisskunig* (1891 [1516]), a fictive autobiography of Maximilian I, the Holy Roman emperor. Ultimately, the ability to heat, cut, beat, and fuse metals passed from armorers to coppersmiths, ornamental ironworkers, and tinsmiths. A contemporary sheet-metal worker sees in Burgkmair's illustration something that is remote in time yet familiar in purpose.

Perhaps most important to mechanics such as Hultgren and Pope is awareness of inheriting an honorable craft tradition. As Ffoulkes observes of the jurisdictional claims of the Armourers' Company (guild): "Under Charles I, in the appeal of the Company to the Crown, leave to use the [trade] mark is requested 'because divers cutlers, smythes, tynkers & other botchers of arms by their unskillfulness have utterly spoiled many arms, armours, etc'" (1912, 120). Seemingly, this is an aside to guild history, but it also sheds light on tinsmiths who, on occasion, take up armor-making or any other "free-time" piece, whether old-fashioned lantern, trinket, or home decoration. As descendants of "tynkers," they do not see themselves as "botchers" but rather as highly skilled metalsmiths. In the same spirit, those who make tin-man trade signs sense that they no longer fashion utilitarian pieces. Instead, they put their hands and minds to an object that speaks to the past and plays the role of symbol within the trade.

79. *The Workshop of Conrad Seusenhofer.*

I have gathered a few stories about tinsmiths from journals, letters, telephone calls, and visits. Sometimes a choice account will fall into my hands without effort, and I am reminded again of my good fortune in friends and fellow workers. For example, folklorist Mary Zwolinski, who is with the Rensselaer County, New York, Council for the Arts, saw tin sculptures on a lawn in Margaretville, New York, while she was employed in Delaware County. Curiosity aroused, she knocked on the cottage door and found a retired tinsmith, the master of a fantasy realm.

Joseph Schoell (1907–93), born in Hungary, had served a rigorous, old-country apprenticeship. Fleeing political persecution in 1956, he migrated with his wife Agnes and two children to Long Island and resumed his trade in the vicinity of

Rockaway and Brighton Beach. Upon retirement, he undertook a second calling—making decorative and whimsical metal objects for his summer house on Route 28. Schoell's tin pieces included a yellow and orange windmill, the Oeden-Burg Castle (reminiscent of his Hungarian hometown), and the *Dragon Family* of fourteen heads—all with sharp teeth. Zwolinski's description of his eight-foot-tall *Statue of Liberty*—a gift to himself celebrating thirty years of American citizenship—is dramatic. *Liberty*'s face is graced with huge blue eyes and long black lashes; she wears a spiked crown, and flowers cover her protruding breasts. A red Bible is in her right hand and a raised torch in the left.

In August 1991 the Delaware County Historical Association exhibited work by several local artists in a show entitled "Folk Art: Tradition and Continuity." Agnes

80. Joseph Schoell's *Miss Liberty.*

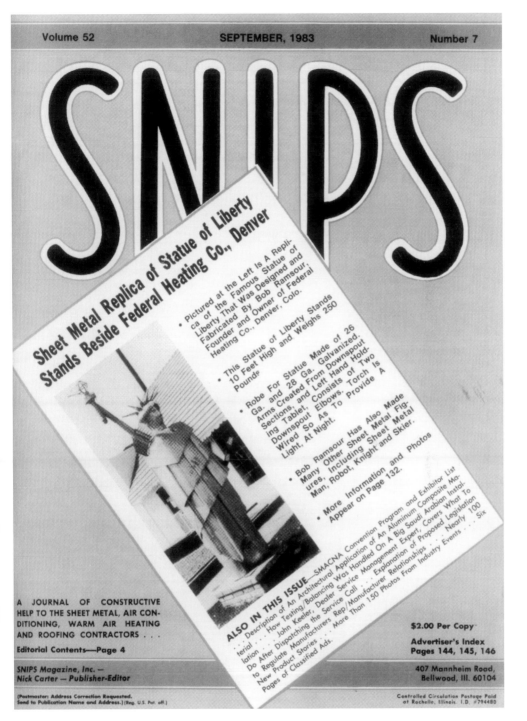

81. Ramsour's *Statue of Liberty.*

and Joseph Schoell attended the opening, Mary Zwolinski wrote to me on November 9, 1999. "He wore a suit for the occasion, and stood for the longest time looking at the things he'd made in the context of a gallery. How lovingly he looked at the pieces, as if he were seeing them for the first time." It is fortunate that Zwolinski met Joseph Schoell and wrote about him, explaining in part his intent in fabricating *Miss Liberty.* Many comparable tinsmiths and their sculptures go unnoticed by scholars or journalists.

Occasionally, a metal craftsman will merit an ephemeral story that deserves an expanded audience. In September 1983, for example, *Snips,* a sheet-metal trade magazine, ran a cover photograph and article on a *Statue of Liberty* figure standing beside the Federal Heating Company in Denver (Carter 1983). Editor Nick Carter took the photographs, interviewed shop's owner-artist Bob Ramsour, and noted the figure's fine detailing. "Instead of the usual sheet metal man gracing the front of a . . . shop, that we periodically see," Carter observed, "we saw a replica of the Statue of Liberty."

82. Bob Ramsour and
Uncle Sam.

The piece was ten feet high, weighed 250 pounds, and had a body made of twenty-six- and twenty-eight-gauge galvanized steel. Carter was especially impressed by its four layers of spiraling robes, "achieved after a lot of trial and error." Ramsour, had, Carter reported, crafted sheet-metal shop figures for a quarter-century: a crouching skier, a knight, a robot, and Uncle Sam.

On July 12, 2001, Bo Ramsour and I spoke of his father's achievement. Subsequently, Bo sent me a photograph of his father standing next to a nine-foot, flag-bedecked Uncle Sam. Bo commented on the vicissitudes it had endured, including vandalism and theft. Some years after the *Snips* feature appeared, David Park Curry added more information (Curry 1987). Ramsour had originally painted the statue white. When media attention surrounded the restoration of Bartholdi's *Statue of Liberty* in 1986, however, the tinsmith repainted his trade-sign piece a minty green to resemble the patinated copper of the original in New York Harbor.

The *Denver Post* pictured Robert Ramsour with the statue after he had made a new head for *Lady Liberty* to replace one that had been stolen ("Another Face-Lift for Lady Liberty" 1986). Undoubtedly, additional accounts exist, oral or published, that would round out the story of this "tin man." Ramsour's replica, although not a man, is as much a trade sign as the others I have discussed, for it advertises a tinshop.

Sheet-metal stories are as varied as the utilitarian gutters or artistic lanterns that tinsmiths fabricate. These trade stories—when read as literary or folk-tales—comment on the making of tin men as diverse as Joseph Schoell's *Miss Liberty,* Bob Ramsour's *Lady Liberty,* Rene Latour's *Cowboy 200,* or John Jordan's *Squire.* The task remains to preserve and present these occupational narratives and ask the questions necessary to inform the inquiry.

83. Adam Brandau and *Big Foot*.

11 QUESTIONS

In portraying tin men and naming some of their makers, I have raised several questions, many of which remain unresolved. Where is the earliest extant American tinshop sign? Is there evidence of nineteenth-century anthropomorphic shop figures? Does a similar classifying scheme apply to all metal men? Do various tin men take their stations along a functional array accepted by initial makers or an esthetic norm favored by current collectors? Ultimately, what do tin men reveal about the creativity and identity of sheet-metal workers?

Coffin (1968), DeVoe (1968; 1981), Gould (1958), Lasansky (1982), and Powers (1957) all provide background reading on early tinware, now prized by antique collectors. Of course, pioneer metalsmiths also worked on buildings, public and private. Shem Drowne of colonial Boston, for example, made the durable grasshopper weather vane for Faneuil Hall, and Thomas Jefferson selected tinplate for the roof when he built his residence at Monticello. These examples of the tinner's craft were duplicated across the land.

This discussion began with accounts of medieval armor, guild-herald figures, domestic weather vanes, and colonial trade signs, implying continuity from such forms to contemporary tin men. Yet I have found no examples of tinshop trade signs in the eighteenth or nineteenth centuries. What explains that lack? How do we link past to present without a chain of evidence from guild emblem to sheet-metal advertising sign?

My chronological pursuit has led to the reluctant conclusion that it is difficult to establish an accurate time-line for American tin men. Some information lies buried in newspaper files. Occasionally, an unusual sign, or the mechanic who made one, catches the eye of a reporter searching for a local-color story. A few tin-

shop owners saved brittle clippings and related ephemera, often undated. Heaphy's in Syracuse kept copies of a picture postcard, issued about 1909, of the shop's
tin man, and in the mid–1930s a report on Stoffer's *Jasper* appeared in a Centralia,
Washington, newspaper. Earlier data, however, has not surfaced.

Matters of age converge with those of category in an attempt to place tin men
in a sequential or functional array. *Snips Magazine* has served the sheet-metal fraternity for six decades. In September 1983 and again in August 1990 editor Nick
Carter used the term *replica* to cover a roundup of figures that readers had crafted.
In a backyard workshop, a Texas shop foreman made a knight; in his Wisconsin
garage, a semi-retired tinner crafted a gladiator; students from St. Mary's County
Technical Center in Maryland built a six-foot-tall tin man; an Indiana shop team
crafted an Oz theater costume; and a shop supervisor in Illinois made Dorothy and
Tin Woodman Halloween costumes.

I suggest that the makers of the knight and the gladiator consciously replicated old forms, perhaps searching books on feudal chivalry or classical history in the
process. Similarly, the Halloween costume designers drew upon visual models
widely seen in popular books and films. By contrast, the students in Maryland
made their tin man as a teaching tool comparable to those in labor-management
apprenticeship classes. Knights, gladiators, and costumes based on *The Wizard of
Oz* have been used infrequently as shop signs. The St. Mary's County Technical
Center figure could be moved to any tinshop and transformed instantly to an advertising role.

Carter, in linking tin-man replicas and Halloween costumes, overcame the lack
of a single term to include figures grouped together across the lines of form, purpose, and appeal. Tinners use metals other than tin to make signs but do not place
mufflers or radiators outside sheet-metal shops. Although tinsmiths step easily
from replicating knights to fabricating figurative trade signs, I do not know of any
knights that are currently displayed as tinshop signs.

"Replica" is a word of partial utility. It also leads to areas of hidden intent by
tinsmiths. What impels one mechanic to cut and join parts to make a knight in a
home shop while another builds a three-dimensional sign at work? Both journeymen fabricate human figures. The knight is a passport to the past in that it is nos-
talgic and signals antiquity. The trade sign identifies itself bluntly as a promotional
icon: "Come inside; let me reveal all within; I symbolize job competence."

Although I have stressed the differences between knights in armor and tin-men
trade signs, I am aware that fabrication techniques are similar. As I suggested in
chapter 10, all tin men—whether clad in armor, dressed as the Tin Woodman of
Oz, or in a space suit—represent a fundamental return to tradition. All speak to the
trade's heritage.

In the categories commonly used in art circles, present-day shop signs rest
ambiguously between the realms of high, formal, or elite art and folk, naive, or self-

taught art. To compound the difficulty in analysis, mass-media or popular art occupies an ever-expanding middle ground that constantly seeks space. By introducing Adam Brandau, I call attention to two tin men. *Big Foot* was not intended as a shop figure, and *Self-Portrait* was intended as a promotional sign. Both gained notice as folk art.

Brandau, an Ohio native born in 1910, learned the tinners' trade from his father Frank in Wellston. At age eight, Adam could solder as well as any man. He joined SMWIA Local 98 in Columbus and eventually traveled to Arizona and Florida for work. In 1939 he opened his own tinshop near Jackson, Ohio, and followed the trade until retirement in 1972. In the new shop, Brandau made a tin man of scraps from an inverted, T-shaped neon sign he had built for a Pomeroy, Ohio, theater. He modeled it after himself and used it to advertise the shop.

About 1984, Brandau sold the sign to an antique picker, apparently from Chil-

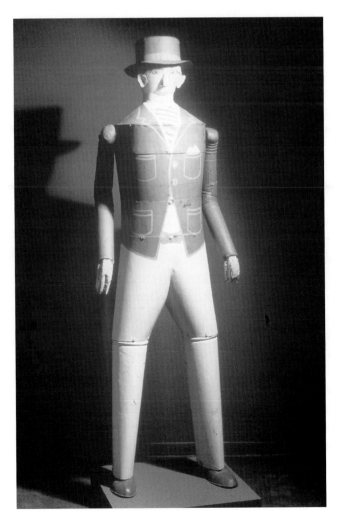

84. Brandau's *Self-Portrait.*

licothe, Ohio. He, in turn, sold it to Darwin Bearley, an Akron folk-art dealer. Bearley sold the piece to the Carl Hammer Gallery in Chicago, and Hammer then sold it to Marna Anderson, a New York antique dealer, who sold it to a private collector. That repetitive process—from maker to picker, dealer, gallery owner, dealer, and collector—is typical of how folk art accrues in monetary value. Although the physical path of a given item can be traced, much else remains obscure—for example, the present location of Brandau's tin man, dates and documentation of the various transactions, and statements concerning the object's appeal. In addition, Brandau told Hammer that he had called his sign *Sam the Tin Man.* What is the significance of his naming act?

Carl Hammer commissioned similar sculptures from Brandau. Thus, more than forty years elapsed between making *Self-Portrait,* his shop sign, and the other pieces. In retirement years free from shop burdens, he devised a fantasy realm filled with cowboys, screen idols, pioneer women, birds, airplanes, ferris wheels, and wind-driven ornaments. Brandau scattered these in his yard, giving neighbors and tourists much pleasure. When a project came to mind, he would draw free-hand patterns on old newspapers, transferring each template onto cardboard, which he would outline against the metal itself. He then cut the metal pieces and soldered them together. Each project was finished with spray paint or auto lacquer in the bold colors that Brandau favored.

Brandau achieved some appreciation of his artistry; unlike many tinners, he also received recognition during his lifetime ("Area Tinner/Folk Artist Sells His Work to Gallery" 1992; Bank and Flanagan 1996; Gilson 1996; McKinniss 1993; Wenstrup 1997). Several of his pieces, including *Big Foot* and a huge companion, *Walking Tall,* were on exhibit at the Riffe Gallery in Columbus, Ohio, in 1996, and Richard and Maggie Wenstrup of New Richmond, Ohio, and Myron Shure of Chicago have given homes to others.

Modest to the end, Brandau seemed pleasantly amused by his transition from tin-knocker to folk artist. It was, he joked, a busted water heater that got him into art. Needing cash for a new one, he sold his first tin man to an antique picker. The anecdote surely cloaks the sources of his artistic impulses, but Brandau's creativity, like that of other tinsmiths, remains unexplored. He died on January 23, 1998.

David Taylor of the Library of Congress's American Folklife Center alerted me to a tin man for sale at Capitol Hill's Eastern Market in March 1996. Tom Rall, a Sunday flea-market auctioneer, had displayed an eighty-one-inch-tall tin man made of galvanized sheet-metal pipes, brushed aluminum, flexed aluminum, and duct tape, all held together by machine screws. The maker, Joel ("Daddy Duct") Galarneau from Arlington, Virginia, had been a heating and ventilating mechanic for twenty-four years. While unemployed, he made several tin men and named his flea-market figure *Buddy* after an actor in a *Wizard of Oz* production.

On sale, *Buddy* sported a tiny, hand-printed label: "A Conversation Piece Folk

85. Joel Galarneau's *Buddy.*

Art Sculpture w/ Adjustable Arms can be used as a garden ornament/scarecrow! $249.00." Put directly, Galarneau needed income in a period of hard times. Would he and Rall have identified the tin man as folk art had it been made as a sign at Galarneau's last place of employment?

Tom Rall knew that Capitol Hill buyers might welcome the sculpture as folk art, a convenient, accordionlike term, without asking questions. The zone of identity that *Buddy* represents includes tin men who resemble shop figures but lack firm evidence of having functioned as trade signs. Rall replied to my questions on May 29, 1988:

> We ended up buying him. Through most of last year he stood in our back yard. He was injured by a falling tree and repaired by Joel after a summer storm. Before Christmas, we moved him to our front yard and dressed him in a Santa's hat. The neighbors seemed to like that, so at Easter we gave him rabbit ears and a basket. We'll probably dress him as Uncle Sam for the Fourth. Every so often we change his position to suggest waving, hugging, or shaking hands. He's become one of the family. Whenever we give directions to our house, we just say you can't miss it because it's the one with the Tin Man in the front yard.

Perhaps the best illustration of an existing shop sign striding across discrete categories of occupation is one atop B.J.'s Welding Shop in North Little Rock, Arkansas. University of California architectural historian Dell Upton, on a cross-country trip in 1997, spotted a spectacular example of vernacular art. The present shop owner, Ken Main, credited the former proprietor, known only as "Big Jim," with fabricating the figure—realistic, functional helmet; welding rod and stinger in left hand; stout, oil-drum torso; and intricate arm and leg joints.

The Welder raises his right hand in a gesture both welcoming and defiant. Those who have picked up the torch will appreciate the stance. Welding is understood as a tool of each trade and belonging to all crafts. It is also a special skill and the jurisdiction of one trade—welders. Although most tinners do some welding, B.J.'s is not a tinshop. Technically, this trade sign does not belong with tin men, yet to an outside observer it is not always clear what sets off metal men from one another.

The matter of niche can be approached from various angles, among them the scholarly efforts to categorize artists who work with metal. The Oakland Museum of California placed metal men and related objects in a provocative exhibit entitled "Hello Again! A New Wave of Recycled Art and Design," which ran from February to July of 1997. The show included a Spam-can truck, metallic robots, a bagpiper, and a window-washer formed from cans. As part of that event, Scott Hanson exhibited an intriguing map of the United States that incorporated forty-eight license plates (Alaska and Hawaii were unrepresented). He cut the plates to outline each geographic border, so individual pieces held designating initials or official state emblems. Map, robot, bagpiper, window-washer, and "Spam truck" could all

86. B.J.'s *The Welder.*

have been created by working tinsmiths. Instead, they were made by artists assaulting the line between esthetic domains.

I doubt whether the Oakland Museum staff, in its search for "Hello Again!" material, encountered a tinshop figure. I have asked whether Gerald McCarthy's *Galvanized Man* would fit within the curatorial bin labeled "recycled art" and featured at the Museum of International Folk Art in Santa Fe (chapter 9). That question underscores conceptual issues inherent for each tin man. Perhaps the curator of a future exhibit, especially someone interested in artisanal traditions, will bring together metal figures from shop and studio and complement them with an interpretive catalog touching upon matters of age, category, and meaning.

Elsewhere, I have discussed various workers' means of expression—ballad, blues, word, tale, custom, belief, ritual, code—and have used "laborlore" as an overarching term to cover these discrete forms (Green 1993). This book extends my study to include physical artifacts. Weather vanes, for example, functioned directly to indicate wind direction and indirectly to reveal the taste of their makers or purchasers. Coppersmiths made the early movable devices in the shape of angels, soldiers, sailors, Indians, and other humans—but apparently not of themselves. No nineteenth-century vanes modeled after their particular makers have turned up in museums or private collections. Tinsmiths did announce wares and skills in the public press. Did such advertising ever picture a shop tin man?

In these times, represented as the Age of Advertising and rewarding the "Big Sell" with national companies demanding attention via television, a figurative store sign only reaches a few souls who pass through a neighborhood. Amana, Carrier, Honeywell, Lennox, Rheem, Trane, and Westinghouse are among the giants that achieve national recognition for heating, cooling, ventilating, and air-conditioning products. Madison Avenue executives far from the shop floor where a tin man might be born handle television commercials or magazine advertising for continental firms.

When a tinshop moves to an industrial park far from an inner city's factory district, it no longer relies on a tin man to advertise. If the shop retains a seldom-seen figurative sign, what does that sign represent—know-how, pride in craft, respect? Frequently, those elements converge, often with a touch of comedy or fantasy. A layout mechanic who uses computer-controled tools does little handwork but senses that a tin man harks back to the past.

Nominally, a tin man announces a shop's presence and its wares. Metaphorically, it displaces time by asking viewers to recall a previous era. *Al, Jordan's Squire, The Dean,* and all the other pieces in these pages are time machines that invoke the past. Handwork governed the shop floor; goods made did not exceed a human scale; and face-to-face transactions among mechanic, proprietor, and customer ruled the day. A sculptured figure represents memory—treasured, romanticized, and sanctified.

Few tinshops, whether large or small, still hold artifactual trade signs—perhaps a hundred. Training centers and union halls may hold an equal number. At best, I can account for fewer than two hundred. That can be measured against a Bureau of Labor Statistics report of June 1998 on employment in the sheet-metal industry: 123,000. Another sign of the scarcity of tin men is the number of shops that display one. In July 1998 the Sheet Metal and Air Conditioning Contractors' National Association reported 1,920 member contractors and estimated some ten thousand unaffiliated shops.

Whether we use a base of shops belonging to the association, BLS employment statistics, or the Sheet Metal Workers' International Association report on paid-up members based on per-capita payment to the national AFL-CIO (ninety-three thousand as of the year 2000) compared to the approximate number of extant tin men, the resulting number is very low. The fact remains that there may never have been a "golden age" of tin men. Yet meaning of such artifacts lies beyond numbers.

To accept that today's tin men symbolize trade heritage rather than advertise shops is to understand why unionists are interested in using them as teaching tools. Apprentices who fabricate tin men very likely graduate to shops that lack one, yet the young mechanics intuit that they have made something sanctioned by time. The skill involved in fashioning a human figure from metal seems timeless.

All tinsmiths with whom I have spoken about tin men have reinforced the notion of tradition. Although few are called upon to fabricate a shop figure, all are confident that they can do so. A mechanic who has knowledge of antiquity has status in the trade. Even a shop sign shaped like a space cadet seems instantly old because it reflects the age of handicraft yet is dressed for intergalactic travel. In today's shops, tin men can be defined as strange—not in appearance but in existence.

A few folk-art enthusiasts prize the ambiguity that envelops a tin man. Curators praise the object in a museum for beauty or rarity, whereas a maker may speak of craftsmanship or skill. Tinsmiths may not employ the language of art, but they are not immune from esthetic codes. They know when they have produced fine work, whether a stately, copper-clad dome, a modern stair finial, a Frank Gehry construct in the National Building Museum, or a Rene Latour geodesic sphere. The passion of a handful of dealers has preserved many of the pieces I have discussed. Like scholars within the academy and outside of it, these dealers add value to tin men no matter how we conceive of purpose—whether advertising sign, artistic trophy, symbol of skill, teaching tool, or passport to antiquity.

Why then do tinsmiths construct tin men? The facile answer would be that their bosses tell them to do so. What, however, is the intent of employers who design and fabricate tin men? The obvious rationale, advertising, hardly makes sense in today's economy.

At another level, a tinsmith may say, "I make tin men as others paint portraits, write poems, compose songs." Yet tinners seldom articulate theories of creativity. They may share the notion that artists are strange, disturbed, rebellious, or unhappy, but they disclaim that craftspeople suffer such afflictions. What is needed are tinners' reports on how and why they generate art. Parallel to such personal views, critics have considerable room to speculate on tinsmith artistry. Although a few tinshop signs have ended in museums or private collections, no tinsmith has achieved wide recognition as a folk artist. The trade magazine *Snips* and the union's *Sheet Metal Workers' Journal* do not comment regularly on aesthetic matters. Mechanics who do artistic work, with few exceptions, do not share the language of art critics.

A comparison could be made between tin men and tobacconist figures. The latter have long been prized as artistic objects by collectors of Americana. Wood-carvers made transitions in response to industrial change: ship figureheads, cigar-store Indians, and carousel animals. Tobacco merchants and circus owners did not carve their own signs, however. They relied on outside craftsmen for these eye-catching products. By contrast, a tinshop called on its mechanics to make tin men. Cigar-store trade signs have been gathered, valued, and studied for more than a century; tin men only since the 1970s. If tin men achieve comparable recognition, tinsmiths will first be drawn into discourse with arbiters of folk-art taste and eventually with art critics at large.

Do tin men contribute to our understanding of work's meaning? Industrialists, labor partisans, and scholars endlessly offer conflicting answers. Work is alienating or life-sustaining, a curse upon humanity or essential in defining the human condition. The visceral debate over work's role will continue in many arenas, whether shop floor, corporate boardroom, or judicial chamber. Seemingly, tin men have little to do with the larger issues in life. Actually, however, as artifacts of material culture, tin men are like the other artistic expressions that enhance everyday existence.

I am conscious that the figures described in these pages do not trumpet overt ideological causes. Mother Jones, Joe Hill, Eugene Debs, or John L. Lewis never built a tin man nor hid a message in its body. Both marchers and spectators at Labor Day parades view them as mascots, more humorous than serious. Even when tin men become teaching tools in apprenticeship schools and wear the SMWIA logo, their purpose remains understated and ambiguous. No tin man sings or leads "Solidarity Forever" or "Which Side Are You On?"

In posing large questions and offering limited answers I am acutely aware that much remains undone. Throughout this book I have called on others to assist in gathering information, with full results or tantalizing leads. In one instance, for example, Andrew Connors, a Smithsonian curator, mentioned that on a trip to Yellowstone Park he had spotted a tin man atop a roof west of the park in Idaho. I reported this clue to Robert McCarl, a Boise folklorist, who set out in search of the proverbial needle in the haystack. Indeed, the tin man did perch on the roof of Jewell Electric in Idaho Falls, an hour's drive from Yellowstone. Before taking up an academic career, McCarl had worked as a production welder in a Portland, Oregon, metal shop. Notwithstanding long familiarity with the trade, he obtained only a few facts from the Idaho Falls firm. Despite its name, Jewell Electric also engaged in sheet-metal work. A former tinsmith named Ernie had fabricated the piece for a parade about 1992. What parade? Could Ernie be reached, and would he discuss his tin man? Who would do so? Was I the only person curious about the Jewell figure?

Without help from Conners and McCarl, I would know nothing of the Jewell shop sign. Yet this tin man, like many others, stimulates additional queries. The

87. Jewell's tin man.

image of tin men in Chinese boxes is apt—each one in descending order asks a question. Answers dissolve into fresh puzzles. Whether in a shop, classroom, union hall, dealer's gallery, museum, or home, questions (and answers) address the larger issues of vernacular culture.

The impulse to fashion the human form in wood, stone, or metal lies deep within the human psyche. When tinners take up snips and hammer to fashion a tin man, they lighten their work day. Such construction at the bench is a conjuring of spirits, an affirmation of creativity, an assertion of trade continuity, and a trumpet call—the shop floor remains more than a place of toil and tears.

Finally, tin men, however mute, both pose and answer questions. I began this study not knowing what might be asked, and I have not found replies to all my queries. Other explorers may follow. The time has come to circle back to my initial encounter with two tin men—sculptured figures—made of galvanized iron and copper.

88. *The Traveling Tinker.*

12   CIRCLE BACK

During the "Working Folk" exhibit in San Francisco's Craft and Folk Art Museum, *Al's the Tin Man* and *Copper Man* stood side by side in a gallery, one dwarfing the other. Yet despite their dissimilar appearances, they seemed to be related. How and why, however, I could not fathom. As their histories became partially known, this book took shape. In it, I have focused on trade signs and teaching tools but drawn freely on a great variety of approaches in vernacular studies.

During the eighteenth and nineteenth centuries, tinsmiths served American communities as all-purpose mechanics. Their ubiquitous ware was cheaper than silver, safer than pewter, and easier to clean than wood. Popular and practical, tin was used in common objects as diverse as pie pans and whale-oil lamps. Beyond providing household goods, tinners engaged in building construction and added features of architectural beauty—bronze gates, zinc statues, and copper friezes— to the landscape.

Present-day sheet-metal mechanics work with complex heating, ventilating, and air-conditioning systems; solar energy equipment; and space-exploration gear. Hammers, snips, and soldering irons have given way to computers and lasers. Whether restoring an ancient gargoyle, cladding a skyscraper, or providing a Silicon Valley factory with a "clean room" (sterile and dust-free), a tinsmith can do the job. Others in the building trades marvel at tin-knockers who can fabricate abstract geometric forms.

Only a few shops possess figurative signs, yet most sheet-metal workers seem acquainted with the custom of creating a tin man. The contrast between general knowledge of the artifact and the limited number of tinners who have actually made one puzzled me. How did tin men become familiar to mechanics who had no models in their shops? Although no easy answer surfaces, few documentary reports from ethnographers or their peers touch the sheet-metal industry to provide leads.

A three-part formula may resolve the seeming contradiction inherent in tinsmiths recognizing tin men but having little practice in making them: long familiarity with fabricating human forms in metal, ready availability of stock parts, and abundant skill in layout and design. When combined, these elements should provide mascots for each shop, yet very few have them—perhaps because owners do not want a tin man. Occasionally, however, an owner does give play to a luxuriant flash, an irrational whim or an unspoken need, and a tin man is born. It will no longer serve an advertising function but rather be a reminder of past days and hand skills. That shift in purpose did not occur overnight, nor did it result from a conscious decision by an employer or mechanic. No one in a shop decreed formally that tin men give up evangelism in favor of symbolism.

Folk-art buffs secretly assume that tinners make tin men to satisfy the possessive needs of collectors. Scholars likewise pretend that tin men exist to pose abstract questions in material-culture studies. The sheet-metal mechanics who actually fabricate shop figures are strangely inarticulate about their artistry. Even when outsiders accept the notion that a secondary purpose has displaced the trade sign's original function, we have a limited grasp of the steps in this change or of the chronology involved.

Attempting to frame a time-line, I hoped to find tin men pictured in books and art catalogs. Although I found armor-clad warriors, domestic weather vanes, and intriguing toys, depictions of tinshop figures before the twentieth century eluded me. Photographs made since, some of which have been reproduced in this volume, are available, however. Looking at art collections and trade guides, I found interior scenes of mechanics at work but no tin men.

In addition to Jost Amman's *Kupfferschmidt,* toiling in a sixteenth-century copper shop (chapter 2), Denis Diderot in his *L'encyclopedie* (1751) offered precise engravings of tinsmiths and the braziers in their shops. Edward Hazen (1836) showed American tin-plate workers with mallets, anvils, or stakes engaged in sheet beating, edge turning, seam locking, and polishing metal products. In these three examples, artists emphasized shop technology and modes of production over portraiture.

James Goodwyn Clonney (1812–67), along with George Caleb Bingham and William Sidney Mount, specialized in everyday, bucolic, and domestic scenes. His genre painting *The Tinsmith* is the earliest American depiction I have seen of an itinerant tinner mending (soldering) a pot or bucket. Three young children observe as he works. I, too, am intrigued and wish to know where and when the artist met the tinsmith. I do not know, however, whether art historians or museum curators can shed light on Clonney's painting. *The Tinsmith* rests in a private collection and has not been reproduced recently.

Related to Clonney's subject, *Harper's Weekly,* on November 26, 1870, featured a cover drawing entitled *The Traveling Tinker* by John Bolles, who made his sketch from life in rural New Jersey. A tinker, portable charcoal stove at his side, kneels on the ground while mending a pot. We no longer see portraits of itinerant workers in the public press. When contemporary sheet-metal mechanics do appear in newspapers, they work with eye-catching abstract designs—curves and asymmetrical angles.

A *Harper's* writer commented nostalgically on Bolles's sketch:

> The itinerant tinker, a few years ago, was an important personage in the rural districts. He traveled from village to village, from farm-house to farm-house, and being generally a good-natured, oldish man, with a talent for conversation and telling stories, and always willing to chat over his puttering work, he was almost as welcome as the traveling peddlar. The growth of villages, and the increasing cheapness of manufacture, have nearly driven him out of business, and he is now rarely met with except in districts remote from large towns. People have discovered that it is cheaper to throw away leaky pans and kettles, and buy new ones, than to have the old tinkered up.

One artist in SMWIA ranks "returned" to the spirit of Clonney and Bolles. Beginning in 1975, John Niro, a retired tinner, donated twenty-six paintings involving tinshops and six drawings to the New York State Historical Association at Cooperstown. None held a tin man, however. Did Niro feel that such pieces were unrepresentative of his trade?

Born in 1906 to Italian and Irish immigrant parents, John Niro, eighteen, broke in on ductwork at the Nathaniel Hawthorne School in Yonkers and joined Local 38 in Westchester County. Depression years saw intermittent employment, non-union work, a stint at running his own shop, and a lapse in SMWIA membership. After wartime work at the Todd Shipyard in Brooklyn, he rejoined the union and transferred to Local 28 in Manhattan. He held every rank from journeyman to draftsmen to shop superintendent and retired in 1972 to Tucson, Arizona. Niro died in 1989.

Niro began to paint with oils as a hobby and progressed to creating a documentary record of a tradesman's life. His storytelling scenes convey personal memories and experiences—shop interiors, installing a metal roof, ductwork in all its phases, furnace work, a copper shop and a cornice shop, layoffs, and retirement. At first glance, the canvasses are realistic in their attention to detail, a mode natural to a mechanic who had long translated blueprints into three-dimensional objects. Viewers may be surprised by the nostalgia that each image evokes; shop interiors are dark, yet a craftman's pride in work lights each scene.

Michael Anne Lynn (1979) has cataloged and described Niro's art. *The Apprentice,* one of his autobiographical pieces, is a sixteen-by-twenty-inch oil. In it, a journeyman and an apprentice (Niro) leave a roofing shop at 7 A.M. The former carries a tool bag slung over his shoulder (reminiscent of the pigskin budget of Shakespeare's day). The apprentice follows, heavily burdened by charcoal fuel, a roll of metal, and a fire pot for heating soldering irons. They seem to be walking directly from shop to job-site or else from shop to trolley line. Niro recalled intense dislike for the tall mechanic with a long stride. "I, loaded down with tools and materials, could hardly keep up with him. . . . However I had to contain my emotions. . . . I knew my 'place in the trade'" (Lynn 1979, 25). This vignette of feeling—fear and duty—animates the painting as it give outsiders a notion of the journeyman's majesty, an aspect of occupational experience.

Although I would welcome seeing one, I have found no nineteenth-century sketch—woodcut, print, or painting—of a sculptured tin man, whether inside, in front of, or atop a sheet-metal shop. The first such art (exclusive of photography) I know of is a drawing of a metal man that appeared in advertising for Pacific Metals Company of San Francisco in June 1937. The firm no longer exists. I have been unable to learn whether the advertisement represents a company logo or an actual figure on the premises. The ad suggests that firms in other part of the country

89. *The Apprentice.*

had tin men that functioned both on location and in public print. Can any such drawings be located?

Because the only tin-men shop signs I have encountered are from the twentieth century, I assume that wooden signboards preceded them. Merchants and artisans have used the word *signboard* in print since 1632. Ambrose Heal (1947) cites 150 trades, among which armorers, braziers, tin platers, pewterers, and wire workers are of interest to contemporary sheet-metal mechanics. Their signs featured crossed keys, frying pans, pewter dishes, teakettles, horns to speak through, bird cages, and the ever-popular lamp and crown (a guild emblem). The ware displayed spoke to production. When did tinsmiths step into their signboards by showing themselves at work?

The words *signboard* and *trade sign* are often exchanged. The former required a painter, the latter, a wood-carver or metal worker. A blacksmith might suspend a horseshoe in front of his smithy, a locksmith might fabricate a large key to announce his shop, or a tinner might cut sheet iron in the form of a fish, bird, animal, or human for display by a tradesman. Museums treasure such nineteenth-century artifacts. I believe that early tinshop trade signs exist but have yet to find one.

Tin men have multiple uses—as shop announcement or symbol of heritage or to display skills. An outdoor trade sign should retain the spirit of early signboards by integrating name and design. George Dean's shop in Terre Haute, Indiana, for example, held a figure with raised, vertical letters spelling DEAN (chapter 9). Louis Stoffer of Centralia, Washington, built a tin man who points to the shop with one hand as he beats a drum with the other (chapter 10). Raised letters on the drum's rim announce the owner's name.

Other tin men relate variously to the names of their shops. Over the entrance to Valley Heating and Air Conditioning Supply in Spring Valley, New York, a sign functions like a traditional signboard. On it, a painted tin man resembles the actual tin figure who stands by the door. Wm. C. Brown and Son of Lowville, New York, places its figure underneath a sign that runs the length of a porch. The Stars and Stripes flank the piece, adding to its importance. Brennan Heating and Air-Conditioning in Jacksonville, Illinois, announces itself with a huge tin man who holds above his head a sign for Brennan's Plaza. The figure has been present in the community for more than a half-century. The Lee-Hi Sheet Metal tin man in Fairfax, Virginia, takes its name from the (Robert E.) Lee Memorial Highway that runs west through northern Virginia (U.S. 50).

These tin men represent trade signs that great numbers of viewers have not seen. *Youbert,* a Cincinnati figure visible from Interstate 75, however, attracts the attention of countless commuters and travelers. The Young and Bertke Air-Systems Company has engaged in industrial sheet-metal work since 1920 and since 1925 has used a drawing of a man made from duct tubing as its logo. Many decades ago

90. Valley Heating.

company tinsmiths enlarged the emblem and made it into an animated sign that was placed on top of the Y&B plant. Fans in the bleachers at nearby Crosley Field, formerly the Cincinnati Reds' home baseball park, could see the sign's image, which appeared to be striding. The onlooker who best guessed the distance the tin man "walked" won tickets for next year's games as part of a Y&B-sponsored competition.

Young and Bertke had to move after the construction of Interstate 75 in 1958 and built a new sign atop its second plant. When a major storm destroyed that sign, David Young, grandson of the founder, fabricated the present giant figure. *Youbert* (the tin man's nickname) is eighteen-and-a-half feet tall and strides vigorously, two yards at a step, with the help of an electric motor. Although he never leaves home, he has circumnavigated the globe three times over.

When *Youbert*'s motor fails, he is still. On one such occasion, commuters used to seeing him daily sent him a get-well card. Folklorist Tim Correll, who remem-

91. Wm. C. Brown and Son.

bers the figure from childhood in Cincinnati, recalls a sense of wonder at the tin man who simultaneously walked and stood still. Years elapsed before Tim recognized the work involved and developed an appreciation of the tin man's meaning. It is likely that more people have been amused by the Y&B tin man, visible from an urban freeway, than by any other in America. Has *Youbert* impressed them with tinshop skill? Is his kinship to figures in training centers and art museums obvious? How does he compare to other local landmarks?

I have used the terms *trade sign* to include all tin men who proclaim a shop presence (although some have ended in the hands of collectors or curators) and *teaching tools* to name sculptures in apprenticeship classes or in related vocational-education settings. Tin men who carry the seal of the Sheet Metal Workers' International Association also advertise, but their chief purpose is to ensure that the trade stays in good hands and that the skill nourished over centuries survives.

Much territory remains open to future explorers. We need biographical ac-

92. Brennan's Plaza.

counts of individual tinsmiths that examine their creativity. An overview of the diverse types of metal men used in trades other than sheet metal also would be of immense help. A search can still be made for tin men whose stories remain unknown. We lack comparative studies of tinshop signs. Perhaps a few folk-art buffs prefer some mystery in their prized objects, as if negative elements add value to their possessions. I find that attitude baffling, for tin men (as well as other work expressions) challenge me to explore matters of origin, use, and meaning.

Some art and antique dealers let goods deliberately pass through their hands without keeping records. Others are indifferent or hostile to extraneous questions. Fortunately, Aarne Anton at the American Primitive Gallery does not belong to that school. He has kept photographs of the tin men he has sold and has encouraged me in my pursuits. Anton recalls buying a tin man that was originally from Zanesville, Ohio. Built about 1950, it held a lightbulb in its grille-box head. It is unclear who has *Lighthead* now and whether the present owner has traced its story.

Lighthead is an example of many shop signs, and the tin men made in apprenticeship classes, whose beginning or present location remains clouded. I am committed to seeking details that demystify the process of fabrication, use, and disposition of such artifacts. I have attempted to trace the path that individual pieces

93. *Lee-Hi Sheet Metal.*

travel, and I share this curiosity with friends. Perhaps if I were a collector I would take pleasure in ownership and not feel impelled to engage in a form of detective work. The desire to know each tin figure's story—to assign meaning—has persisted throughout my research for this book.

The process of discovery seems obvious, yet it is marked by casual encounters and focused inquiry. Endless telephone calls and letter-writing in pursuit of tin men may seem obsessive to some and frivolous to others. Yet the accumulation of details about particular artifacts is preliminary to expansive knowledge about sheet-metal culture. One begins with a tin man and does not know the outcome of the search—biographical detail, institutional history, or ethical purpose.

As my research neared an end, Salt Lake City folklorist Hal Cannon, on a visit to San Francisco, brought me news (and slides) of several tin men and a tire-rim man that cast light on many of the issues touched upon in this book. Previously, he has collected western lore and has pioneered in the public presentation of such culture by inaugurating the Cowboy Poetry Gathering at Elko, Nevada. Thus, he approached undiscovered sheet-metal art as it compared to well-known cowboy ballads, legends, and material artifacts.

I judged the tire-rim construct to be outside this book's boundaries, but it reminded me of the arbitrary nature of any set of definitions. In Salt Lake City Local

94. The Young and Bertke animated sign.

312's hall, a twenty-inch cowboy perched atop a filing cabinet. The wee wrangler with gun, spurs, and Stetson seemed more playful than heroic. Unlike many tin men fabricated by apprentices as a proof piece, this figure had been made by Terry Larsen, a retired SMWIA member in Apache Junction, Arizona. In my opinion, the buckaroo resembles a tommy-knocker, the leprechaunlike spirit in hard-rock mines who simultaneously tricks miners and warns them of impending disasters. Is my analogy far-fetched, or did a diminutive cowboy in a region of silver and copper mines take on a second occupation?

Both Cannon and I talked to Larsen by telephone, and we hope that someone will visit him and document his amazing handiwork. Like most sheet-metal mechanics, Terry Larsen worked a lifetime without special attention to his latent artistry or trade's traditions. In 1994, however, he detected signs of muscular dystrophy and retired from Utah to Arizona. To keep his hands occupied, he made a Tin Woodsman from *The Wizard of Oz*. That choice of subject is not unusual, but Larsen's use of material (soup, juice, and kipper cans) is. In Apache Junction, Larsen has fabricated some 250 items of various metals—cowboys, cowgirls, Indians, sheriffs, prospectors, scarecrows, fishermen, cactuses, and carousels. He has scattered them widely to friends in Salt Lake City and elsewhere, to collectors through casual contact, and by auction at local health and charitable foundations.

Simultaneous with his visit to the Salt Lake SMWIA local, Hal Cannon conducted a series of interviews with union officers, apprentices, journeymen, retirees, and

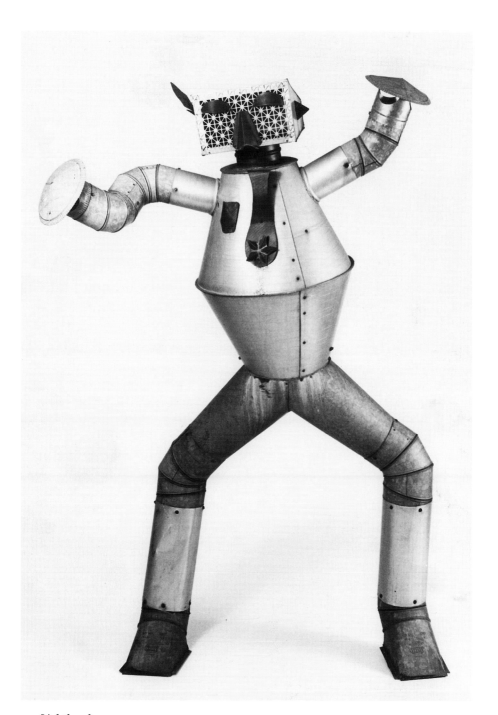

95. *Lighthead.*

employers for a program about sheet-metal artistry, aired on National Public Radio's *Marketplace* on December 6, 1999. The broadcast opened with the Tin Woodman's search for a heart—not the pulsing organ sustaining life, but the craft heritage that binds tinkers and tin-knockers together. Drawing upon interviews, Cannon used excerpts from visits with Alvin Joseph, eighty-eight, who had started in the trade in Birmingham, England; Steve Bunting, owner of the Schoppe Company, the oldest sheet-metal firm in Utah; Robbie Hatch, an apprentice doing ductwork on a modern high-rise office building in Provo, Utah; and myself as a folklorist.

Each participant commented on old and new shop customs. Joseph recalled hammering out Jaguar and Spitfire body parts by hand. Hatch noted that as a young construction hand and recently married, he found the demanding Provo job "a home away from home." Bunting, faced with computer-driven changes in his industry, speculated on the decline in craft pride exemplified by the demands put upon new workers. The program concluded with the thought that tinners

96. *Little Cowboy.*

would continue to search for heart, essentially a constant in redefining meaning in chosen work.

In addition to work on his radio production, Cannon assisted me in searching for tin men. He sent photographs of the Schoppe Company's four-foot-tall tin man made of standard parts. The piece now hangs on the shop's wall, permitting tinners to decorate it with a beard and accessories for Christmas. Cannon also interviewed Don Warinski, who had built the tin man in anticipation of a visit from a fifth-grade class. Don added a three-foot-tall metal owl, feathered and able to deliver Halloween candy to the children. In addition, Cannon photographed two of Terry Larsen's humorous figures, a cowboy and a fisherman, retained by the R. M. Chris Sheet Metal in West Jordan, Utah, near Salt Lake City. A few of Larsen's other pieces can be found in Utah, but the Chris figures are likely his only ones that function as tinshop trade signs. Another piece at the Ron Case Roofing Company is a Tin Woodman with funnel hat and axe. Perhaps inadvertently, he masks some ambivalence in design or purpose. The figure stands on a float parked in front of the plant, much like a huge logo, and advertises Case's sturdy roofs in various community parades.

Edward Armour, Local 312 organizer, indicated to Cannon that members contemplated making a tin man for a future parade float, but they would not use an Oz template. "We'll do it right." Did that comment mean Armour was displeased with a fantasy realm, or did he imply that the union should stand for values more significant than those of Oz? Possibly, Armour intended only that the local's figure deserved skill in its making greater than that accorded a Tin Woodman. There is much to be learned about how tinners view their own symbols.

Following Cannon's leads, I telephoned Michael Cooper, Salt Lake's apprentice-training officer, on October 4, 1999, to ask about additional tin men in Utah. His reply was startling. He had in storage and planned to display a little copper man that David Turner, a retired SMWIA official, had given the local. I knew it to be one of sixteen made by Pete Lyszewski at the annual AFL-CIO Union Industries Show (chapter 10). Pete had kept only one copper man at home. Of the many given away over the years, this is the first that I have traced.

Like many training officers for the SMWIA, Cooper had impressive experience. He knew the trade from the shop floor up. He had worked on air scrubbers (on the giant stacks) at Kennicott Copper. (I am curious about whether Kennicott's recent workers know of Wobbly Joe Hill's role in Utah copper mines and smelters.) Cooper expressed pride in his apprentices, who had won prizes in regional and national competitions. Above all, he was conscious of, and accepted responsibility for, continuing the traditions of his trade and his union.

In chapter 4, I defined the tin-can art pursued by hobbyists as being beyond the scope of this volume. Yet when I learned of Terry Larsen's use of cans along with other pieces of metal for his miniature pieces, I departed from my self-imposed standards. His cowboys live in a union hall and a modern sheet-metal shop in Utah; they also rest in these pages.

I have no facile explanation for why I am flexible about boundaries. Ideally, this book is focused on its subject as well as broad in its range of contents. Leads on lightly treated areas are found in the References. Bobby Hansson (1966), for example, has provided a fine survey of tin-can art. Although I leave the subject to him, I do note that the line dividing tin-can men from tin men requires constant attention and analysis. In a search for Alabama tinshop trade signs, for example, folklorist Joey Brackner visited SMWIA Local 48 in Birmingham and found a tin-can man made by retired member George Trigg. In a radically different setting, sociologist Bill Friedland found a little tin-can figure hanging from a tree in the campus garden of the University of California at Santa Cruz. It seemed to represent pagan or environmental beliefs, but when traced to its maker, Anna Wilks, she revealed no such mystery. Instead, she pointed to her neighbor, Stacey Grant, who had made tin-can pieces for a decade.

Two incomplete stories underscore this book's unresolved problems and open-ended challenges. Michael Hall opened the path for many explorers of tinsmith artistry. Among other leads, he found J&J Metal Products Company in Warren, Michigan. Its owner, called "Jim," asserted his originality in crafting a half-dozen tin men since 1984 and in protecting them by copyright. Hall noted Jim's four decades at the trade and his artistry. Hall also used two photographs of J&J pieces—*Find Us Fast* and *Summer Figure*—in a Cincinnati exhibition catalog (Metcalf and Hall, eds. 1986) and a *Metalsmith* article (Hall 1988).

Wishing to add to Hall's report, I reached Tom ("Jim") Kehoe by telephone on February 24, 1998, only to learn that he had moved his shop to nearby Clinton Township, Michigan. He seemed more protective of his tin men than other mechanics I have met. I shared that information with Oscar Paskal, a retired auto worker in Detroit, who visited Kehoe and noted the shop's tin-man logo outlined in neon in J&J's window and an ambulatory tin man on a wheeled contraption outside the shop. It took some fifteen years to move from Hall's to Paskal's findings. I am pleased that some of Kehoe's story is known, but much remains hidden. Where have Keohoe's tin men gone? Does he still plan to make new figures, and to what does he attribute his creativity?

In discussing Dan Collier's *Star Wars*–derived hybrid piece—part tin, part fiberglass—in chapter 5, I reported that he had seen, in childhood, a rider mounted on horseback used as a tinshop sign in San Bruno, California. Collier led me to Bob Quintero, who worked in the Dan Marelich shop in the 1950s. In turn, Bob referred me to Mary Marelich in Capitola, California. By telephone on October 19, 1998, she confirmed that her husband had indeed made a splendid trade sign for his shop, which was located close to the Tanforan Race Track. He sold the business many years ago, however, when Dennis Sammut bought the property to establish

97. *Find Us Fast.*

a popular casino, Artichoke Joe's, for those unable or unwilling to travel to Reno or Las Vegas. When Sammut demolished the tinshop to enlarge his casino, he did not destroy its distinctive trade sign. Rather, he had an exact duplicate horse and rider made and moved the pair to a secluded corral in Woodside, an hour's drive south of San Francisco. The pair, like horses put out to pasture, can not reflect on their fate. They might well have lived on in the Smithsonian Institution or a similar museum or been secreted in the home of a private collector.

We may never learn why Sammut preserved Marelich's tin man and had a tinsmith fabricate a companion. It is unlikely that I shall unearth the pair's full story, but I am pleased to have made a beginning. Several problems similar to the unanswered queries posed by the Marelich-Sammut pieces remain.

Sheet-metal mechanics constitute a small but vital portion of the American work force; they have received little attention in literary and artistic domains. If the Hollywood producers of *The Grapes of Wrath* or *On the Waterfront* had pictured their heroes as tin-knockers, Henry Fonda or Marlon Brando would have crafted a dazzling tin man. Ralph Ellison's *Invisible Man* spoke to only one aspect of American invisibility. Workers and their emblems need daylight as well.

Architect Frank Gehry used metal forms and material in 1988 to celebrate the centennial of the Sheet Metal Workers' International Association. For that occasion, Gehry designed a unique structure, confident that SMWIA mechanics would be able to give substance to his abstraction. The same exciting partnership is open to other artists and sculptors.

Sheet-metal workers heat and cool libraries, schools, museums, and think tanks of every persuasion. The intellectual issues of concern within these institutions need not be foreign to tin-knockers. Although my prime subject in these pages is

98. Outside the shop.

a set of physical artifacts, I have also considered the cultural matters that surround tinners and tin men. Such concerns may themselves be inferred from governing objects or practices. The Elizabethan artist who created a woodcut of a jolly tinker for a broadside ballad, for example, assumed that readers and singers had knowledge of a tinsmith's duties. Poets, playwrights, graphic artists, and filmmakers contribute to and extend such knowledge. Perhaps the guiding images held by and about tin-man fabricators will be detailed on another occasion; such a study may lead in surprising directions.

John Bunyan's fame rests on *The Pilgrim's Progress.* That allegory may seem an unlikely source for tin-man lore, but Bunyan worked as a tinker before he found outlet in preaching and writing. Did he see hellfire in the flames of the forge? Did he ever craft a demonic figure from metal? Such speculation aside, we know that tinkers had low status in Bunyan's day. Christopher Hill describes the itinerant menders of pots carousing, drabs and doxies by their sides, in the ale house (1989, 135–38).

Hill also traces the traditional, at times erotic, joke about tinkers making more holes than they repair to George Gascoigne's satiric poem *The Steele Glas* (1973 [1576]). In addition, he cites *The Tincker of Turvey* (1630), based on Chaucer's *Canterbury Tales,* to demonstrate beliefs held by Bunyan's contemporaries. Such find-

99. Out to pasture.

ings intrigue me and fan my curiosity about how such lore stands behind the varied shop signs I have found. It is easy to see a Tin Woodman, robot, or cowboy as a visible model for a tinshop trade sign. It is challenging, however, to know whether contemporary craftsmen still have images of drunken, lecherous tinkers.

I pose larger issues than the fate of particular tin men. If such matters are explored, it will take tinners, scholars, folk-art dealers, collectors, curators, apprenticeship training instructors, and labor officials together to dig out the full significance of tinshop and classroom figures. What follows are a few paragraphs on the responsibility of unionists.

Among the matters that union members face (although they often do not articulate it) is organized labor's role in the cultural arena. Some think that unions should stick to bread-and-butter issues (economic, social, and political); others maintain that unions cannot survive without attention to the identity and creativity of their members. Between those polar positions lie a wide range of possible actions.

Do union-staff educators and journal editors have a duty to consider members' artistry? How do esthetic, semantic, or moral problems intersect with labor's central concerns—wages, hours, and conditions of employment? What portion of dues money should go toward creative endeavors? Such questions may seem far-removed from this book's focus, yet they intrude as each tin man becomes known. The chain that links an individual tinsmith's sculpture to labor's larger goals may seem nonexistent or insubstantial. My task, however difficult, is to make that connection tangible and intelligible.

Scott Thurnan, SMWIA Local 66 organizer for the state of Washington, described a former business agent who had cleared the hall of all junk, including the tin man made by apprentice Jack Miller and teacher Bob Hansen in 1951. En route to the town dump, member Ted Eastman, owner of a Lynwood, Washington, shop, rescued Hansen and Miller's *Lance Man* (chapter 7). Re-named *Ski Poles* and nearly a half-century old, it stands secure in the Kenwood, Washington, hall. Thurnan's story is a metaphor for the ambiguous relationship of tin men to trade unionism. An apprentice built the tin man as part of his assimilation of trade competence and introduction to heritage. An officer junked the piece out of ignorance of tradition and contempt for antiquity. A member rescued it out of appreciation of ornamentation and respect for creativity. Craft artistry triumphed over careless pragmatism in Local 66, but how often does the reverse prevail?

In this book, I have called upon the preservationist impulses of sheet-metal workers. I do not know how many persons have destroyed tin men or how many museum curators or private collectors have rescued such objects. I remain committed to the proposition, however, that all individuals who take pleasure or comfort in tin men should join forces in unlocking their secrets. Tin men equate with ballads, blues, stories, sayings, rituals, riddles, customs, codes, and other expressive forms of laborlore. Although they are not easily apparent, a tin man, like any other artistic piece, is an outlet for creative energy, a mark of defiance, an affirmation of community, and a summation of a worker's experience.

Companion studies on muffler and tin-can men, abstract and recycled-scrap sculptures, and humanity in metal form across the lines of trade would be ideal. I do not assert that a piece of recognized folk art is more beautiful, valuable, or significant than a trade-sign figure. In addition to having significant social meaning, the latter, and their classroom companions, challenge us to see them as symbolic of a trade and expressions of workers' artistry.

Leaving aside esthetic and philosophic matters, I circle back to my initial meeting with *Al's the Tin Man* and *Copper Man* in the San Francisco Craft and Folk Art Museum. There, they combined shop-floor geometry and trade-union imagery in an occupational pageant. Each challenged me to examine facile codes, question the lines that divide artists from workers, and raise again the troubling matter of how contemporary society handles labor's concerns.

Al and his copper buddy asked me to jump about from museum gallery to union hall, folk-art bookstore, academic library, classroom, toy shelf, and tinshop. In those diverse places I met many old friends and made new ones who were generous beyond expectations. Above all, they invited me to rethink fixed assumptions on blue-collar artistry and welcome fresh approaches to overlooked artifacts.

When the Fort Mason exhibit ended, Caskey and Lees carted *Al's the Tin Man* back to Topanga, some twenty miles from his original place in a Melrose Avenue tinshop. After a few years, the antique dealers sold *Al* to the Carl Hammer Gallery in Chicago. In turn, Hammer sold it to a private collector. I do not know whether the present owner cares that *Al*'s story is still incomplete or whether that person is curious about the sequence transforming a functional trade sign into a prized objet d'art. By contrast, Lewis Wittlinger's *Copper Man* has returned from the Craft and Folk Art Museum to San Francisco Local 104's inner sanctum, thus rejoining related gifts made for and by graduating apprentices to symbolize the wedding of craft wizardry and union belief.

I have read the shop-sign *Al* and Local 104's *Copper Man* as complex texts that hold diverse purposes and hidden meanings. One, at time of fabrication, attracted commercial hustle. The other, with a union logo stamped on his chest, advanced social issues. *Al,* facing an urban street, was a brother to the giant loggers, cowboys, and riverboatmen along U.S. highways. *Copper Man,* cloistered in a union hall, asks for attention to the links that tie teaching tool to trade sign.

With luck and care, tin sign and copper symbol will escape rust and stain. I pray that each wards off the wrecker's ball, junker's torch, and vandal's hand. Each, with brothers and sisters from the Atlantic to the Pacific, deserves a long life and quiet chance to reflect on a venerable trade's mystery.

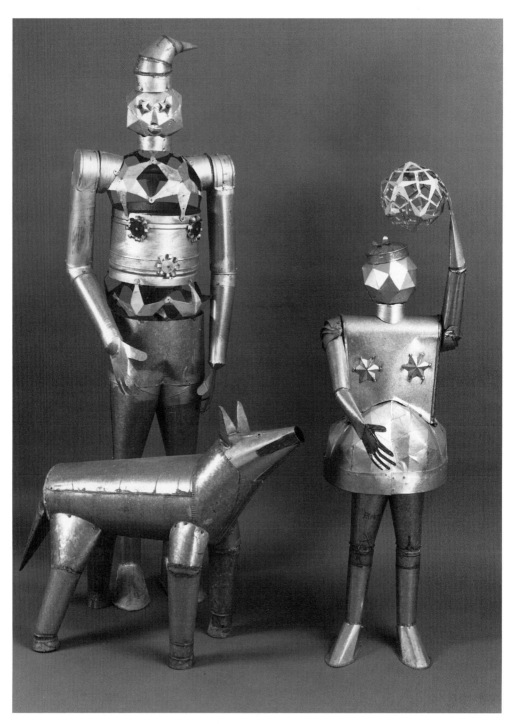

100. Rene Latour's *Clown, Dog,* and *Girl with Ball.*

APPENDIX: INVENTORY

This inventory is of tin-man trade signs and related teaching tools usually made in apprenticeship classes, including items made of sheet metal (galvanized iron or steel), stainless steel, copper, aluminum, zinc, and alloys. I exclude figures made of mufflers, pipes, gears, tanks, radiators, and parts fabricated by auto mechanics, plumbers, electricians, and ironworkers. In some cases, a combination shop, such as sheet metal–plumbing or sheet metal–roofing, has a tin man that I include. Recycled or found-object art and folk or fine-art, metal-sculptured figures should be listed by others.

The inventory does not include all pieces mentioned in this book, although they were made by tinsmiths. Nor does it list replica figures such as knights made at home or at work. Tin-can art presents a classificatory challenge; I do list a few tin-can men.

I have identified tin men by photographs in my files and photographs published in books, museum catalogs, newspaper or journal articles, and shop advertisements. I have retained tin-men names given by sheet-metal workers, authors, editors, collectors, curators, or dealers. My arrangement is alphabetical by location, Akron, Ohio, to Woodside, California. I do not know the location of some items that have been either lost or destroyed or are in private hands.

Akron, Ohio, Local 70: Tin man made for Labor Day parade float, 1986. "Local 70 Members Keep Busy," *Sheet Metal Workers' Journal* 78 (April 1987): 12.

Albion, Iowa: Civil War drummer, *Moses,* made by Donco Air Products employees and displayed on premises.

Anchorage, Alaska: Five-button figure made by Marvin Munger for Western Sheet Metal Works, 1959, and on shop roof. M. J. Gladstone, *A Carrot for a Nose* (New York: Scribner's, 1974), 40; [Phil Airulla], "'Tin Men': The Sheet Metal Worker's Human Touch in Metal," *Sheet Metal Workers' Journal* 87 (Jan.–Feb. 1996): 4–8.

Angels Camp, Calif.: Made for Angels Sheet Metal, 1992, and on the front of the shop building.

Arlington, Va.: Robot-like tin man, eight feet tall, probably made in Kansas City ca. 1950.

Originally attached to the front of an unknown tinshop. Purchased by Darrell Dean at Hillsville, Va., flea market.

Atlanta, Ga., Local 85: Tin man with ventilator head made for Labor Day parade, 1983; a second figure with Local number, MR 85, on chest, made for Labor Day 1986. "Pictured Is the Local 85, Atlanta, Georgia Float," *Sheet Metal Workers' Journal* 74 (Oct. 1983): 9; "Local 85 Participants in Labor Day Parade," *Sheet Metal Workers' Journal* 74 (Nov.–Dec 1983): 18; "Local 85 Float Takes First Place in Labor Day Parade," *Sheet Metal Workers' Journal* 77 (Nov. 1986): 13.

Berea, Ky.: Little man with safety goggles and protective earmuffs purchased by Larry Hackley at Heartland Antiques Show, Richmond, Ind., from a dealer who brought it from New England.

Birmingham, Ala., Local 48: Tin-can man made by retiree George Trigg and exhibited in the union hall.

Boise, Idaho, Local 213: Two made by apprentices between 1947 and 1949 and exhibited at the Idaho State Fair. "Idaho Local Exhibits Apprenticeship Work," *Sheet Metal Workers' Journal* 41 (Feb. 1950): 14.

Boise, Idaho: Made by Wayne Van Cleave at Quality Heating and exhibited at the 1993 home show.

Boston, Mass., Local 17: Made by apprentices in western Massachusetts Local 63, Springfield, then "captured" and held in Local 17's eastern Massachusetts training center in Dorchester. [Phil Airulla], "'Tin Men': The Sheet Metal Worker's Human Touch in Metal," *Sheet Metal Workers' Journal* 87 (Jan.–Feb. 1996): 4–8.

Buffalo, N.Y., Local 71: Copper and tin men made by Peter Lyszewski for union apprenticeship classes and in community-sponsored vocational-education schools. Copper men also made regularly between 1974 and 1989 during the annual AFL-CIO Union Industries Show and used as gifts. The total number and location of each are unknown except for one in the Lyszewski home in Buffalo and one in the Salt Lake City Joint Apprentice Training Center. "Sheet Metal Craftsmanship Demonstrated at 1979 AFL-CIO Union Industries Show," *Sheet Metal Workers' Journal* 70 (May 1979): 17; "SMWIA Skills and Craftsmanship Demonstrated at 1980 AFL-CIO Union Industries Show," *Sheet Metal Workers' Journal* 71 (July 1980): 10; Joseph Ritz, "'The Lantern Man' Cast a Glow with Handicraft," *Buffalo News,* June 15, 1987, B8.

Burlingame, Calif.: A life-sized tin man with white gloves and huge red heart was photographed by Tom Carey in Feb. 2000 in the window of American Cancer Discovery Shop. The tin man sold, and there is no trace of its maker or present owner.

Canton, N.Y.: A figure made by Milford Howe for his hardware store and tinshop ca. 1940 was purchased by Kate and Allan Newell in 1983 at the Howe estate auction.

Centralia, Wash.: *Jasper,* made by Louis Stoffer in 1932 for his original downtown shop, is now in a new shop lobby outside town. *Daily Chronicle* (Centralia, Wash.) ca. 1937, reprinted in part in "Iron Man Now Has Been Living Indoors for Thirty-nine Years," *Daily Chronicle,* July 4, 1976 (advertisement).

Centralia, Wash.: A man beating a drum, made by Louis J. Stoffer in 1984, is now on the lawn and pointing to shop.

Chicago, Ill., Local 73: Six figures were made for a St. Patrick's Day parade float, 1988, and are also used at other events. They are held at the apprenticeship school in Bellwood, Ill. "Committee Awards First Prize to Local 73," *Sheet Metal Workers' Journal* 79 (Dec. 1988): 17; [Phil Airulla], "'Tin Men': The Sheet Metal Worker's Human Touch in Metal," *Sheet Metal Workers' Journal* 87 (Jan.–Feb. 1996): 4–8; Archie Green, "Tin Men on Parade," *Labor's Heritage* 10 (Spring–Summer 1999): 34–47.

Chicago, Ill.: On the roof of Kirby's Sheet Metal. Photograph by Bucky Halker.

Chicago, Ill.: A menacing figure made ca. 1945 in a Halstead Avenue shop was described as a "Bear's linebacker" by Hall. Photographed in a shop window by Roger Brown. Robert Hemphill and Julia Weissman, *Twentieth-Century American Folk Art and Artists* (New York: E. P. Dutton, 1974), 79; Michael D. Hall, "This Side of Oz: A Heart for the Tin Man," *Metalsmith* 8 (Spring 1988): 24.

Chicago, Ill.: A tin woman made by Local 73 apprentices. [Nick Carter], "Local 73 Apprentice Coordinator Keith Switzer. . . ." *Snips* (April 1988): 97 (photo).

Cincinnati, Ohio: The huge, animated figure powered by an electrical motor gear-reducer is part of a roof sign at Young and Bertke Co. (sheet metal and air systems). Various other stationary signs are also on the building; *Youbert* was developed from a logo registered in 1925. David Wecker, "Landmark Walks, Walks, but Gets Nowhere," *Cincinnati Post,* n.d., 1C; Archie Green, "Tin Men on Parade," *Labor's Heritage* 10 (Spring–Summer 1999): 41.

Cleveland, Ohio, Local 33: Members displayed two tin men and demonstrated metalworking skills while visiting the Mount Pleasant Historical Society. "Tin Men Visit Historic Village," *Sheet Metal Workers' Journal,* 81 (May 1990): 21.

Clinton Township, Mich.: Tin man pictured at J&J Metal Products, Warren, Mich., made by owner Tom Kehoe and identified as *Summer Figure.* Michael D. Hall, "This Side of Oz: A Heart for the Tin Man," *Metalsmith* 8 (Spring 1988): 27.

 a. A second man marked by telephone-book advertising on his chest: *Find Us Fast.* Eugene Metcalf and Michael Hall, eds., *The Ties That Bind: Folk Art in Contemporary American Culture* (Cincinnati: Contemporary Arts Center, 1986), 46.

 b. A third man in the shop window marked with *J&J* on his chest. Eugene Metcalf and Michael Hall, eds., *The Ties That Bind: Folk Art in Contemporary American Culture* (Cincinnati: Contemporary Arts Center, 1986), 46.

 c. The shop moved from Warren, Mich., to its present location, where the fourth man is on a wheeled contraption and moved inside shop each night.

Cold Spring, N.Y.: Life-sized figure for sale in 1999 by Tin Man Antiques and Fine Art.

Columbus, Ohio, Local 24: Three tin men made by apprentices held at the local's hall.

Denver, Colo., Local 9: *Union Family* (*Daddy, Mommy, Baby Boy,* and *Baby Girl*) made by Colorado apprentices. Also two little men, three feet tall, pulled in wagons by youngsters at parades. Held in apprenticeship center. "SMWIA Float at Colorado State Fair," *Sheet Metal Workers' Journal,* Nov. 1986, 10.

Denver, Colo.: A replica of the Statue of Liberty fabricated by Bob Ramsour of Federal Heating in 1983. Originally painted white but subsequently painted mint green to resemble Bartholdi's original. A seven-foot figure of Uncle Sam made by Bob Ramsour in the 1970s. [Nick Carter], "Ramsour of Federal Heating, Denver, Makes Replica of Statue of Liberty for Shop Front," *Snips* (Sept 1983): 132–34; "Another Face-Lift for a Lady Liberty," *Denver Post,* Oct. 29, 1986, 1; *An American Sampler: Folk Art from the Shelburne Museum* (Washington, D.C.: National Gallery of Art, 1987), 38.

Denver, Colo.: A seven-foot figure of Uncle Sam made by Bob Ramsour in the 1970s.

Des Moines, Iowa, Local 45: Smiling sheet-metal robot made for display at AFL-CIO Union Industries Show in Des Moines, 1961. "Local 45 Captures the Crowd," *Sheet Metal Workers' Journal* 52 (Dec. 1961): 20.

Detroit Locals 281 and 292: Float of *Metal Dingers Band* in 1949 Labor Day parade included a large tin man. Labor Day parade in 1951 featured a tin man riding a metal-sculptured horse. "Detroit Labor Day Parade Units," *Sheet Metal Workers' Journal* 40 (Oct. 1949): 14; "I.A. Float Detroit Prize Winner," *Sheet Metal Workers' Journal* 42 (Oct. 1951): 14.

Duluth, Minn.: Life-sized, Tin Woodman–like figure on the roof of D. G. Solem and Sons made ca. 1994 by foreman Brian Linn. A smaller man is mounted on an abandoned well-casing in the yard of Linn's house behind the tinshop.

Eugene, Ore., Local 16: Figure wearing cowboy hat and boots and made by apprentices in Medford, Ore., in 1975 is held at Lane Community College, Eugene, by Perry McGill, program director of the Southwest Oregon Sheet Metal Training Trust.

Fairfax, Va.: A greeter, arms outstretched, is on the roof of Lee-Hi Sheet Metal.

Falls Church, Va.: *Mr. Dixie* was made for the Dixie Sheet Metal Works in 1962 and stands in front of the shop. Jeff Bagato, "Tin Man," *Washington Post Magazine,* Aug. 28, 1994, 7; Alan Jabbour, "The American Folklife Center: A Twenty-Year Retrospective," *Folklife Center News* 18, 1–2 (1996): 4; Jeff Bagato, "Unusual Suspects," *Washington Post Weekend,* Sept. 1, 2000, 32.

Farmingdale, N.J., Local 27: A four-foot-tall figure is held at the Southern New Jersey Training Center.

Flint, Mich.: A stainless-steel man was made at Dee Cramer, Inc. for trade-fair display in 1990 and is displayed in the shop's showroom. "Off to the Show," *Flint Journal,* March 9, 1990, 1; [Nick Carter], "Stainless Steel Tin Man Fabricated by Dee Cramer, Inc. for Display at Flint Fair," *Snips* (April 1990): 118–19.

Goshen, Mass.: Made by George Duensser for the Hampshire Engineering Service, Haydenville, in 1952 and repaired several times. It stands in front of the Good Time Stove Co. on Route 112. Chris Burrell, "Goshen's Towering Tin Man," *Daily Hampshire Gazette,* July 3, 1991, 15; Kim Winters, "Tin Man Gets a Heart," *Daily Hampshire Gazette,* Dec. 21, 1996.

Grand Rapids, Mich., Local 410: Oz-like Tin Woodman, axe in hand, was made by fourth-year apprentices and shown at the Saginaw County United Way "Have a Heart" campaign. "His Heart Is in the Right Place," *Sheet Metal Workers' Journal* 73 (Nov. 1982): 16.

Grosse Point Park, Mich.: A tin man with wooden cut-out hands covered in tin. Made ca. 1970s at Royal Oaks, Mich., and held by Michael and Peggy Hennigen.

Hartford, Conn., Local 40: A figure flanked by the SMWIA and SMACNA logos displayed at the 1987 Connecticut State Fair. "Local 40 Booth at State Fair a Success," *Sheet Metal Workers' Journal* 78 (May 1987): 23.

Hermiston, Ore.: Two figures on are on the roof of Road Runner Sheet Metal and date to 1955 and 1998. The first (in a cowboy hat) was made by Wayne Hamilton to advertise his shop. In retirement Hamilton teaches apprentices, who made second man (in a baseball hat) for the present shop. Richard Rockwell, "Tin Man Survives More Than Fifty Years Later," *Hermiston Herald,* n.d.

Idaho Falls, Idaho: Made by a sheet-metal worker named Ernie for a parade in 1992 and now mounted on top of Jewell Electric, a firm that includes air-conditioning work.

Jacksonville, Fla.: *Tin Man Jr.* made with Crown Products fittings pictured at Fort Lauderdale meeting. [Nick Carter], "Presenting Final Photos Taken at Florida A.C. Contrs. Ass'n Conference and Trade Show," *Snips* (Aug. 1990): 166.

Jacksonville, Ill.: Made by R. W. Brennan in 1982, the figure is at an outdoor plaza in front of Brennan Heating and Air Conditioning. Brennan's grandson made a little tin man in 1996.

Kennewick, Wash., Local 66: A man, three feet tall, was made by apprentices and instructor Paul Smith. It is held by Frank Worthington, coordinator of the Southeast Washington–Northeast Oregon Sheet Metal Training Trust.

Las Vegas, Nev., Local 88: A broad-shouldered man holding lunchbox and a blueprint roll was made by apprentices and is held in the local's training center.

Leonardtown, Md.: Made by Larry Brabec's students at St. Mary's County Technical Center, 1989. [Nick Carter], "Presenting a Round-Up of Tin Man Replicas and Costumes Fabricated by Various Sheet metal Craftsmen," *Snips* (Aug. 1990): 16–22.

Lewiston, Maine: A smiling tin man on stilts holds an overhead sign: "General Insulation Company: HVAC Insulations, Accessories & Gasketing Materials."

Los Angeles, Calif., Local 108: Made by Lloyd Rademacher, JATC administrator, but left unfinished at his death on Feb. 11, 1997.

Lowville, N.Y.: Made for Wm. C. Brown and Son Heating and Plumbing and stands on the shop's porch.

Merced, Calif.: De Wing Sheet Metal had a tin man on the canopy over its shop door from 1945. In 1952 the owner, Carl De Wing, built a stainless-steel man, which was kept in the shop until De Wing's retirement in 1976 and then donated to Merced Community College. De Wing Sheet Metal advertisement, *Farmer-Labor News* (Modesto, Calif.), March 16, 1951, 11; "Longtime Sheet Metal Contractor De Wing Retires," *Sun-Star* (Merced, Calif.), Jan. 22, 1976, n.p.

Milwaukee, Wis., Local 124: *Mr. Sheet Metal,* a robot figure made by apprentices, is displayed at the Wisconsin Sheet Metal Contractors Association. "'Mr. Sheet Metal,' Robot Made at No. 124," *Sheet Metal Workers' Journal* 42 (May 1951): 17.

Milwaukee, Wis.: Created by the sheet-metal division (John Lipski, Tim Peterson, and Bob Menden) for the Christmas parade in 1991, the figure was held in the lobby of the Master Lock Co. before being retired in 1998.

Milwaukee, Wis.: *Fred,* one of many inventory display figures made at the Williamson Co. in Hillsboro, Ohio, a duct-work manufacturer, for Harding Heating and Cooling in Troy, Ohio, in 1974. Held in the Milwaukee Art Museum. Milwaukee Art Museum, *Common Ground/Uncommon Vision: The Michael and Julie Hall Collection of American Folk Art* (Milwaukee: The Museum, 1993), 133.

Milwaukee, Wis.: *The Greeter,* made by Bruno Poldinsek for Duquet and Sons Heating, Highland, Mich., ca. 1982, is held in the Milwaukee Art Museum. Michael D. Hall, "This Side of Oz: A Heart for the Tin Man," *Metalsmith* 8 (Spring 1988): 26; Milwaukee Art Museum, *Common Ground/Uncommon Vision: The Michael and Julie Hall Collection of American Folk Art* (Milwaukee: The Museum 1993), 134.

Mount Vernon, N.Y.: Made by Artie Tartaglia and Anthony Infalice about 1975, a figure is in the graffiti-scrawled shop window of Cornely Brothers.

New York, N.Y., Local 28: Made by apprentices and instructor Nick Maldarelli for the Labor Day 1998 parade float, the figure is held at the training center in Jamaica, N.Y. Archie Green, "Tin Men on Parade," *Labor's Heritage* 10 (Spring–Summer 1999): 44.

New York, N.Y.: Made by George Dean for his outside shop sign, Terre Haute, Ind., ca. 1956, and in the collection of Elli Buk, New York City. Archie Green, "Tin Men on Parade," *Labor's Heritage* 10 (Spring–Summer 1999): 39.

New York, N.Y.: David Owen, "The Sultan of Stuff," *The New Yorker,* July 19, 1999, 53 (a profile of Alex Shear). The caption of the photograph indicates that Shear has thirty-five tin men. Photographer Chris Callis posed him with twelve of them, three of which do not fit this inventory. Of the remaining nine, I can identify several made by sheet-metal workers, probably as trade signs. Specifically, one with claw hands and a thermostat on its chest was purchased at a Massachusetts flea market by Aarne Anton of the American Primitive Gallery and sold to Shear. Another was originally purchased by Linda Franklin's father at a Hillsville, Va., flea market, eventually sold to Anton, and the resold to Shear.

New York, N.Y.: A Viking-like figure with a horned helmet was made in Ohio ca. 1945 and sold by Aarne Anton to a Manhattan restaurant.

New York, N.Y.: Cowboy with number 200 on his chest. Made in Ormond Beach, Fla., by Rene Latour for his backyard shop in 1976. Purchased by Aarne Anton and then sold to Bert Hemphill, who donated it to American Museum of Folk Art.

New York, N.Y.: *The Dandy* was made by David Goldsmith for his West End Sheet Metal and Roofing Works in Long Island City, N.Y., ca. 1930. Purchased by antique dealer Gerald

Kornblau about 1968 and then sold to Elaine Cooper. Subsequently sold again to a private collector, Ralph Esmerian, in New York City. Now in American Museum of Folk Art. Amherst College, *American Folk Art* (Amherst: The College, 1974), fig. 120; Robert Bishop, *American Folk Sculpture* (New York: E. P. Dutton, 1974), 38–39; M. J. Gladstone, *A Carrot for a Nose* (New York: Scribner's, 1974), 41; Jean Lipman, *Provocative Parallels* (New York: E. P. Dutton, 1975), 40; Jean Lipman and Helen Franc, *Bright Star: American Painting and Sculpture since 1776* (New York: E. P. Dutton, 1976), 83; Jean Lipman, Elizabeth V. Warren, and Robert Bishop, *Young America: A Folk-Art History* (New York: Hudson Hills Press in association with the Museum of American Folk Art, 1986), 148; Jean Lipman et al., *Five Star Folk Art: One Hundred American Masterpieces* (New York: Abrams, 1990), 122; Michael D. Hall, "This Side of Oz: A Heart for the Tin Man," *Metalsmith* 8 (Spring 1988): 22–27; Stacey Hollander, *American Radiance: The Ralph Esmerian Gift to the American Folk Art Museum* (New York: Abrams, 2001), 550; Whitney Museum of American Art, *Two Hundred Years of American Sculpture* (Boston: Godine, 1976), 106.

North Little Rock, Ark.: An oil-drum figure on a shop roof holds a welding torch. It was made ca. 1960 by the original owner of B.J. (Big Jim's) Welding.

Novato, Calif.: Made by Grant Garl for Aaero Heating and Sheet Metal ca. 1979, it is on a back wall inside the shop.

Oak Forest, Ill.: Made for King Heating and Air Conditioning ca. 1971, the figure has a crown on its head and a *K* on its chest. It is on the roof of the building.

Oak Harbor, Wash.: The roof-line trade sign of man on horse at Lueck Sheet Metal was designed by Stener Johnson. "At the Sign of the Tin Horse," *Sheet Metal Workers' Journal* 42 (Oct. 1951): 15.

Pacifica, Calif.: Made by Matt Addiego for Coast Sheet Metal, Heating and Mechanical ca. 1992, the figure was in the shop's window. After the firm changed hands, the figure vanished.

Parkersburg, W.V. Local 299: A cartoonlike tin man was shown at a Jaycee Exposition. "An Apprenticeship Training Display," *Sheet Metal Workers' Journal* 60 (July 1969): 15.

Pasco, Wash.: A six-foot-tall man is held at Columbia Community College.

Peoria, Ill.: A copper man, nine feet tall, was made by Ray Mackie and Frank Matulis of A. J. Fritch Sheet Metal Shop. "L.U. 1 Craftsmen Make Real Sheet Metal Man," *Sheet Metal Workers' Journal* 62 (Jan. 1971): 11.

Peoria, Ill., Local 1: A robotlike sheet-metal figure was made by apprentices ca. 1970; a copper man was made in 1998 by fourth-year apprentices. Both are in the union hall.

Phoenix, Ariz., Local 359: Cowboy with Stetson at the Union Industries Show in 1967. "Sheet Metal Exhibit Attracts Attention at Show," *Sheet Metal Workers' Journal* 58 (July 1967): 13.

Pittsburgh, Pa., Local 12: A football player was made by apprenticeship instructor Frank Cardiello. "Pittsburg Local Holds Diamond Jubilee Dinner," *Sheet Metal Workers' Journal* 46 (Dec. 1955): 12.

Pulaski, Va.: A tin man made of standard parts in a third-generation family tinshop was loaned to the Blue Ridge Institute at Ferrum College in Ferrum, Va., for an exhibit: "Roadside Attractions: Folk Art along the Byways." "Tin Man Shop Sign by Robert J. Kirkner," *Folk Art Finder* 20 (Summer 1999): 13; "Tin Man and Yard Dog," *Berea College Appalachian Center News Letter* (Summer 1999).

Raleigh, N.C.: Made for N. B. Handy, a furnace-fitting wholesaler ca. 1973, the figure is on the merchandise floor.

Reno, Nev., Local 26: Two tin men are held at the local's training center.

Rhinebeck, N.Y.: Made in Ormond Beach, Fla., by Rene Latour for Ormond Sheet Metal and Roofing in 1961, purchased by Aarne Anton, and sold to Stephen Mazoh, Rhinebeck, N.Y.

Richmond, Va., Local 15: A sheet-metal robot was made by third-year apprentices. "Richmond L.U. 15 Apprentices Build Sheet Metal Robot," *Sheet Metal Workers' Journal* 64 (June 1973): 22.

Sacramento, Calif., Local 162: *Willie Bend* wears a hard hat and has flag decals on its chest. It was made by fifth-year apprentices in 1996 and is held in the local's training center.

Sacramento, Calif.: *The Sheriff,* made ca. 1997 for Perfection Home Systems, was exhibited at home shows and occasionally loaned out.

Salt Lake City, Utah, Local 312: A copper man made by Pete Lyszewski, Buffalo, N.Y., is held at the Utah Sheet Metal Education and Training Trust.

Salt Lake City, Utah, Local 312: A cowboy made by Terry Larson, Apache Junction, Ariz., is held in the union's hall.

Salt Lake City, Utah: A tin man hangs on a wall inside the shop of the Schoppe Co.

Salt Lake City, Utah: A tin man was on a parade float outside the Ron Case Roofing Co.

Sandusky, Ohio, Local 65: Apprentice Don Ahner and instructor Charles Gundlach turned out a life-sized robot. "Apprentice Builds Sheet Metal Robot," *Sheet Metal Workers' Journal* 46 (Dec. 1955): 8.

San Francisco, Calif., Local 104: A copper man sixteen inches tall was made by Lewis Wittlinger for apprenticeship students ca. 1979 and held in the union's hall. C. Kurt Dewhurst, "Working Folk: Artists at Work," in *A Report* 13, no. 2 (1995): 4; Archie Green, "Tin Man and Copper Man: Trade Sign and Union Symbol," *Commemorating One Hundred Years of Excellence in Craftsmanship, 1896–1996* (San Francisco: Building and Construction Trades Council), 97; Archie Green, "Tin Men on Parade," *Labor's Heritage* 10 (Spring–Summer 1999): 42.

San Francisco, Calif.: A metal man appeared in advertising for the Pacific Metals Co. Whether it was an advertising logo or whether an actual tin man existed is unknown. "The 'Metal Man' Congratulates the Class of June, 1937," *The Mission* (Mission High School yearbook).

San Jose, Calif., Local 104: A figure inspired by C-3PO in *Star Wars,* made of sheet metal and fiberglass by Dan Collier as a Halloween costume in 1977, is displayed in the lobby of the local's San Jose training office, where it is on permanent loan.

Santa Fe, N.M.: A figure was on the roof of Tin Man Supply.

Seattle, Wash., Local 99: Made by apprentice Jack Miller in 1951, the original held a lance. The figure was altered ca. 1970, however, to hold ski poles. It is now in the shop at the union hall and training center of Local 66 (Kirkland, Wash.). "Edison School Robot to 'Explain' Display at Centennial Show," *Seattle Times,* Oct. 28, 1951, 10; "No. 99 Apprentice Makes Robots," *Sheet Metal Workers' Journal* 43 (April 1952): 9; [Phil Airulla], "'Tin Men': The Sheet Metal Worker's Human Touch in Metal," *Sheet Metal Workers' Journal* 87 (Jan.–Feb. 1996): 4–8.

Sebastopol, Calif.: Made by John Jordan for King and Jordan Sheet Metal Work ca. 1948, the figure is now on top of Glenn's Metal Works. Hanafi Russell, "Tin Man Lives," *Sebastopol Times,* Jan. 10, 1980, 1; [Phil Airulla], "'Tin Men': The Sheet Metal Worker's Human Touch in Metal," *Sheet Metal Workers' Journal* 87 (Jan.–Feb. 1996): 4–8; Timothy Correll and Patrick Polk, eds., *The Cast-Off Recast: Recycling and the Creative Transformation of Mass-Produced Objects* (Los Angeles: UCLA Fowler Museum of Cultural History, 1999), 38.

Sparrow Bush, N.Y.: Made for John Coda and Son, sheet-metal supplies, and on the roof of its building.

Spokane, Wash., Local 212: Made for a Labor Day float in 1983, the figure is an unusual "happy-faced" tin man with guitars, banjo, and string bass. The instruments were retained at training center, but the tin man subsequently "got away." "Local 212 Displays Skills in Labor Day Parade," *Sheet Metal Workers' Journal* 74 (Nov.–Dec. 1983): 18.

Spring Green, Wis.: A cowboy was made for Tri-County Heating and Sheet Metal. Michael D. Hall, "This Side of Oz: A Heart for the Tin Man," *Metalsmith* 8 (Spring 1988): 27.

Spring Valley, N.Y.: Made for Valley Heating and Air Conditioning Supply.

St. Croix Falls, Wis.: Made by Harold Bishop and David Carlson for the Tin Man Shop ca. 1967.

Ste. Genevieve, Mo.: Made for Schweiss Plumbing, Heating and Air Conditioning. "New Location," *Ste. Genevieve Herald,* July 8, 1998, 3.

St. Louis, Mo., Local 36: The local holds two tin-man costumes that apprentices wear on occasion and pose in front of a replica of the Gateway Arch in front of the training center. "Dale Luttrell Helps Celebrate Expansion of Steelworkers Training Facility," *Ste. Genevieve Herald,* May 31, 2000; "Technology Advances Metal Work," *St. Louis Post Dispatch,* June 4, 2000.

Syracuse, N.Y.: Two (possibly more) made by tinsmiths at D. J. Heaphy and Son:

    a. One with *Heaphy the Tinman* painted on its chest. With frequent repaintings, the words vary. Placed in front of the shop and pictured on a postcard ca. 1908. Replaced and rebuilt after being hit by a car. Donated to the Onondaga Historical Association. Dick Chase, "After Decades at Work, Tin Man Retires to Museum," *Herald-American,* Jan. 11, 1998; Archie Green, "Tin Men on Parade," *Labor's Heritage* 10 (Spring-Summer 1999): 40.

    b. A figure with no sign on its chest. Exhibited at the Everson Museum of Art in 1996. Michael Davis and Roland Sweet, "Tin Kin," *New Times,* May 1, 1985, 9.

Syracuse, N.Y.:

    a. A figure for the Saya Heating and Sheet Metal Co. is named *Superman.*

    b. Lincoln Supply Co.

    c. A tin woman in the window of Krell Distributing Co. All pictured in Michael Davis and Roland Sweet, "Tin Kin," *New Times,* May 1, 1985, 9.

Tucson, Ariz.: Made by Dave Carlson, Sr., and Clarence R. McSherry in 1997 and in the showroom of the Carlson Co.

Washington, D.C.: Made by Gerald McCarthy for his shop in Ogdensburg, N.Y., ca. 1950. The words "Plumbing, Heating, Cooling" are painted on chest of the figure, named *Galvanized Man* in the catalog of the Hemphill exhibit at the Heritage Plantation in Sandwich, Mass., in 1974. Now in the Smithsonian Institution's National Museum of American Art. Milwaukee Art Museum, *American Folk Art: The Herbert Waide Hemphill, Jr. Collection* (Milwaukee: The Museum, 1981), 90; Lynda Roscoe Hartigan, *Made with Passion* (Washington, D.C.: Smithsonian Institution Press, 1990), 89; M. M. Esterman, *A Fish That's a Box* (Arlington: Great Ocean Publishers, 1990), 17; Charlene Cerny and Suzanne Seriff, *Recycled, Re-Seen: Folk Art from the Global Scrap Heap* (New York: Abrams, 1996), 42.

Washington, D.C.: A figure resembling a pot-bellied stove was made in Maine, purchased by Aarne Anton and sold to Herbert Waide Hemphill, Jr., and then acquired by the Smithsonian Institution from Hemphill's estate. Lynda Roscoe Hartigan, *Made with Passion* (Washington, D.C.: Smithsonian Institution Press, 1990), 3

Washington, D.C.: A man with arms, legs, and neck made from flexible tubing was sold to Darwin Bearley, Akron, by an Ohio antique picker. Bert Hemphill then purchased the figure from Bearley at a Massachusetts sale. In turn, the Smithsonian Institution acquired it from Hemphill's estate. Eugene Metcalf and Michael Hall, eds., *The Ties That Bind: Folk Art in Contemporary American Culture* (Cincinnati: Contemporary Arts Center, 1986), 13.

Washington, D.C.: A tin man, origin unknown, was acquired by the Smithsonian Institution from the estate of Herbert Waide Hemphill, Jr.

Washington, D.C.: A small copper man, origin unknown, held by Estelle E. Friedman.

Washington, D.C.: Three pieces held by Al Marzorini, a private collector:

    a. A life-sized figure, made in Oregon, wearing red hat made from a funnel;

    b. Little man one inch in size, source unknown;

    c. A life-sized figure made in central Pennsylvania.

Waterloo, Iowa, Local 197: Apprentices pose with little man made of standard fittings. "Waterloo, Iowa, Local Has Active Apprentices," *Sheet Metal Workers' Journal* 43 (Nov. 1952): 23.

Watertown, N.Y.: Made by Leon Derouin for Derouin's Plumbing and Heating in 1980.

West Allis, Wis.: Made in Abbotford, Wis., tinshop ca. 1975 and purchased by Fred Stonehouse for his garden.

West Hampton, N.Y.: *Tiny Tin* made by a foreman for Herman Dominick's shop in the Bronx ca. 1939 and then transferred in 1960 to the Spring Valley, N.Y., shop. Two others were made in Spring Valley by Irving Dominick. Original sold to James Kronen; acquired by Muriel Karasik and sold by her to private collector in West Hampton. Location of the two other replacements unknown. Cathy Maroney, "From Metal to Works of Art," *Journal News,* ca. 1982, 4.

West Jordan, Utah: A cowboy and a fisherman made by Terry Larsen, Apache Junction, Ariz., are held at R. M. Chris Sheet Metal. The cowboy is pictured in company catalogs.

Wichita, Kans., Local 29: Figure made by Don Hansen for Labor Day parade floats in 1984 and 1985. "Local 29 Captures First Prize in Wichita Labor Day Parade," *Sheet Metal Workers' Journal* 75 (Nov. 1984): 13; "Local 29 Takes First Place in Wichita Labor Day Parade," *Sheet Metal Workers' Journal* 76 (Nov. 1985): 20; "Local 29 Celebrates Fiftieth Anniversary with Gala Event," *Sheet Metal Workers' Journal* 78 (Jan. 1987): 18; Leo Meyer, *Training Modules: Youth to Youth* (Washington, D.C.: Sheet Metal Workers' International Association, 1993), 57.

Wichita, Kans., Local 29: Three tin men were made by apprentices in 1995. [Phil Airulla], "'Tin Men': The Sheet Metal Worker's Human Touch in Metal," *Sheet Metal Workers' Journal* 87 (Jan–Feb 1996): 4–8.

Wichita, Kans., Local 29: Seven men were made by apprentices in 1996. Art Garcia, "Building Tin Men, and More," *Wichita Eagle,* July 25, 1998, A14; Archie Green, "Tin Men on Parade," *Labor's Heritage* 10 (Spring–Summer 1999), 43.

Wichita, Kans., Local 29: Four men were made by apprentices in 1997. Art Garcia, "Building Tin Men, and More," *Wichita Eagle,* July 25, 1998, A14; Archie Green, "Tin Men on Parade," *Labor's Heritage* 10 (Spring–Summer 1999), 43.

Wichita, Kans., Local 29: One man, who has a Native American silhouette, was made by an apprentice in 1999.

Woodside, Calif.: A man on horseback was made for Marelich Sheet Metal, San Bruno, Calif., about 1950 and put on top of that shop. When the building was sold and replaced by Artichoke Joe's, a card room, the new owner made an exact duplicate of the trade sign and placed both figures in his coral.

Location unknown for the following items:

Al's the Tin Man: Made for Al's Sheet Metal Shop, Los Angeles. Inherited by son of owner. Sold to an antique dealer, who sold it to Caskey and Lee, Topanga, Calif. Purchased by Carl Hammer Gallery, Chicago, and sold to an unidentified private collector. [Phil Airulla], "'Tin Men': The Sheet Metal Worker's Human Touch in Metal," *Sheet Metal Workers' Journal* 87 (Jan.-Feb. 1996): 4–8.

Lighthead, a man with electric light in head. Made near Zanesville, Ohio, ca. 1950, and purchased (and sold) by Aarne Anton.

Self-Portrait: Made by Adam Brandau in Jackson, Ohio, in 1939. Purchased by an antique picker and sold to Darwin Bearley, an Akron dealer, then to the Carl Hammer Gallery in Chicago, which in turn sold it to Marna Anderson, a New York dealer, who sold it to unidentified private collector.

Uncle Sam: Made by Brian French, shop and site unnamed. Michael D. Hall, "This Side of Oz: A Heart for the Tin Man," *Metalsmith* 8 (Spring 1988): 22–27.

101. A tin man points the way.

ILLUSTRATION SOURCES

1. *Vulcan,* engraving, ca. 1650, source unknown. Courtesy of David Taylor.
2. Museum buddies, 1995. Courtesy of Louanne Green.
3. *Al's the Tin Man,* in [Phil Airulla], "'Tin Men': The Sheet Metal Worker's Human Touch in Metal," *Sheet Metal Workers' Journal* 87 (Jan.–Feb. 1996): 4–8. Courtesy of Caskey Lees.
4. *Copper Man,* San Francisco Local 104 Hall, in C. Kurt Dewhirst, "Working Folk: Artists at Work," *A Report* 13(2) 1995 (publication of the San Francisco Craft and Folk Art Museum). Courtesy of Louanne Green.
5. Louis Gold and apprentices, 1988. Courtesy of Louis Gold.
6. *Flexible Tube Man,* Bert Hemphill Collection, in *The Ties That Bind: Folk Art in Contemporary American Culture,* ed. Eugene Metcalf and Michael Hall (Cincinnati: Contemporary Arts Center, 1986).
7. Tinman and Tools, in Charles Tomlinson, *Illustrations of Useful Arts, Manufactures, and Trade* (London: Society for Promoting Christian Knowledge, 1858).
8. *Der Kupfferschmidt,* in Jost Amman and Hans Sachs, *Stadebuch* (1568, reprint New York: Dover, 1973).
9. Union banner, Liverpool, 1821, in Ted Brake, *Men of Good Character: A History of the National Union of Sheet Metal Workers, Coppersmiths, Heating and Domestic Engineers* (London: Lawrence and Wishart, 1985).
10. Pressed-tin trade sign, 1897. Courtesy of the Heritage Plantation of Sandwich, Cape Cod, Mass.
11. *Habit de ferblanquier,* in Nicholas de Larmessin, *Les costumes grotesques et les métiers XVII siècle* (1695, reprint Paris: Veyrier, 1974).
12. *Un cofretier* (Ein Flaschner), in Martin Engelbrecht, *Assemblage nouveau des manouvries habilles* (New collection of clothing of the trades) (Augsberg: Augustae Vindelicorum, 1730).
13. *Une cofretiere* (Eine Flaschnerin), in Martin Engelbrecht, *Assemblage nouveau des manouvries habilles* (New collection of clothing of the trades) (Augsberg: Augustae Vindelicorum, 1730).
14. *Pot to Mend* by Marcellus Laroon, 1687, in *The Criers and Hawkers of London: Engravings*

and Drawings by Marcellus Laroon, ed. Sean Shesgreen (Stanford: Stanford University Press, 1990).

15. *Pots and Kettles to Mend,* in Thomas Rowlandson, *Rowlandson's Characteristic Sketches of the Lower Orders . . .* (London: Leigh, 1820).

16. W. W. Denslow's Tin Woodman in L. Frank Baum, *The Wonderful Wizard of Oz* (Chicago: Hall, 1900).

17. Sapolio advertisement in *McClure's Magazine,* Dec. 1900, 177.

18. "Professor Bugs Mechanical Men of 2029." Courtesy of Urban Archives, Temple University, Philadelphia, Pa.

19. Angels Camp tin man. Courtesy of Jerri Mills.

20. Canton tin man, Newell Collection, Canton, New York. Photo © Martha Cooper.

21. Tank, tinsmith Brian Linn, and tin man, Duluth, Minn. Courtesy of Sal Salerno.

22. *Harvey Gallery.Com,* Lahaska, Pa. Courtesy of Mark Lerner.

23. *Grinder Man,* in Jean Lipman, Elizabeth V. Warren, and Robert Bishop, *Young America: A Folk-Art History* (New York: Hudson Hills Press in association with the Museum of American Folk Art, 1986). Courtesy of America Hurrah Antiques, New York City.

24. *The Toastmaster,* Chicago, ca. 1900, in collection of Estelle Friedman, Washington, D.C. Courtesy of Michael D. Hall.

25. Strike 'Em Out baseball players. Courtesy of Penny and Allan B. Katz Americana, Woodbridge, Conn.

26. *The Bearded One* by Francis Bellimer, Bristol, N.H. Courtesy, Aarne Anton, American Primitive Gallery, New York City.

27. *Moses.* Courtesy of Larry Raymon.

28. World's largest tin soldier, in "Local 280 Members Create World's Largest Tin Soldier," *Sheet Metal Workers' Journal* 91 (Jan.–Feb. 2001): 6–10 and cover photograph.

29. *I'm Your Man,* in collection of Hill Gallery, Birmingham, Mich. Courtesy of Michael D. Hall.

30. *Jordan's Squire* on roof, Sebastopol, Calif. Courtesy of Henry Anderson.

31. *Jordan's Squire,* Sebastopol, Calif., in [Phil Airulla], "'Tin Men': The Sheet Metal Worker's Human Touch in Metal," *Sheet Metal Workers' Journal* 87 (Jan.–Feb. 1996): 4–8 and cover photograph.

32. Glenn's Metal Works business card. Courtesy of Dick Aldrich.

33. *Aaero Man,* Aaero Heating and Sheet Metal, Novato, Calif. Courtesy of Louanne Green.

34. Dan Collier's C-3PO, held at Local 104 Hall, San Jose, Calif. Courtesy of Louanne Green.

35. *Mr. Dixie,* Dixie Sheet Metal Works, Falls Church, Va. Courtesy of David Taylor.

36. Rene Latour in his garage shop, Ormond Beach, Fla. Courtesy of Ormond Loomis.

37. Latour's first trade sign, Ormond Beach, Fla., 1961. Courtesy of Martin Kline, Rhinebeck, N.Y.

38. Latour's copyright claim, May 15, 1961. Courtesy of Aarne Anton, American Primitive Gallery, New York City.

39. Latour's *Cowboy 200,* American Museum of Folk Art, New York City. Courtesy of Aarne Anton, American Primitive Gallery, New York City.

40. Latour's *Sphere-Headed Man.* Courtesy of Penny and Allan Katz Americana, Woodbridge, Conn.

41. Postcard for D. J. Heaphy and Son, Syracuse, N.Y., ca. 1909. Courtesy of Dennis Heaphy.

42. Folk art at the Everson Museum of Art, 1996. Courtesy of Everson Museum of Art.

43. Heaphy's tin man, Syracuse, N.Y., in Archie Green, "Tin Men on Parade," *Labor's Heritage* 10 (Spring–Summer 1999): 34–47. Photo © Martha Cooper.

44. A. O. Doughty's mailbox, Rayville, La. Courtesy of Susan Roach.

45. *The Goggle-Wearer.* Courtesy of Hackley Gallery, Berea, Ky., photograph by Jason Gibson.

46. *Tin Man* and *Copper Man,* Local 1, Peoria, Ill. Courtesy of Mike Matejka, *Livingston and McLean Counties Union News.*

47. *Lance Man* and Jack Miller, Seattle Local 66, in [Phil Airulla], "'Tin Men': The Sheet Metal Worker's Human Touch in Metal," *Sheet Metal Workers' Journal* 87 (Jan.–Feb. 1996): 6. Courtesy of Jack Miller.

48. St. Patrick's Day float, 1988, Chicago Local 73, in [Phil Airulla], "'Tin Men': The Sheet Metal Worker's Human Touch in Metal," *Sheet Metal Workers' Journal* 87 (Jan.–Feb. 1996): 7. Courtesy of James Slovey.

49. Wagon men made by Denver Local 9 apprentices. Courtesy of Gene Yale.

50. Local 29 Labor Day float, Wichita, Kans., in "Local 29 Takes First Place in Wichita Labor Day Parade," *Sheet Metal Workers' Journal* 76 (Nov. 1984): 20.

51. Dan Ruebbelke's class projects, in Art Garcia, "Building Tin Men, and More," *Wichita Eagle,* July 25, 1998, A14.

52. Labor Day robots, Local 220, Aurora-Elgin, Ill., in "First Prize Winner in Labor Day Parade," *Sheet Metal Workers' Journal* 60 (March 1969): 11.

53. Living tin men, Eastern Massachusetts Local 17, in [Phil Airulla], "'Tin Men': The Sheet Metal Worker's Human Touch in Metal," *Sheet Metal Workers' Journal* 87 (Jan.–Feb. 1996): 8

54. Local 28 in Labor Day parade, New York City. Courtesy of Joe Doyle.

55. Local 28 at Festival of American Folklife, 2001. Courtesy of Paula Johnson.

56. Lion's head at Sheet Metal Workers' International Association Centennial, 1988. Courtesy of the National Building Museum, Washington, D.C., photograph by Walter Smalling, Jr.

57. St. Louis Local 36 apprentices "dress up." Courtesy of Dan Andrews.

58. *Hephaistos* by Steele Savage, in Homer, *The Illiad,* ed. Alston Chase and William Perry, 1950. Courtesy of Little, Brown.

59. *Elizabethan Tinker,* woodcut on broadside, 1616, in *The Pepys Ballads,* ed. W. G. Day (Cambridge, Eng.: D. S. Brewer, 1987).

60. Lucy the Elephant, Margate, N.J. Postcard from the Save Lucy Committee.

61. *The Dean* by George Dean, Terre Haute, Ind., in Archie Green, "Tin Men on Parade," *Labor's Heritage* 10 (Spring–Summer 1999): 34–47. Courtesy of Michael Tingley.

62. *The Dandy,* West End Sheet Metal, New York, in Michael D. Hall, "This Side of Oz: A Heart for the Tin Man," *Metalsmith* 8 (Spring 1988): 23. Courtesy of Michael D. Hall.

63. *Galvanized Man* and companions, Santa Fe, N.M. Courtesy of Joyce Ice.

64. *Marla* by Irving Dominick, Spring Valley, N.Y., in Lynda Roscoe Hartigan, *Made with Passion* (Washington, D.C.: Smithsonian Institution Press), 1990. Courtesy of Smithsonian American Art Museum, Gift of Herbert Waide Hemphill, Jr.

65. *Tiny Tin.* Courtesy of Aarne Anton, American Primitive Gallery, New York City.

66. *Goshen Man* at the Good Time Stove Co., Rt. 112, Goshen, Mass. Courtesy of Kristin O'Connell.

67. *Thermostat Man,* collection of Alex Shear, New York City. Courtesy of Aarne Anton, American Primitive Gallery, New York City.

68. *The Drummer,* Louis Stoffer and Son, Centralia, Wash. Courtesy of Karin Nelson.

69. *Jasper,* Centralia, Wash. Courtesy of Louis J. Stoffer.

70. Iron man, in "Iron Man Now Has Been Living Indoors for Thirty-nine Years," advertisement in Centralia, Wash., *Daily Chronicle,* July 4, 1976.

71. *Tin Man,* St. Croix Falls, Wis. Courtesy of John Turner.

72. Tucson tin man. Courtesy of Dave Carlson.

73. *Stainless-Steel Man,* Dee Cramer Inc., Flint, Mich., in "Off to the Show," *Flint Journal,* March 9, 1990, 1.

74. Announcement. Courtesy of Pete Lyszewski.

75. Plans for *Copper Man,* Pete Lyszewski. Courtesy of Pete Lyszewski.

76. Pete Lyszewski's *Copper Man.* Courtesy of Pete Lyszewski.

77. AFL-CIO Union Industries Show, Denver, in "Sheet Metal Craftsmanship Demonstrated at 1979 AFL-CIO Union Industries Show," *Sheet Metal Workers' Journal* 70 (May 1979): 17.

78. Scott Hultgren and his knight. Courtesy of Scott Hultgren.

79. *The Workshop of Conrad Seusenhofer,* a woodcut by Hans Burgkmair, in Maximillian I, *Der Weisskunig* (1525, reprint Vienna: Tempsky, 1891).

80. Joseph Schoell's *Miss Liberty.* Courtesy of Mary Zwolinski, Rensselaer County Council for the Arts, Troy, N.Y.

81. Ramsour's *Statue of Liberty,* Federal Heating and Supply, Denver. Courtesy of Bo Ramsour and Nick Carter.

82. Bob Ramsour and *Uncle Sam.* Courtesy of Bo Ramsour.

83. Adam Brandau and *Big Foot,* Riffe Gallery, in Nancy Gilson, "Scrap-Metal Sculptor," *Columbus Dispatch,* March 14, 1996, 6E. Photograph by Fred Squillante. Reprinted, with permission, from the *Columbus Dispatch.*

84. Brandau's *Self-Portrait,* Jackson, Ohio, 1939. Courtesy of the Carl Hammer Gallery, Chicago.

85. Joel Galerneau's *Buddy,* Tom Rall Collection, Arlington, Va. Courtesy of David Taylor.

86. B.J.'s *The Welder,* North Little Rock, Ark. Courtesy of Dell Upton.

87. Jewell's tin man, Idaho Falls, Idaho. Courtesy of Bob McCarl.

88. *The Traveling Tinker* by John Bolles, in *Harper's Weekly,* Nov. 26, 1870.

89. *The Apprentice* by John Niro, in Michael Lynn, "The Works of John Niro: Scenes of the Sheet Metal Worker's Trade," master's thesis, SUNY, Oneonta, 1979. Courtesy of the New York State Historical Association, Cooperstown, N.Y.

90. Valley Heating, Spring Valley, N.Y. Courtesy of Aarne Anton, American Primitive Gallery, New York City.

91. Wm. C. Brown and Son, Lowville, N.Y. Photo © Martha Cooper/Traditional Arts in Upstate New York.

92. Brennan's Plaza, Jacksonville, Ill. Courtesy of Mary Lee Brennan.

93. *Lee-Hi Sheet Metal,* Fairfax, Va. Courtesy of David Taylor.

94. Young and Bertke animated sign, Cincinnati, Ohio, in Archie Green, "Tin Men on Parade," *Labor's Heritage* 10 (Spring–Summer 1999): 34–47. Courtesy of Tim Correll.

95. *Lighthead.* Courtesy of Aarne Anton, American Primitive Gallery, New York City.

96. *Little Cowboy* by Terry Larsen, Apache Junction, Ariz., Salt Lake City Local 312 Hall. Courtesy of Hal Cannon.

97. *Find Us Fast,* J&J Metal Products, Warren, Mich., in *The Ties That Bind: Folk Art in Contemporary American Culture,* ed. Eugene Metcalf and Michael Hall (Cincinnati: Contemporary Arts Center, 1986).

98. Outside the shop, J&J Metal Products, Clinton Township, Mich. Courtesy of Oscar Paskal.

99. Out to pasture. Dan Marelich's former shop sign and a companion, Woodside, Calif. Courtesy of Louanne Green.

100. *Clown, Dog,* and *Girl with Ball.* Courtesy of Myron Shure, Chicago, and Aarne Anton, American Primitive Gallery, New York City.

101. A tin man points the way. Trade sign at General Insulation Co., Lewiston, Maine. Courtesy of Bob Eskind.

REFERENCES

[Airulla, Phil]. 1996. "'Tin Men': The Sheet Metal Worker's Human Touch in Metal." *Sheet Metal Workers' Journal* 87 (Jan.–Feb.): 4–8 and cover photo.

An American Sampler: Folk Art from the Shelburne Museum. 1987. Washington, D.C.: National Gallery of Art.

"American Sheet Metal Worker Meets with Polish Solidarity Union Leader Lech Walesa." 1981. *Sheet Metal Workers' Journal* 72 (July): 9.

Amherst College. 1974. *American Folk Art.* Amherst, Mass.: The College (exhibition catalog).

Amman, Jost, and Hans Sachs. 1973 (1568). *Standebuch* (The book of trades). Introduction by B. A. Rivkin. New York: Dover.

"Another Face-Lift for a Lady Liberty." 1986. *Denver Post,* Oct. 29, 1 (photo).

"Apprentice Builds Sheet Metal Robot." 1955. *Sheet Metal Workers' Journal* 46 (Dec.): 8.

"An Apprenticeship Training Display." 1969. *Sheet Metal Workers' Journal* 60 (July): 15.

Ardery, Julia. 1998. *The Temptation: Edgar Tolson and the Genesis of Twentieth-Century Folk Art.* Chapel Hill: University of North Carolina Press.

"Area Tinner/Folk Artist Sells His Work to Gallery." 1992. *Wellstone* (Ohio) *Telegram,* June 3.

"At the Sign of the Tin Horse." 1951. *Sheet Metal Workers' Journal* 42 (Oct.): 15.

Aydelotte, Frank. 1913. *Elizabethan Rogues and Vagabonds.* Oxford: Oxford University Press.

Bagato, Jeff. 1994. "Tin Man." *Washington Post Magazine,* Aug. 28, 7.

———. 2000. "Unusual Suspects." *Washington Post Weekend,* Sept. 1, 31–34.

Bailey, Clayton. 1981. *The Robot Builder's Manual.* Port Costa, Calif.: Wonder of the World.

Bank, Liz, and Michael Flanagan. 1996. *In Their Own Time: The Art of Carl McKenzie and Adam Brandau.* Columbus: Riffe Gallery.

Baum, L. Frank. 1900. *The Wonderful Wizard of Oz.* Chicago: Hall.

———. 1973. *The Annotated Wizard of Oz.* Introduction, notes, and bibliography by Michael P. Hearn. New York: Clarkson Potter.

Berry, W. T., and H. E. Poole. 1966. *Annals of Printing.* Toronto: University of Toronto Press.

Bishop, Robert. 1974. *American Folk Sculpture.* New York: E. P. Dutton.

———, and Patricia Coblentz. 1981. *A Gallery of American Weathervanes and Whirligigs.* New York: E. P. Dutton.

Bloch, Chayim. 1972. *The Golem: Legends of the Ghetto of Prague.* Trans. Harry Schneiderman. Blauvelt, N.Y.: Freedeeds Library.

Boardman, Kathryn Ann. 1981. "The Tin and Sheet Metal Shop of the Fred McGown Corporation Cooperstown, New York." Senior research paper, SUNY, Oneonta.

Brake, Ted. 1985. *Men of Good Character: A History of the National Union of Sheet Metal Workers, Coppersmiths, Heating and Domestic Engineers.* London: Lawrence and Wishart.

Brewington, Marion. 1962. *Shipcarvers of North America.* Barre, Mass.: Barre Publishing.

Bruno, Leonard. 1995. *The Tradition of Technology.* Washington, D.C.: Library of Congress.

Burrell, Chris. 1991. "Goshen's Towering Tin Man." *Daily Hampshire Gazette* (Northhampton, Mass.), July 3, 15.

Cannon, Hal. 1999. "Tin Men Notes" and "Tape Log." Unpublished typescript, author's files.

[Carter, Nick]. 1983. "Ramsour of Federal Heating, Denver, Makes Replica of Statue of Liberty for Shop Front." *Snips,* Sept., 132–34.

———. 1988a. "Sheet Metal Craftsmanship Exhibition Opens in Washington, D.C." *Snips,* Feb., 18–26.

———. 1988b. "Local 73 Apprentice Coordinator Keith Switzer Shows Tin Woman" *Snips,* April, 97 (photo).

———. 1988c. "Sheet Metal Craftmanship Exhibition Opens in Washington, D.C." *Snips,* Feb. 1988, 18–26.

———. 1990a. "Presenting Final Photos Taken at Florida A.C. Contrs. Ass'n Converence and Trade Show." *Snips,* Aug., 166.

———. 1990b. "Presenting a Round-Up of Tin Man Replicas and Costumes Fabricated by Various Sheet Metal Craftsmen." *Snips,* Aug., 16–22.

———. 1990c. "Stainless Steel Tin Man Fabricated by Dee Cramer, Inc. for Display at Flint Fair." *Snips,* April, 118–19.

Case, Dick. 1998. "After Decades at Work, Tin Man Retires to Museum." *Herald-American* (Syracuse, N.Y.), Jan. 11.

Cerny, Charlene, and Suzanne Seriff. 1996. *Recycled, Re-Seen: Folk Art from the Global Scrap Heap.* New York: Abrams.

Chase, David, and Carolyn Laray. 1988. *Sheet Metal Craftsmanship: Progress in Building.* Washington, D.C.: National Building Museum.

Chase, George D. 1914. "Further Word-Lists, Maine." *Dialect Notes* 4, pt. 2, 151–53.

Cirker, Blanche. 1962. *1800 Woodcuts by Thomas Bewick and His School.* New York: Dover.

The Cobler of Canterburie; or, An Inuectiue against Tarltons Newes out of Purgatorie. 1852 (1590). London: J. E. Taylor.

Coffin, Margaret. 1968. *The History and Folklore of American Country Tinware, 1700–1900.* Camden, N.J.: Nelson.

"Committee Awards First Prize to Local 73." 1988. *Sheet Metal Workers' Journal* 79 (Dec.): 17.

Correll, Timothy, and Patrick Polk, eds. 1999. *The Cast-Off Recast: Recycling and the Creative Transformation of Mass-Produced Objects.* Los Angeles: UCLA Fowler Museum of Cultural History.

———. 2000. *Muffler Men.* Jackson: University Press of Mississippi.

Curry, David Park. 1987. "Rose-Colored Glasses: Looking for 'Good Design' in American Folk Art." In *An American Sampler: Folk Art from the Shelburne Museum.* Washington, D.C.: National Gallery of Art.

Dabakis, Melissa. 1999. *Visualizing Labor in American Sculpture.* New York: Cambridge University Press.

"Dale Luttrell Helps Celebrate Expansion of Steelworkers Training Facility." 2000. *Ste. Genevieve* (Mo.) *Herald,* May 31.

Davis, Michael, and Roland Sweet. 1985. "Tin Kin." *New Times* (Syracuse, N.Y.), May 1, 9.

Day, W. G., ed. 1987. *The Pepys Ballads.* Facsimile volume 1. Cambridge, Eng.: D. S. Brewer.

DeCarlo, Tessa. 1997. "Putting a Mixer in a Museum and Asking, What Is Art?" *New York Times,* June 22, H38.

Dekker, Thomas. 1966 (1603). *The Wonderfull Yeare.* Ed. G. B. Harrison. New York: Barnes and Noble.

Demer, John. 1973. "How Tinsmiths Used Their Tools." *Chronicle of the Early American Industries Association* 26 (Dec.): 49–57.

———. 1974a. "Jedediah North and His Tool Business." *Chronicle of the Early American Industries Association* 27 (Dec.): 59–66.

———. 1974b. "Tinners' Tools and Their Manufacture." *Chronicle of the Early American Industries Association* 27 (April): 1–7.

"Detroit Labor Day Parade Units." 1949. *Sheet Metal Workers' Journal* 40 (Oct.): 14.

DeVoe, Shirly S. 1968. *The Tinsmiths of Connecticut.* Middletown: Wesleyan University Press.

———. 1981. *The Art of the Tinsmith: English and American.* Exton, Pa.: Schiffer.

Dewhurst, C. Kurt. 1995. "Working Folk: Artists at Work." In San Francisco Craft and Folk Art Museum, *A Report* 13(2): 4.

Diderot, Denis. 1959. *A Diderot Pictorial Encyclopedia of Trades and Industries.* Ed. Charles Gillispie. New York: Dover (facsimile reproduction of plates from 1751–53).

Dietsch, Deborah. 1988. "Precious Metals." *Architectural Record* 176 (June): 138–39.

Ditchfield, P. H. 1904. *The City Companies of London.* London: J. M. Dent.

"Edison School Robot to 'Explain' Display at Centennial Show." 1951. *Seattle Times,* Oct. 28, 10.

Engelbrecht, Martin. 1730. *Assemblage nouveau des manœuvries habilles* (New collection of clothing of the trades). Augsberg: Augustae Vindelicorum.

Epstein, Rachel. 1996. *Mailbox, U.S.A.* Salt Lake City: Gibbs Smith.

Esterman, M. M. 1990. *A Fish That's a Box.* Arlington, Va.: Great Ocean Publishers.

Ffoulkes, Charles. 1912. *The Armourer and His Craft.* London: Methuen.

"First Prize Winner in Labor Day Parade." 1969. *Sheet Metal Workers' Journal* 60 (March): 11.

Flower, Philip W. 1880. *A History of the Trade in Tin: A Short Description of Tin Mining and Metallurgy.* London: George Bell and Sons.

"Frank Nolden Passes On." 1932. *Labor Gazette* (Peoria, Ill.), Jan., n.d.

Fried, Frederick, and Mary Fried. 1978. *America's Forgotten Folk Arts.* New York: Pantheon.

Friedley-Voshhardt Co. 1926. *Architectural Sheet Metal, Ornaments, Statuary, Spun Work . . . Catalogue 50.* Chicago: The Company.

"From a Bygone Labor Day." 1958. *Sheet Metal Workers' Journal* 49 (Sept.): 8.

"From 'Tin Knocker' to Air Balancer on Washington's Mall." 1973. *Sheet Metal Workers' Journal* 64 (Sept.): 10–11.

Garcia, Art. 1998. "Building Tin Men, and More." *Wichita* (Kans.) *Eagle,* July 25, A14.

Gascoigne, George. 1973 (1576). *The Steele Glas.* New York: De Capo Press.

Gayle, Margot, David W. Look, and John G. Waite. 1992. *Metals in America's Historic Buildings: Uses and Preservation Treatments.* 2d ed. Washington, D.C.: National Park Service.

Geerlings, Gerald. 1929. *Metal Crafts in Architecture.* New York: Scribner's.

A General Description of All Trades. . . . 1747. London: Waller.

Gilson, Nancy. 1996. "Scrap-Metal Sculptor." *Columbus* (Ohio) *Dispatch,* March 14, 6E.

Gladstone, M. J. 1974. *A Carrot for a Nose.* New York: Scribner's.

Gorman, John. 1973. *Banner Bright.* London: Allen Lane.

Gould, Mary Earle. 1958. *Antique Tin and Tole Ware.* Rutland, Vt.: Charles Tuttle.

Grego, Joseph. 1880. *Rowlandson the Caricaturist.* 2 vols. New York: Bouton.

Green, Archie. 1993. *Wobblies, Pile Butts, and Other Heroes: Laborlore Explorations.* Urbana: University of Illinois Press.

———. 1996a. "Tin Man and Copper Man: Trade Sign and Union Symbol." *Commemorating One Hundred Years of Excellence in Craftsmanship, 1896–1996.* San Francisco: Building and Construction Trades Council.

———. 1996b. *Calf's Head and Union Tale: Labor Yarns at Work and Play.* Urbana. University of Illinois Press.

———. 1998. "Rene Latour: Metal Sculpture." In *Florida Folklife: Traditional Arts in Contemporary Communities,* ed. Stephen Stuempfle. Miami: Historical Museum of Southern Florida.

———. 1999. "Tin Men on Parade." *Labor's Heritage* 10 (Spring–Summer): 34–47.

Greene, Robert. 1966 (1592). *The Second Part of Conny-Catching.* Ed. G. B. Harrison. New York: Barnes and Noble.

Hall, Michael D. 1988. "This Side of Oz: A Heart for the Tin Man." *Metalsmith* 8 (Spring): 22–27.

Hansson, Bobby. 1996. *Fine Art of the Tin Can.* Asheville, N.C.: Lark Books.

"Happy Hundredth Sheet Metal Workers No. 1." 1988. *Labor* (Peoria, Ill.), March 17, 1.

Harkins, William. 1962. *Karel Capek.* New York: Columbia University Press.

Harman, Thomas. 1930 (1566). *A Caveat or Warning for Common Cursetors, Vulgarley Called Vagabonds.* In *The Elizabethan Underworld,* ed. A. V. Judges. New York: E. P. Dutton.

Hartigan, Lynda Roscoe. 1990. *Made with Passion:* Washington, D.C.: Smithsonian Institution Press.

Hazen, Edward. 1836. *Panorama of Professions and Trades.* Philadelphia: Uriah Hunt. Reprinted 1981 as *Popular Technology; or, Professions and Trades.* Albany, N.Y.: Early American Industries Association.

Hazlitt, W. Carew. 1892. *The Livery Companies of the City of London.* London: Swan Sonnenschein.

Heal, Ambrose. 1947. *The Signboards of Old London Shops.* London: Batsford.

Hemphill, Herbert, and Julia Weissman. 1974. *Twentieth-Century American Folk Art and Artists.* New York: E. P. Dutton.

Hendrickson, Paul. 1988. "The Tinmen: Silhouettes in Sheet Metal." *Washington Post,* Jan. 25, C1.

The Herbert Waide Hemphill, Jr. Collection of Eighteenth-, Nineteenth-, and Twentieth-Century American Folk Art. 1974. Sandwich, Mass.: Heritage Plantation of Sandwich.

Hibbard, G, R. 1951. *Three Elizabethan Pamphlets.* London: Harrap.

Hill, Cristopher. 1989. *A Tinker and a Poor Man.* New York: Knopf.

Hindley, Charles. 1969 (1884). *A History of the Cries of London, Ancient and Modern.* 2d ed. Detroit: Singing Tree Press.

"His Heart Is in the Right Place." 1982. *Sheet Metal Workers' Journal* 73 (Nov.): 16.

"Hobbyist Demonstrates Art." 1955. *Sheet Metal Workers' Journal* 46 (Jan.): 16.

Hollander, Stacy C., ed., with Gerard C. Wertkin and John Bigelow Taylor. 2001. *American Radiance: The Ralph Esmerian Gift to the American Folk Art Museum.* New York: Abrams.

Homer. 1950. *The Illiad.* Ed. Alston Chase and William Perry. Boston: Little, Brown.

———. 1962. *The Illiad of Homer.* Ed. Richmond Lattimore. Chicago: University of Chicago Press.

Hunt, Marjorie. 1999. *The Stone Carvers: Master Carvers of Washington National Cathedral.* Washington, D.C.: Smithsonian Institution Press.

"I. A. Float Detroit Prize Winner." 1951. *Sheet Metal Workers' Journal* 42 (Oct.): 14.

"Idaho Local Exhibits Apprenticeship Work." 1950. *Sheet Metal Workers' Journal* 41 (Feb.): 14.

"Illinois Member Fashions Armor Suit for Grandson." 1964. *Sheet Metal Workers' Journal* 55 (Feb.): 12–13.

"Iron Man Now Has Been Living Indoors for Thirty-nine Years." 1976. *Daily Chronicle* (Centralia, Wash.), July 4 (advertisment in bicentennial edition).

Jabbour, Alan. 1996. "The American Folklife Center: A Twenty-Year Retrospective." *Folklife Center News* 18(1–2): 3–19.

Judges, A. V. 1930. *The Elizabethan Underworld*. New York: E. P. Dutton.

Kazin, Michael, and Steven Ross. 1992. "America's Labor Day: The Dilemma of a Workers' Celebration." *Journal of American History* 38 (March): 1294–323.

Kennedy, Peter, ed. 1975. *The Folksongs of Britain and Ireland*. New York: Schirmer Books.

Kidd, Archibald. 1949. *History of the Tin-Plate Workers and Sheet Metal Workers and Braziers Societies*. London: National Union of Sheet Metal Workers and Braziers.

Kirby, Doug, Ken Smith, and Mike Wilkins. 1992. *The New Roadside America: The Modern Traveler's Guide to the Wild and Wonderful World of America's Tourist Attractions*. Rev. ed. New York: Simon and Schuster.

Klamkin, Charles. 1973. *Weather Vanes: The History, Design, and Manufacture of an American Folk Art*. New York: Hawthorne Books.

Kussi, Peter. 1990. *Toward the Radical Center: A Karel Capek Reader*. Highland Park, N.J.: Catbird Press.

"Labor Day Paraders Sport Tin Umbrellas." 1966. *Sheet Metal Workers' Journal* 57 (June): 20.

Larmessin, Nicolas de, and Gerard Valck. 1969. *Fantastic Costumes of Trades and Professions*. London: Holland Press.

Larmessin, Nicolas de. 1974 (1695). *Les costumes grotesques et les métiers XVII siècle* (Fantastic costumes of the trades and professions of the seventeenth century). Paris: Henri Veyrier.

Lasansky, Jeannette. 1982. *To Cut, Piece, and Solder: The Work of the Rural Pennsylvania Tinsmith, 1778–1908*. Lewisberg, Pa.: Oral Traditions Project.

Lipman, Jean. 1974. *Provocative Parallels*. New York: E. P. Dutton.

———, and Helen Franc. 1976. *Bright Star: American Painting and Sculpture since 1776*. New York: E. P. Dutton.

———, Elizabeth V. Warren, and Robert Bishop. 1986. *Young America: A Folk-Art History*. New York: Hudson Hills Press in association with the Museum of American Folk Art.

———, et al. 1990. *Five Star Folk Art: One Hundred American Masterpieces*. New York: Abrams.

"Local 29 Captures First Place in Wichita Labor Day Parade." 1984. *Sheet Metal Workers' Journal* 75 (Nov.): 13.

"Local 29 Celebrates Fiftieth Anniversary with Gala Event." 1987. *Sheet Metal Workers' Journal* 78 (Jan.): 18.

"Local 29 Takes First Place in Wichita Labor Day Parade." 1985. *Sheet Metal Workers' Journal* 76 (Nov.): 20.

"Local 33 Happenings." 1989. *Sheet Metal Workers' Journal* 80 (March): 21.

"Local 33 'Tin Man' in Cleveland Labor Day Parade." 1990. *Sheet Metal Workers' Journal* 81 (Jan.): 22.

"Local 40 Booth at State Fair a Success." 1987. *Sheet Metal Workers' Journal* 78 (May): 23.

"Local 43 Members Restore 'Lucy' the Elephant." 1978. *Sheet Metal Workers' Journal* 69 (Oct.): 10–11.

"Local 45 Captures the Crowd." 1961. *Sheet Metal Workers' Journal* 52 (Dec.): 20.

"Local 70 Members Keep Busy." 1987. *Sheet Metal Workers' Journal* 78 (April): 12.

"Local 85 Float Takes First Place in Labor Day Parade." 1986. *Sheet Metal Workers' Journal* 77 (Nov.): 13.

"Local 85 Participants in Labor Day Parade." 1983. *Sheet Metal Workers' Journal* 74 (Nov.–Dec.): 18.

"Local 212 Displays Skills in Labor Day Parade." 1983. *Sheet Metal Workers' Journal* 74 (Nov.–Dec.): 18.

"Local 280 Members Create World's Largest Tin Soldier." 2001. *Sheet Metal Workers' Journal* 91 (Jan.–Feb.): 6–10, cover photo.

"Longtime Businessman Succumbs." 1978. *Sun-Star* (Merced, Calif.), Feb. 11, 13.

"Longtime Local Sheet Metal Contractor De Wing Retires." 1976. *Sun-Star* (Merced, Calif.), Jan. 22, n.p.

"L.U. 1 Craftsmen Make Real Sheet Metal Man." 1971. *Sheet Metal Workers' Journal* 62 (Jan.): 11.

"L.U. 220 Double Winner in Aurora, Ill." 1970. *Sheet Metal Workers' Journal* 61 (Feb.): 7.

Lynn, Michael Anne. 1979. "The Works of John Niro: Scenes of the Sheet Metal Worker's Trade." Master's thesis, SUNY, Oneonta.

Marling, Karal Ann. 1984. *The Colossus of Roads: Myths and Symbols along the American Highway.* Minneapolis: University of Minnesota Press.

Maroney, Cathy. 1982. "From Metal to Works of Art." *Journal News* (Rockland and Westchester Counties, N.Y.), n.d., n.p.

Maximilian I, Holy Roman Emperor. 1516. *Der Weisskunig.* Vienna: Tempsky, 1891.

McCarl, Robert. 1974. "The Production Welder: Product, Process and the Industrial Craftsman." *New York Folklore Quarterly* 30(4): 243–53.

McKinniss, Barbara. 1993. "Tin Man of Jackson." *The Messenger* (Athens, Ohio), June 13, D1.

Meadows, Cecil A. 1957. *Trade Signs and Their Origin.* London: Routledge and Kegan Paul.

"Member Puts Skills to Good Use during Retirement." 1968. *Sheet Metal Workers' Journal* 59 (Nov.): 46.

Mercey, Arch. 1980. *The Sheet Metal Workers' Story.* Washington, D.C.: Sheet Metal Workers' International Association.

"The 'Metal Man' Congratulates the Class of June, 1937." 1937. *The Mission* (Pacific Metals Company advertisement in Mission High School [San Francisco] yearbook).

Metcalf, Eugene, and Michael Hall, eds. 1986. *The Ties That Bind: Folk Art in Contemporary American Culture.* Cincinnati: Contemporary Arts Center.

Meyer, Leo. 1993. *Training Modules: Youth to Youth.* Washington, D.C.: Sheet Metal Workers' International Association.

Milgrom, Melissa. 1998. "The Nostalgia Broker: Alex Shear's Obsession with Consumerism Has Created a Mirror of Modern America." Web-site at <http://www.cigaraficionado.com> accessed Aug. 1, 2001.

Milwaukee Art Museum. 1981. *American Folk Art: The Herbert Waide Hemphill, Jr. Collection.* Milwaukee: The Museum.

———. 1993. *Common Ground/Uncommon Vision: The Michael and Julie Hall Collection of American Folk Art.* Milwaukee: The Museum.

Mish, Charles C., ed. 1963. *Short Fiction of the Seventeenth Century.* New York: New York University Press.

"'Mr. Sheet Metal,' Robot Made at No. 124." 1951. *Sheet Metal Workers' Journal* 42 (May): 17.

Mulholland, James. 1981. *A History of Metals in Colonial America.* University: University of Alabama Press.

National Museum of American Art. 1995. *National Museum of American Art.* Washington, D.C.: The Museum.

"Neon Sign Fabrication." 1958. *Sheet Metal Workers' Journal* 49 (July): 4–5.

"New Location." 1998. *Ste. Genevieve* (Mo.) *Herald,* July 8, 13.

"No. 99 Apprentice Makes Robots." 1952. *Sheet Metal Workers' Journal* 43 (April): 9.

"Off to the Show." 1990. *Flint* (Mich.) *Journal,* March 9, 1 (Matthew Goebel photo).

"Old-Timers." 1949. *Sheet Metal Workers' Journal* 40 (Sept.): 7.

On the Cutting Edge. 1988. Washington, D.C.: Sheet Metal Workers' International Association.

"One If by Land." 1975. *Sheet Metal Workers' Journal* 66 (July): 6–8.

"On the Welding Edge." 1988. *Sheet Metal Workers' Journal* 79 (April): 10–14.

"Ornamental Sheet Metal Work Monument to Artistic Skills in Era of Decorative Design." 1967. *Sheet Metal Workers' Journal* 58 (May): 12–13.

Osborn, Judy. 1963. "Champaign Man Makes Miniature Suit of Armor for His Grandson." *Champaign-Urbana* (Ill.) *Courier,* April 25, 18.

Owen, David. 1999. "The Sultan of Stuff." *The New Yorker,* July 19, 52–63.

"Pay No Attention to That Man behind the Curtain." 1994. *New York Times,* June 29 (photo of Alex Shear's zinc-coated tin men on National Mall).

Peterson, Charles, ed. 1976. *Building Early America: Contributors toward the History of a Great Industry.* Radnor, Pa.: Chilton.

"Pictured Is the Local 85, Atlanta, Georgia Float." 1983. *Sheet Metal Workers' Journal* 74 (Oct.): 9.

Pinto, Vivian de Sola, and Allan Rodway, eds. 1957. *The Common Muse: An Anthology of Popular British Ballad Poetry, XVth-XXth Century.* London: Chatto and Windus.

"Pittsburg Local Holds Diamond Jubilee Dinner." 1955. *Sheet Metal Workers' Journal* 46 (Dec.): 12.

Powers, Beatrice. 1957. *Early American Decorated Tinware.* New York: Hastings House.

"Putting on the Ritz at Labor Day Parade." 1961. *Sheet Metal Workers' Journal* 52 (Aug.): 22.

Reif, Rita. 1974. "Antiques: Folk Art Show." *New York Times,* June 29, 26.

———. 1999. "There Can Be Art in Car Parts, Too: Take Muffler Men." *New York Times,* Nov. 21, 45.

"Richmond L.U. 15 Apprentices Build Sheet Metal Robot." 1973. *Sheet Metal Workers' Journal* 64 (June): 22.

Ritz, Joseph. 1987. "'The Lantern Man' Cast a Glow with Handicraft." *Buffalo News,* June 15, B8.

Roach, Susan. 2001. "Making the 'Biggest Tin Man': A Folk Artist–Folklorists' Partnership." Unpublished typescript, author's files.

Rockwell, Richard. 199?. "Tin Man Survives More Than Fifty Years Later." *Hermiston* (Ore.) *Herald,* n.p.

Rollins, Hyder E., ed. 1929–32. *The Pepys Ballads.* 8 vols. Cambridge: Harvard University Press.

Rowlandson, Thomas. 1799. *Cries of London.* London: Ackermann.

———. 1820. *Rowlandson's Characteristic Sketches of the Lower Orders. . . .* London: Leigh.

Russell, Hanafi. 1980. "Tin Man Lives." *Sebastopol* (Calif.) *Times,* Jan. 10, 1.

Salzman, L. F. 1923. *English Industries of the Middle Ages.* Oxford: Oxford University Press.

Sessions, Ralph. 2000. "The Shipcarvers' Art: Shop and Cigar Store Figures in America." Ph.D. diss., City University of New York.

Shakespeare, William. 1963. *The Winter's Tale.* Ed. J. H. P. Pafford. London: Methuen.

———. -95. *The Winter's Tale.* Ed. John F. Andrews. London: J. M. Dent.

"Sheet Metal Craftsmanship Demonstrated at 1979 AFL-CIO Union Industries Show." 1979. *Sheet Metal Workers' Journal* 70 (May): 17.

"Sheet Metal Exhibit Attracts Attention at Show." 1967. *Sheet Metal Workers' Journal* 58 (July): 13.

"Sheet Metal Exhibit Hit of AFL-CIO Union Industries Show in Detroit, Michigan." 1995. *Sheet Metal Workers' Journal* 86 (May–June): 28–29.

"Sheet Metal Signposts of Freedom." 1974. *Sheet Metal Workers' Journal* 65 (Aug.): 6–8.

Sheffield, Helen. 1984. "Simple Rules Govern Mailbox Decor." *News-Star-World* (Monroe, La.), Feb. 2, D1.

Shesgreen, Sean, ed. 1990. *The Criers and Hawkers of London: Engravings and Drawings by Marcellus Laroon.* Stanford: Stanford University Press.

"Shine? Yes, If You Use Sapolio."y900. *McClure's Magazine* 16 (Dec.): 177 (advertisement inside back cover).

Simon, Stephanie. 1999. "Metal Behemoths Punctuate Prairie Vistas in North Dakota." *Los Angeles Times,* Aug. 24, A5.

"SMWIA Float at Colorado State Fair." 1986. *Sheet Metal Workers' Journal* 77 (Nov.): 10.

"SMWIA Skills and Craftsmanship Demonstrated at 1980 AFL-CIO Union Industries Show." 1980. *Sheet Metal Workers' Journal* 71 (July): 10.

Snaije, Olivia. 1997. "Collector of Americana with Eye for the Absurd." *Christian Science Monitor,* Sept. 23.

Souvenir Pictorial History of Local Union No. 104 . . . . 1910. San Francisco: Local 104.

Spielvogel, Rochelle. 1985. "Typescript Biography of David Goldsmith and Related Correspondence." Author's files.

Stanley, Edward [Lord Derby]. 1864. *The Iliad of Homer Rendered into English Blank Verse.* London: Murray.

Stuempfle, Stephen, ed. 1998. *Florida Folklife: Traditional Arts in Contemporary Communities.* Miami: Historical Museum of Southern Florida.

"Technology Advances Metal Work." 2000. *St. Louis Post Dispatch,* June 4, suburban journal section.

The Tincker of Turvey, His Merry Pastime in His Passing from Billinsgate to Graves-End. 1963 (1630). In *Short Fiction of the Seventeenth Century,* ed. Charles C. Mish. New York: New York University Press.

"Tin Man Shop Sign by Robert J. Kirkner." 1999. *Folk Art Finder* 20 (Summer): 13 (photo and caption).

"Tin Man and Yard Dog." 1999. *Berea College Appalachian Center News Letter.* Summer.

"Tin Men Visit Historic Village." 1990. *Sheet Metal Workers' Journal* 81 (May): 21.

Tomlinson, Charles. 1858. *Illustrations of Useful Arts, Manufactures, and Trade.* London: Society for Promoting Christian Knowledge.

"The Traveling Tinker." 1870. *Harper's Weekly,* Nov. 26 (headnote for cover drawing by John Bolles).

Tuer, Andrew. 1883. *London Cries.* London: Field and Tuer.

———. 1884. *Quads for Authors, Editors, and Devils.* London: Field and Tuer.

———. 1885. *Old London Street Cries and the Cries of Today.* London: Field and Tuer.

"Turning in the Wind." 1965. *Sheet Metal Workers' Journal* 56 (Dec.): 17.

Vlach, John Michael. 1981. *Charleston Blacksmith: The Work of Philip Simmons.* Athens: University of Georgia Press.

Warner, Anne, ed. 1984. *Traditional American Folk Songs from the Anne and Frank Warner Collection.* Jeff Warner assoc. ed. Syracuse: Syracuse University Press.

"Waterloo, Iowa, Local Has Active Apprentices." 1952. *Sheet Metal Workers' Journal* 43 (Nov.): 23.

Weber, Nicholas Fox. 1993. "Connecticut Folk Tale." *Architectural Digest* 50 (March): 98–105.

Webster, Mary. 1970. *Francis Wheatley.* London: Routledge and Kegan Paul.

Wecker, David. 199?. "Landmark Walks, Walks, but Gets Nowhere." *Cincinnati Post,* n.d., 1C.

Wenstrup, R. L. 1997. "Adam Brandau." *Folk Art Finder* 18 (Jan.): 19.

Whitney Museum of American Art. 1976. *Two Hundred Years of American Sculpture.* Boston: Godine.

Winters, Kim. 1996. "Tin Man Gets a Heart." *Daily Hampshire Gazette* (Northhampton, Mass.), Dec. 21.

Zahner, L. William. 1995. *Architectural Metals.* New York: Wiley and Sons.

Zwolinski, Mary. 1991a. Paragraph on and photos of Joseph Schoell and his work. In *Innovative Traditions* (exhibition catalog, Delaware County, N.Y., Historical Society).

———. 1991b. "The Tin Sculpture of Joseph Schoell." *New York Folklore Newsletter* 12 (Fall): 4–5.

———. 1991c. Unpublished paper on Joseph Schoell. Author's files.

INDEX

Archie Green lives in San Francisco and is a long-time member of the United Brotherhood of Carpenters and Joiners of America. In 1982 he retired as professor of English and folklore at the University of Texas, Austin. He has written *Only a Miner* and *Wobblies, Pile Butts, and Other Heroes* in addition to *Calf's Head and Union Tale: Labor Yarns at Work and Play,* and *"Torching the Fink Books" and Other Essays on Vernacular Culture.* He is also editor of *Songs about Work.* In the decade between 1967 and 1976, he lobbied for the American Folklife Preservation Act. From its inception, he has been active in the John Edwards Memorial Forum, an archival association treating vernacular music.

Folklore and Society

The University of Illinois Press
is a founding member of the
Association of American University Presses.

Composed in 9.5/14 ITC Stone Serif
with ITC Stone Sans display
by Paula Newcomb
at the University of Illinois Press
Designed by Paula Newcomb
Manufactured by Thomson-Shore, Inc.
University of Illinois Press
1325 South Oak Street
Champaign, IL 61820-6903
www.press.uillinois.edu